AF739840

State and Society Responses to Social Welfare Needs in China

This volume examines the shifting role of the state and social organizations (e.g. NGOs) in providing social services in contemporary China. A series of case studies identifies a dynamic whereby the state increasingly withdraws from social service provision, with social organizations taking up the slack. An interdisciplinary line-up of contributors explore this dynamic, and how it affects the state–society relationship and the quality of social services provided.

Based on current research, this book engages existing debates over state–society relations, offering a new thematic framework to evaluate this relationship. Drawing on the framework, each chapter explores a particular aspect of social service provision, including orphan care, migrant labor protection, and infectious disease control. Differentiating between case studies of crisis and non-crisis social service provision situations, this volume argues that state and social organizations engage in ongoing negotiations to achieve shared social service provision goals – a dynamic largely controlled by the state. However, during crises, the controlled relationship may alter as the priority becomes addressing the immediate demand for essential social services. The result is the potential for a rapid change in relations between the state and social organizations.

State and Society Responses to Social Welfare Needs in China is important reading for scholars interested in politics, public administration and social policy and welfare in China.

Jonathan Schwartz is Associate Professor of Political Science at SUNY New Paltz. His research focuses on factors influencing policy implementation.
Shawn Shieh is Associate Professor of Political Science at Marist College in Poughkeepsie, New York. He is engaged in two projects in China, one on corruption and the other on NGOs.

Routledge contemporary China series

1 **Nationalism, Democracy and National Integration in China**
Leong Liew and Wang Shaoguang

2 **Hong Kong's Tortuous Democratization**
A comparative analysis
Ming Sing

3 **China's Business Reforms**
Institutional challenges in a globalised economy
Edited by Russell Smyth and Cherrie Zhu

4 **Challenges for China's Development**
An enterprise perspective
Edited by David H. Brown and Alasdair MacBean

5 **New Crime in China**
Public order and human rights
Ron Keith and Zhiqiu Lin

6 **Non-governmental Organizations in Contemporary China**
Paving the way to civil society?
Qiusha Ma

7 **Globalization and the Chinese City**
Fulong Wu

8 **The Politics of China's Accession to the World Trade Organization**
The dragon goes global
Hui Feng

9 **Narrating China**
Jia Pingwa and his fictional world
Yiyan Wang

10 **Sex, Science and Morality in China**
Joanne McMillan

11 **Politics in China since 1949**
Legitimizing authoritarian rule
Robert Weatherley

12 **International Human Resource Management in Chinese Multinationals**
Jie Shen and Vincent Edwards

13 **Unemployment in China**
Economy, human resources and labour markets
Edited by Grace Lee and Malcolm Warner

14 **China and Africa**
Engagement and compromise
Ian Taylor

15 **Gender and Education in China**
Gender discourses and women's schooling in the early twentieth century
Paul J. Bailey

16 **SARS**
Reception and interpretation in three Chinese cities
Edited by Deborah Davis and Helen Siu

17 **Human Security and the Chinese State**
Historical transformations and the modern quest for sovereignty
Robert E. Bedeski

18 **Gender and Work in Urban China**
Women workers of the unlucky generation
Liu Jieyu

19 **China's State Enterprise Reform**
From Marx to the market
John Hassard, Jackie Sheehan, Meixiang Zhou, Jane Terpstra-Tong and Jonathan Morris

20 **Cultural Heritage Management in China**
Preserving the cities of the Pearl River Delta
Edited by Hilary du Cros and Yok-shiu F. Lee

21 **Paying for Progress**
Public finance, human welfare and inequality in China
Edited by Vivienne Shue and Christine Wong

22 **China's Foreign Trade Policy**
The new constituencies
Edited by Ka Zeng

23 **Hong Kong, China**
Learning to belong to a nation
Gordon Mathews, Tai-lok Lui, and Eric Kit-wai Ma

24 **China Turns to Multilateralism**
Foreign policy and regional security
Edited by Guoguang Wu and Helen Lansdowne

25 **Tourism and Tibetan Culture in Transition**
A place called Shangrila
Åshild Kolås

26 **China's Emerging Cities**
The making of new urbanism
Edited by Fulong Wu

27 **China–US Relations Transformed**
Perceptions and strategic interactions
Edited by Suisheng Zhao

28 **The Chinese Party-State in the 21st Century**
Adaptation and the reinvention of legitimacy
Edited by André Laliberté and Marc Lanteigne

29 **Political Change in Macao**
Sonny Shiu-Hing Lo

30 **China's Energy Geopolitics**
The Shanghai cooperation organization and Central Asia
Thrassy N. Marketos

31 **Regime Legitimacy in Contemporary China**
Institutional change and stability
Edited by Thomas Heberer and Gunter Schubert

32 **U.S.–China Relations**
China policy on Capitol Hill
Tao Xie

33 **Chinese Kinship**
Contemporary anthropological perspectives
Edited by Susanne Brandtstädter and Gonçalo D. Santos

34 **Politics and Government in Hong Kong**
Crisis under Chinese sovereignty
Edited by Ming Sing

35 **Rethinking Chinese Popular Culture**
Cannibalizations of the canon
Edited by Carlos Rojas and Eileen Cheng-yin Chow

36 **Institutional Balancing in the Asia Pacific**
Economic interdependence and China's rise
Kai He

37 **Rent Seeking in China**
Edited by Tak-Wing Ngo and Yongping Wu

38 **China, Xinjiang and Central Asia**
History, transition and crossborder interaction into the 21st century
Edited by Colin Mackerras and Michael Clarke

39 **Intellectual Property Rights in China**
Politics of piracy, trade and protection
Gordon Cheung

40 **Developing China**
Land, politics and social conditions
George C. S. Lin

41 **State and Society Responses to Social Welfare Needs in China**
Serving the people
Edited by Jonathan Schwartz and Shawn Shieh

State and Society Responses to Social Welfare Needs in China

Serving the people

Edited by Jonathan Schwartz and Shawn Shieh

Routledge
Taylor & Francis Group
LONDON AND NEW YORK

First published 2009
by Routledge
2 Park Square, Milton Park, Abingdon, Oxon OX14 4RN

Simultaneously published in the USA and Canada
by Routledge
270 Madison Ave, New York, NY 10016

Routledge is an imprint of the Taylor & Francis Group, an informa business

© 2009 Selection and editorial matter, Jonathan Schwartz and Shawn Shieh; individual chapters, the contributor.

Typeset in Times by Wearset Ltd, Boldon, Tyne and Wear
Printed and bound in Great Britain by TJI Digital, Padstow, Cornwall

All rights reserved. No part of this book may be reprinted or reproduced or utilized in any form or by any electronic, mechanical, or other means, now known or hereafter invented, including photocopying and recording, or in any information storage or retrieval system, without permission in writing from the publishers.

British Library Cataloguing in Publication Data
A catalogue record for this book is available from the British Library

Library of Congress Cataloging-in-Publication Data
State and society responses to social welfare needs in China: serving the people/edited by Jonathan Schwartz and Shawn Shieh.

p. cm.
Includes bibliographical references and index.

1. Public welfare–China. 2. China–Social policy. I. Schwartz, Jonathan. II. Shieh, Shawn.

HV418.S73 2009
361.951–dc22

2008050127

ISBN10: 0-415-45224-4 (hbk)
ISBN10: 0-203-93119-X (ebk)

ISBN13: 978-0-415-45224-3 (hbk)
ISBN13: 978-0-203-93119-6 (ebk)

We dedicate this book to our wives, Linda Brotman and Betsy Shieh, whose support, patience and understanding were central to its successful completion.

Contents

Illustrations

Figures

Table

Contributors

Timothy Hildebrandt is a Ph.D. Candidate of Political Science at the University of Wisconsin–Madison.

Joan Kaufman, MA, M.S., Sc.D. is Director of the AIDS Public Policy Project at the John F. Kennedy School of Government, Harvard University, Lecturer in Social Medicine at Harvard Medical School, and Senior Scientist at the Brandeis University Heller School for Social Policy and Management.

Catherine H. Keyser, Ph.D. is Associate Professor of Political Science at Drew University, Madison, New Jersey.

André Laliberté, Ph.D. is Associate Professor at the University of Ottawa's School of Political Studies.

Jonathan Schwartz, Ph.D. is Associate Professor of Political Science and Asian Studies at the State University of New York, New Paltz.

Shawn Shieh, Ph.D. is Associate Professor of Political Science at Marist College, Poughkeepsie, New York.

Marsha Smith, Ph.D. is Professor of Sociology and Director of the East Asian Studies Program at Augustana College, Rock Island, Illinois.

Jennifer L. Turner, Ph.D. is director of the China Environment Forum at the Woodrow Wilson Center, Washington, DC, and editor of the *China Environment Series*.

Hong Zhang, Ph.D. is Associate Professor of East Asian Studies at Colby College.

Foreword

The impetus for this project arose from a panel at the 2006 Association for Asian Studies (AAS) Annual Conference in San Francisco. The panel drew together scholars looking at various aspects of China's social service provision situation in interesting and interrelated ways. Following the panel, we concluded that herein was the basis for an interesting and worthwhile volume. With the enthusiastic support of existing panel members and some new additions, we began the process, presenting a second time at the 2007 Boston AAS as part of our effort to ensure the coherence of the volume.

As a result of these efforts and the cooperation of our contributors, we have completed what we believe is a coherent and informative study of the changing nature of social service provision in China. We thank the anonymous reviewers for their feedback, and our editors at Routledge – Stephanie Rogers and Sonja van Leeuwen – for their support in seeing this volume through to publication.

Jonathan Schwartz and Shawn Shieh

Abbreviations

ACFTU	All-China Federation of Trade Unions
ARV	anti-retroviral
BRA	Bureau for Religious Affairs
BSR	Business for Social Responsibility
CANGO	China Association for NGO Cooperation
CASAPC	Chinese Association of STD and AIDS Prevention and Control
CBA	Chinese Buddhist Association
CCAA	Chinese Center for Adoption Affairs
CCF	China Charity Foundation
CCM	Country Coordinating Mechanism
CCP	Chinese Communist Party
CCYL	Chinese Communist Youth League
CDC	Center for Disease Control
China CARES	China Comprehensive AIDS Response
CLAPV	Center for Legal Aid to Pollution Victims
CNEU	civil, non-enterprise unit
CPPCC	Chinese People's Political Consultative Conference
CSO	civil society organization
CSR	corporate social responsibility
CWI	child welfare institute (i.e. orphanage)
CWWN	Chinese Working Women Network
CYDF	China Youth Development Foundation
DFID	Department for International Development (United Kingdom)
DPP	Democratic Progressive Party (Taiwan)
EED	Evangelischer Entwicklungsdienst
ENGO	environmental non-governmental organization
EU	European Union
FCC	Families with Children from China
FDI	foreign direct investment
FIE	foreign-invested enterprise

FON	Friends of Nature
FPA	Family Planning Association
GFATM	Global Fund for AIDS, TB and Malaria
GIPA	greater involvement of people living with AIDS
GONGO	government-organized non-governmental organization
ICCO	International Committee for the Care of Orphans
ICO	Institute of Contemporary Observation
IDU	injecting drug user
IED	Institute for Environment and Development
ILO	International Labour Organization
IMF	International Monetary Fund
INGO	international non-governmental organization
IPEA	Institute of Public and Environmental Affairs
LDC	less developed country
LPM	Law on the Protection of Minors
MEP	Ministry of Environmental Protection
MOCA	Ministry of Civil Affairs
MOH	Ministry of Health
MSM	men who have sex with men
MWDC	Migrant Worker Documentation Center
NCAIDS	National Center for AIDS Prevention and Control
NGNCE	non-governmental, non-commercial enterprise
NIS	newly independent states
NPC	National People's Congress
NPO	non-profit organization
OHEC	Occupational Health Education Center
PLA	People's Liberation Army
PLWHA	people living with HIV/AIDS
PRA	Participatory Rural Appraisal
PRC	People's Republic of China
PRD	Pearl River Delta
RC	residence committee
RDA	Rural Development Association
ROC	Republic of China (i.e. Taiwan)
RWKA	Rural Women Knowing All
SAI	Social Accountability International
SARS	severe acute respiratory syndrome
SMEs	small and medium-sized enterprises
SMFTU	Shenzhen Municipal Federation of Trade Unions
SNISD	South-North Institute for Sustainable Development
SO	social organization
SOE	state-owned enterprise
STD	sexually transmitted disease
SWA	Social Work Association

SWI	social welfare institute
TNC	The Nature Conservancy
UNDP	United Nations Development Programme
VC	village committee
WTO	World Trade Organization

Part I

Introduction

1 State and society responses to China's social welfare needs

An introduction to the debate

Shawn Shieh and Jonathan Schwartz

Introduction

In May 2007, the European Union (EU) and the United Nations Development Programme (UNDP) signed an agreement with the Chinese government to support a large-scale initiative to strengthen the rule of law and civil society participation in China. The initiative, Governance for Equitable Development, will contribute US$10.5 million over a four-year period to support reforms in the law-making and judicial process and in civil society participation. About half of the program's US$10.5 million budget will be devoted to strengthening the legal framework for civil society organizations (CSOs) and improving communication and coordination between CSOs, the government and other social actors. In explaining the need for such an initiative, Khalid Malik, the UNDP's Resident Representative in China, noted a shift in the Chinese government's attitude toward CSOs: "Increasingly, the government recognizes the strengths of CSOs or non-governmental organizations (NGOs) in reaching out to disadvantaged groups, especially in areas such as reducing poverty, addressing environmental challenges, and preventing and building awareness on HIV/AIDS" (UNDP-China website).

The above initiative and Mr. Malik's remarks are reminders of the substantial changes that have taken place in China's political landscape over the past decade as the state increasingly acknowledges and welcomes the role of social organizations in addressing China's social problems. This volume explores the rapidly changing relationship between the state and social organizations, with an emphasis on NGOs as they work, sometimes together and at other times at cross purposes, in addressing the country's social welfare needs.[1] It looks at the extent to which this relationship has changed during the reform period, the varied interactions that take place between state and social organizations in addressing China's social welfare needs, and the implications this evolving relationship has for state–society relations and social welfare provision in China. Each contributor explores the evolution of state–society relationships in different areas of social service provision. An important distinction of the volume, and one that we explore later in the chapter, is the difference in the nature of social welfare provision in crisis and non-crisis situations.

This study has two main objectives: first, to explore the evolving roles of state and social organizations in providing social services in the reform era; and second, to evaluate the impact of these changing roles on state–society relations and social welfare provision in China.

China's rapid economic reforms, coupled with the steady dismantling of the Chinese socialist welfare system, have resulted in declining social service provision by the Chinese state. Concurrently, a host of additional challenges have resulted in social problems and needs that must be addressed, such as rising unemployment, growing inequality, an aging population, at-risk children, gender and labor rights issues, and health and environmental problems. Responding to the gap in social service provision, Chinese social organizations have begun to take a growing role in providing social services. A wide range of social organizations have stepped into this newly available space to address these problems and needs. However, these organizations are constrained by a lack of resources and support, and an overly restrictive and ambiguous legal environment. The result is a patchwork of initiatives that fail to address the needs of the majority of the population adequately. One broad question this book explores is how effective the newly evolving relationship between the state and social organizations has proven in addressing China's social welfare needs.

The growing and widespread participation of social organizations in the public arena in turn has important long-term consequences for state–society relations. Most studies looking for signs of a burgeoning civil society in China have focused on the private business sector and trade and professional associations, which increased in number rapidly during the 1980s (Wank 1995; White *et al.* 1996; Pearson 1997; Foster 2002; Dickson 2003; Kennedy 2005). Social organizations devoted to social service provision have received far less attention, primarily because they did not begin emerging in significant numbers until the early and mid-1990s. Yet social organizations engaged in social service provision are becoming an important part of the public sphere dedicated to addressing social goals and influencing public policy, and could be important precursors of a more dynamic and assertive civil society in China (Howell 2004: 145). In their attempt to accelerate market-oriented reforms and promote the goal of "small government, big society" (*xiao zhengfu, da shehui*), the Chinese leadership has grown more tolerant of social organizations engaged in social service provision. These organizations, in turn, have responded by proliferating rapidly over the past decade (Wang and Gu 2000: 15–16; Howell 2004: 146–7). The chapters in this volume indicate that social organizations are becoming increasingly autonomous and independent of the state, linking with international NGOs and with other sectors of society, particularly intellectuals and students. This volume looks at some of the potential consequences these trends are having for China's political and social development.

The remainder of this chapter is divided into four sections. In the following section, we define the terms "social welfare," "social organizations," and "NGOs" and engage with the debate over conceptions of civil society in China. In the second section, we consider the impact of crisis and non-crisis situations on the division of roles between the state and social organizations in providing social services. In the third section, we introduce the organizing themes addressed in the book, while in the concluding section we summarize the various arguments made by the contributors to this volume.

Social welfare needs and social organizations in China

Following Elisabeth Croll (1999), we define social welfare (*shehui fuli*) broadly to include social insurance (*shehui baoxian*), social services (*shehui fuwu*), and social relief (*shehui jiuji*). Social insurance refers to arrangements for retirement pensions and medical treatment; unemployment, maternity, sickness, and work-related injury or disability benefits; and subsidies for widows and orphans. Social services involve specialized support for the elderly, disabled, and abandoned as well as services such as education, health and housing, and legal services. Social relief refers to assistance for elderly and disabled people without income or other forms of familial support, as well as relief in response to natural and human-caused crises such as floods, earthquakes, and environmental disasters.

This broad definition of social welfare means we are interested in a large spectrum of social organizations that do not fit neatly within conventional categorizations of social welfare or social service organizations. Thus, some organizations classified by Wang and Sun (2002: 234–70) in Table 1.1 as primarily cultural/religious or self-governing organizations are also involved in providing social services such as education and poverty relief. Examples of these types of organizations are provided in chapters by Laliberté (Chapter 6, religious organizations) and Schwartz (Chapter 7, village and residence committees). There are also social organizations working on HIV/AIDS (see Chapter 8 by Kaufman), migrant labor (see Chapter 4 by Zhang and Smith), and environmental issues (see Chapter 5 by Hildebrandt and Turner) that are involved in activities that go beyond conventional notions of social service delivery to include activities such as advocacy work.[2]

A thornier issue is how to define the term "social organizations."[3] For the purposes of this volume, we define social organizations as organizations that are distinct from the state and provide social services. We recognize the difficulty of drawing a clear distinction between the state and social organizations, particularly in the Chinese setting, where many social organizations are a creation of the Party-state. We therefore include within the rubric of "social organizations" a wide variety of organizations that range from quasi-state actors, which we discuss further in the next paragraph, to what are conventionally defined as NGOs. A conventional NGO is defined as an organization that is non-profit, largely self-governing, and voluntary in nature (White *et al.* 1996; Ma 2004). This definition of conventional NGOS assumes that NGOs have a significant, though not absolute or even near absolute, degree of autonomy and independence from the state. Other defining characteristics of NGOs include having a staff and specific, long-term goals related to protecting and advancing their constituents' interests and values.[4] Our focus is on domestic NGOs based in China, although we recognize that domestic NGOs increasingly have important links with overseas organizations. In order to include the large

Table 1.1 Classification of NGOs based on their function

Type	*Definition*	*Examples*
Recreational organizations (*xingqu huodong zuzhi*)	Organizations established by members who share a common interest or hobby	Mountaineering associations, stamp-collecting associations
Interest group organizations (*liyi qunti zuzhi*)	Organizations which seek the common good for members of the interest group	Trade unions, self-employed and private enterprise associations, professional associations
Social service organizations (*minjian shehui fuwu zuzhi*)	Organizations whose main purpose is to meet social needs and provide services to society	Foundations for poverty relief, private educational institutions, community service organizations
Social welfare organizations (*shehui gongyi zuzhi*)	Organizations that provide services and advocate for society as a whole or specific groups in need of help	Women's Federation, Communist Youth League, Red Cross, environmental organizations
Self-governing organizations (*minjian zizhu zuzhi*)	Organizations that meet the needs of their members	Village committeees, urban residents, committees, community management committees
Cultural/religious organizations (*wenhua qunti zuzhi*)	Organizations based on religious beliefs, ethnicity or region	Buddhist organizations, Christian churches, native-place associations
Scientific and technological organizations (*kexue jishu minjian zuzhi*)	Organizations that promote scientific and technical research and knowledge	Science and technology associations

Source: Adapted from Wang and Sun (2002: 230-70).

number of grassroots organizations that have emerged in China, our definition encompasses organizations that are not formally registered.

To clarify the distinction between the state and social organizations, we provide a spectrum of the many types of organizations in China, and their relative autonomy from the state, in Figure 1.1. On the left-hand end of the spectrum reside government agencies that are part of the state bureaucracy. In addition to government agencies, the state end of the spectrum includes public institutions (*shiye danwei*) such as state-run universities and hospitals, and state-owned enterprises. While these latter two are somewhat removed from the state because they are not directly linked to the bureaucracy, they are funded and staffed by the state and must submit to supervision by state and party organs.[5] To the right of the state on this spectrum lie a diverse collection of groups that comprise what we term "social organizations." These range from quasi-state organizations, such as mass organizations and village and neighborhood committees, to NGOs and networks, which appear on the right-hand end of the spectrum.

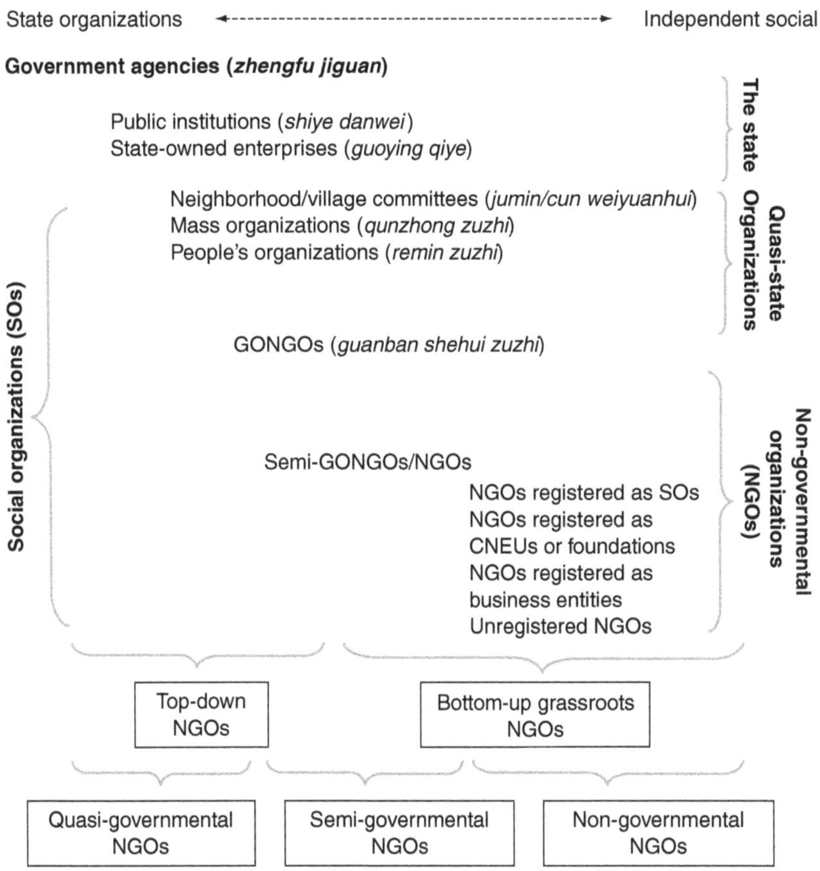

Figure 1.1 NGOs in China and their relationship to the state.

Note

The spectrum describes the degree of independence from the state, where 0 signifies total state control (i.e. no civil society activism) and 5 signifies an active and completely autonomous civil society. GONGO, government-organized non-governmental organization; CNEU, civil, non-enterprise unit; SO, social organization.

We can further unpack the category of NGOs by distinguishing between registered and unregistered NGOs. In terms of registered NGOs, Chinese regulations differentiate between three kinds: social organizations (SOs) (*shehui tuanti*), which are essentially membership organizations; civil, non-enterprise units (CNEUs) (*minjian feiqiye danwei*), which operate as non-profit service providers; and foundations (*jijinhui*). The Chinese government defines SOs in the 1998 "Regulations for Registration and Management of SOs" as "non-profit organizations that are voluntarily founded by Chinese citizens for their common will and operated according to their charters." The 1998 "Provisional Regulations for the Registration and Management of Civil, Non-enterprise Units" distinguish CNEUs as "social entities that are organized by enterprises, non-commercial institutions, and other social forces with non-state funds that engage in not-for-profit social services."[6] Generally, CNEUs are income-earning institutions such as non-state-run schools, hospitals, research institutions, and other organizations that provide a social or professional service. The 2004 "Regulations on Administration of Foundations" distinguish between public fundraising foundations and non-public fundraising foundations. A China Development Brief analysis of these foundations notes that the latter category "seems basically designed to cover privately endowed family or corporate grant making foundations – what one might be tempted to call 'real foundations,'" while those in the former category seem more like operational NGOs such as Oxfam, Save the Children, and the Salvation Army in that they both raise money and spend it on their own projects ("Blurred Law" 2004). All of these NGOs – SOs, CNEUs, and foundations – must register with the Ministry of Civil Affairs or a local civil affairs bureau, and must have a professional supervising body (*yewu zhuguan bumen*), usually a governmental agency, a state-owned enterprise, or a public institution (*shiye danwei*) such as a university. Generally speaking, because the regulations governing SO management and adherence to political and moral principles are stricter, SOs are more tightly regulated than CNEUs (Ma 2004: 68).

In terms of their relationship with the state, these NGOs occupy a range of positions on the spectrum ranging from those with close ties with the state to grassroots NGOs with few or no ties to the state. The former generally were established by governmental units that also serve as their supervising body. These spin-off organizations are referred to in the literature as government-organized NGOs (GONGOs), "top-down" (*zishang erxia*) NGOs, or "quasi-governmental" NGOs, and they are closely dependent on the state for personnel, funding. and management (Wang 2002: 4; Meng 2002: 14; Schwartz 2004; Cooper 2006). Their leader may be a state official and they may be fully state funded. There also exist SOs and CNEUs further removed from the state and thus further to the right on the spectrum. These may be spin-offs of a GONGO or an NGO that received permission to be based in a state unit, but whose management, leadership, and funding may be only peripherally connected to that unit. These are sometimes referred to as "semi-governmental" NGOs (semi-GONGOs). In addition, there exist SOs and CNEUs that are essentially grassroots organizations with few ties to the state. These are sometimes referred to as "bottom-up" NGOs or autonomous NGOs (Wang 2002: 5–6; Meng 2002: 14). An example is what Caroline Cooper calls "working NGOs," which register as CNEUs and are formed by semi-GONGOs that become their supervising body. Cooper argues that these NGOs remain independent in terms of leadership and direction and are able to "achieve the highest degree of legal NGO autonomy currently available in China. Funds are raised from international sources while state and university money is rejected. Good relations, however, are maintained with obliquely overseeing state or university bodies" (2004: 122–3).

The other category of NGOs comprises those that are not registered with the Ministry of Civil Affairs (MOCA). Like the registered NGOs, this group of NGOs also occupy a range of positions on the spectrum. Closer to the state end of the spectrum are NGOs that reside within government agencies, state-owned enterprises, and public institutions such as universities. These are sometimes placed in the GONGO or semi-GONGO category. However, unlike the GONGOs and semi-GONGOs discussed above, they are not formally registered with a state organ, though they are affiliated (*guakao*) with a state unit. An example is the Center for Legal Aid to Pollution Victims (CLAPV), which Schwartz (2004: 44) puts in the semi-NGO category. Further to the right of the spectrum are NGOs that have registered as business entities with the Industrial and Commercial Administration. Cooper (2006: 122) and Zhao (2000) argue that these business NGOs enjoy greater autonomy than NGOs registered as SOs or CNEUs because they do not need a supervisory body to register, nor do they have to draft and submit monthly reports on their activities and finances.[7] Zhao (2000: 45) cites the example of an environmental NGO, Global Village (*diqiu cun*), that registered as a business in order to avoid having a supervisory body and thus gain greater autonomy. On the other hand, as others have pointed out, business NGOs face a distinct disadvantage in that they are required to pay taxes and undergo annual audits (see Turner 2004).

Finally, furthest removed from the state are NGOs and both real and virtual networks that are neither legally registered nor associated with a government unit. Cooper (2006: 123) refers to these to as underground NGOs. An example of this form of NGO is Zhao Xiumei's "volunteer associations" (*zhiyuan lianheti*) engaged in environmental protection. These are not legally registered but may associate with other organizations and networks (2000: 44).

NGOs and the debate over civil society in China

The quasi- or semi-governmental status of many NGOs in China has led to a debate among scholars as to whether Chinese NGOs can be considered truly non-governmental and thus expressions of an independent civil society. One reason for this debate has to do with differing definitions of civil society. This debate is usefully framed by the distinction between sociological and political conceptions of the term. The sociological definition views civil society as an intermediate associational sphere situated between the state and the building blocks of society (individuals, families, and firms). Civil society organizations are therefore separate from the state, enjoying a level of autonomy from the state, and are formed voluntarily by people in order to protect or advance their interests and values (White 1996: 197–8; Yu: 1–2; Misztal 2001; Gellner 1994; Shigetomi 2002: 10–13). By contrast, the political definition identifies civil society organizations as components of a social force in opposition to the state resulting in, or by nature a part of, the democratization process. Drawing on the Eastern European experience, scholars adhering to the political definition of civil society argue that democratization arises over time as a result of individuals combining their otherwise disparate grievances against the state, and learning norms of democratic interaction in the process (Di Palma 1991: 75–7).[8] These groups eventually create institutions capable of resisting the authoritarian state (White 1996; Wiktorowicz 2000: 43).

Clearly, one's choice of definition has significant implications for how state–society interactions are perceived and evaluated, as well as for what organizations can be considered components of civil society. In emphasizing an organization's autonomy from, and opposition to, the state, and civil society's function of advancing democratic change, the political definition is more restrictive of the kinds of organizations that would qualify as a NGO. As a result, many Chinese organizations long considered NGOs would not qualify. By contrast, the sociological definition includes consideration of organizations that over time may constitute both a challenge to the state and a supporter of shared goals with the state (Cooper 2006: 114; Tong 1994: 334). This definition emphasizes relative levels of autonomy and de-links civil society from democratization, thus broadening the realm of organizations that may be considered NGOs.

In this volume, we rely on the sociological definition of civil society. We argue that it is neither possible nor desirable to set clear limits on what defines an NGO. As becomes clear in Figure 1.1, organizations such as public institutions and mass organizations are tied to the state and are clearly *not* non-governmental in nature. And yet, neither can they be viewed as inherently *of* the state. Drawing distinctions becomes all the more difficult when considering GONGOs and semi-GONGOs. These too are removed from the state by varying degrees. While some GONGOs are closer cousins of public institutions and mass organizations than they are of NGOs, others are becoming increasingly independent of the state.

An additional attraction of the sociological definition is that the legal and political status of many Chinese NGOs is in constant flux. In some cases, GONGOs established by the state have become increasingly independent. In other cases, grassroots organizations that started out with no ties to the state have become more dependent on local or central state agencies. In positing autonomous associations independent from and in opposition to the state, the political definition of civil society does a poor job of capturing the reality of associational life in China, where organizations often seek a close, symbiotic relationship with the state at either the central or the local level. Furthermore, the political definition assumes that more autonomy from the state translates into greater influence, whereas, as a number of scholars point out, autonomy from the state in China often results in decreased influence (Wank 1995; Gallagher 2004; Wexler *et al.* 2006).[9] Indeed, many Chinese NGOs view connections with the state as vital if they are to enjoy any success in social service provision and in their advocacy work.

Ultimately, we agree with Gallagher (2004: 422) that worrying about whether NGOs are really autonomous expressions of "civil society" distracts us from the more interesting questions that are central to this volume: how do NGOs interact with the state and how does their changing relationship affect social service provision?

State–civil society interactions in crisis and non-crisis situations

A central component of our analytical framework is the distinction we draw between the roles played by state and non-state entities in crisis and non-crisis situations. Crises are commonly defined as non-linear events that change existing patterns in a dramatic fashion. Generally, descriptions of crises are limited to international, economically related impacts on the state (Strecker-Downs and Saunders 1998–99: 5–8; Goertz and Diehl 2000: 31; Lindenberg 1990). Thus, an example of a crisis would include the impact of collapsing markets for primary export goods or International Monetary Fund (IMF) structural adjustment loans on domestic political conditions. However, while useful to understanding the impacts of economic developments, this conception of crisis ignores the multiplicity of potential non-economic crises. Moving beyond the economic perspective, Stern defines crises as "a decision making situation, deriving from a change in the external or internal environment of a collectivity, characterized by three necessary and sufficient perceptions on the part of the responsible decision makers: A threat to basic values, urgency and uncertainty" (1999: 8). Thus, crises may include economically related events such as ascension to major international treaties (e.g. the World Trade Organization), as well as earthquakes or other natural disasters or disease outbreaks (Fidler 2003: 7; Lardy 2002/2003: 265; Fewsmith 2001: 586–9).[10] Zhong Kaibin identifies severe acute respiratory syndrome (SARS), avian flu, and the 2005 Songhua River benzene spill as examples of human-caused and natural disasters constituting major crises (2007: 91).

Because of their relative lack of resources and their weak adjustment capabilities, crises are especially challenging for less developed countries (LDCs). Furthermore, such countries' leaders are especially vulnerable to the impacts of crises because they constitute the likeliest target of unrest generated by sudden declines in well-being that may arise as a result of a crisis (Krasner 1985: 4–6).

One often noted impact of crises on LDCs is the emergence, or strengthening, of NGOs. In most Eastern European states, the crisis was driven by the liberalizing reforms initiated from outside by Moscow under Gorbachev (McFaul 2002: 234). Ultimately, these NGOs made important contributions to bringing about regime collapse among Eastern European communist regimes. Since China was not a Soviet satellite state, an equivalent crisis did not occur (though the impact of the collapsing Soviet Union on the Chinese state should not be minimized). Nonetheless, China's leadership has had to cope with other forms of crisis. In fact, the frequency of major crises has increased over the past thirty years as a result of rapid economic, social, and environmental changes even as Chinese crisis management capacity has declined owing to the reform and opening of the recent decades (Zhong 2007: 91).

In this volume, we argue that the changing nature of state–society relations should be understood as occurring simultaneously, in two separate ways. In non-crisis situations, as the state sheds responsibilities for social services, or new demands for social services arise, these responsibilities are taken up by civil society organizations. This describes a negotiated and occasionally conflictual process in which cooperation between the state and social organizations is built over time. By contrast, in crisis situations the state's inability to fulfill its responsibilities to the public is suddenly and starkly brought to light. In these situations, the state responds both by recentralizing power and focusing on resolving the specific crisis. At the same time, the state turns to social organizations to assist in meeting immediate demands for assistance, resulting in an expansion of political space for non-state actors.

By exploring these two distinct processes, this volume sheds light on the complexity of the state–society relationship, suggesting that changes in the relationship are not advancing solely in a linear fashion; during crises, non-linear shifts occur.

Organizing themes

This volume builds on previous studies that focus on state and society responses to the powerful political, economic, and social forces created by China's reform and opening (e.g. Wong 1994; White *et al.* 1996; Howell 2004; Saich 2000; Ma 2004). These studies illustrate how the gradual withdrawal and redefinition of the state's social management role has occurred alongside the growth of a burgeoning and diverse collection of NGOs in a wide range of sectors in both urban and rural areas. These twin trends – the withdrawal of the state and the growth of NGOs – have accelerated noticeably over the past ten years and are the focus of the main themes that have been taken up by each of the contributors to this volume. These themes are: (1) changes in the roles played by the state and social organizations in providing social services; (2) the evolving nature of interactions between the state and NGOs in social service provision; and (3) the ramifications of these changes for state–society relations and social service provision in China.

Changes and continuities in the state–NGO division of labor during the reform period

One theme this volume explores is what has changed and what has not changed in terms of the roles of the state and social organizations in providing social services. How, for example, has the state's role changed as it withdraws from direct provision of social services via the work unit and moves toward a welfare system funded by a combination of state, enterprise, and individual contributions and based on market norms of profit and competition (Solinger 2004; Gu and Zhang 2006)? A look at recent reforms in unemployment insurance and the national health insurance show the state engaged in the monumental task of replacing the old enterprise- or work unit-based social service provision system in an effort to construct a system that provides for all urban residents, regardless of their employment status.

The decentralizing thrust of the reforms also requires us to acknowledge that what we call the "state" actually consists of different levels of government and an array of government agencies with different roles and interests when it comes to the role of social organizations in providing social services. How have those roles and interests changed? Studies suggest that local governments have taken on a more prominent role as more responsibilities for social service provision have been decentralized to them. Local governments are asked to carry out experiments with social programs, and to bear more of the burden of funding and provision of social services (Croll 1999: 694). Yet there is also evidence that local and central interests are not fully aligned, and that local agencies are selective in implementing regulations governing the role of social organizations, sometimes to their advantage and other times to their disadvantage.[11]

In addition, how have social services changed? The chapters in this volume suggest that new services such as outreach to those infected with HIV/AIDS, legal education for migrants, foster care for abandoned children, and environmental advocacy are emerging alongside traditional services such as flood and poverty relief and public health.

At the same time, we want to be mindful of areas where the influence of the old system lingers. The pull of the enterprise-based system, for instance, can be seen in the implementation of unemployment and health care programs, where one's access to these services depends on the ability and willingness of one's employer or previous employer to contribute. In the case of the new social health insurance program, many people have chosen not to participate in the new initiative because they would rather rely on the health care provided by their work unit. Another continuity carried over from the Maoist welfare regime is the privileging of workers from the state-owned enterprises and urban residents who hold urban residency permits (*hukou*). Like the old system, the new system provides a "parsimonious, residual allocation … to the truly poor" (Solinger 2005: 86). The difference between now and twenty years ago is that the pool of people slipping through the social safety net has grown and includes "workers from firms that have collapsed, peasant migrants to the cities, workers from heavily indebted enterprises and able-bodied poor" (Solinger 2005: 96), as well as the self-employed, children and students (Gu and Zhang 2006).

The nature of interactions between the state and social organizations

A second theme has to do with the evolving nature of interactions between state and social organizations. As noted, since the 1990s there has been a blossoming of social organizations and networks that have taken on responsibilities that were once the sole responsibility of the state.

As argued above, we believe the sociological definition of civil society more effectively explains the nature of the state–society relationship in China than does the political definition. While the political definition of civil society posits a conflictual relationship between the state and civil society that contributes to the birth of a democratic system, the sociological definition identifies civil society as less confrontational with, and, when convenient to its goals, even cooperative with, the state (Brook and Frolic 1997: 8, 12–13; Ding 2000: 115–29). This reflects joint recognition of shared goals.

The sociological definition is modified by scholars who argue that the state-led civil society argument ignores state weakness and the ability of non-state organizations to influence policy-making processes while pursuing the interests of their own members (Saich 2000: 125; Tong 2005: 186). As the state increasingly turns to social organizations to take on additional responsibilities, it withdraws from the political space it once dominated (see Figure 1.2). In the process, non-state actors search for opportunities to embed themselves within the state, and to influence it, while drawing on the state's resources. The state–civil society relationship is a "negotiated," symbiotic one, with non-state actors and the state benefiting from the interactions.

The result is an important change in the state–society relationship whereby Chinese NGOs are expanding their roles and increasing their independence from the state, even as the state grows increasingly dependent on NGOs. Nor is this a process that can be reversed, as NGOs become increasingly unlikely to return willingly to state domination.

The rapid growth of these formal and informal organizations and networks leads us to ask several questions about the nature of interactions between social organizations and the state. How do these organizations engage the state and seek to influence it in the sphere of social service provision? To what extent do these organizations function within the framework of the law, and to what extent do they resort to extra-legal means? What relationships have they established with other social organizations and networks working either in the same sector or in different sectors? To what extent is there collaboration and coordination between labor, business, social service organizations, religious groups, and intellectuals? Finally, how has the state responded to the increasing number of social organizations? How has the state sought to regulate and institutionalize the role and status of these organizations, and what have been the consequences of these efforts?

The implications of state–NGO interactions for social service provision in China

The last theme addressed in this volume returns to the broader questions raised at the outset of this chapter. What are the long-term implications for state–society relations of the state's ongoing efforts to address the social welfare needs of its population? As we noted earlier, China's reforms have created a host of social problems that have left many in a more vulnerable position than before the reforms began. At the same time, the state has cut back on many services offered under the old work unit-based system, and relied increasingly on market mechanisms, social organizations, families, and individuals to provide those services. NGOs are thus part of a broader effort to put in place a more comprehensive social welfare system to replace the "iron rice bowl" of the pre-reform years. The

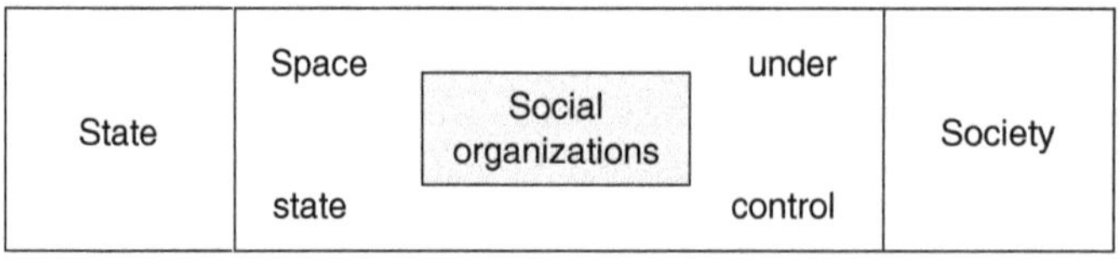

Figure 1.2 NGOs take over tasks in the public sphere that once were a state responsibility.

question is, how well is this supposed "partnership" between the state and NGOs working? Are NGOs playing a role that complements and enhances the state's social programs?

Chapter summary

This volume starts with a theoretical chapter by Shieh (Chapter 2) outlining a framework for understanding the state–social organization interactions in this volume. The remaining chapters are organized according to the crisis/non-crisis distinction discussed earlier. The non-crisis cases (Keyser, Chapter 3; Zhang and Smith, Chapter 4; and Hildebrandt and Turner, Chapter 5) come first, followed by the crisis cases (Laliberté, Chapter 6; Schwartz, Chapter 7; and Kaufman, Chapter 8). The volume ends with a concluding chapter summarizing what we learn about our organizing themes and questions from these cases.

Chapter 2 (by Shieh) outlines an approach to analyzing state–society interactions that differs from previous approaches such as corporatism and civil society. Unlike these frameworks, which tend to simplify the dynamic, multifaceted nature of state–society relations in China, this approach examines state–society interactions through three modes: regulation, negotiation, and societalization. Regulation refers to the mode in which the state controls and manages NGOs involved in the provision of social services. Negotiation is the mode in which state and NGOs interact with one another in the provision of social services. Societalization refers to the mode whereby NGOs provide social services through initiatives in which the state is not an active partner.

Shieh finds that while the regulation of NGOs has grown more systematic and comprehensive over time, it is restrictive and has not been effective in regulating a rapidly growing NGO community. Instead, regulation has deterred many NGOs from registering and driven them into an informal sector where they operate as businesses or as unregistered NGOs. This trend has in turn made the other two modes – negotiation and societalization – more important. Of the two, negotiation has emerged as the more important as NGOs seek out ties with state and quasi-state organizations in an effort to be effective in a restrictive regulatory environment. There is substantial evidence that NGOs that negotiate good relationships with the state can have greater influence on and autonomy from the state. The societalization mode, however, is becoming increasingly important. Signs of societalization can be found in the growth of unregistered NGOs, of social and virtual networks among NGOs, of funding from non-governmental and international sources, and of media coverage of NGOs. Ultimately, though, the societalization mode is constrained by a restrictive regulatory environment and lack of funding and other resources for many grassroots NGOs without ties to the state.

Starting off the non-crisis section is Keyser's chapter, which examines the range of responses by the state and NGOs, both international and domestic, in addressing the needs of one group of at-risk children: orphans. She finds that significant gaps in providing for the needs of orphans have appeared during the reform period, and that a number of quasi-state, non-state, and international organizations have stepped in to try to fill these gaps, particularly since the mid-1990s, when the problem of orphan care was highlighted in a BBC documentary on state orphanages in China. The result is a patchwork of arrangements ranging from negotiated relationships between state orphanages or quasi-state organizations and NGOs at the local level, to unregistered international non-governmental organizations (INGOs) and NGOs working on their own while avoiding the state. The challenge of addressing the needs of orphans has been exacerbated by a regulatory environment that is incomplete, restrictive, and ambiguous. This environment has made it difficult not only for central and local state agencies to coordinate on identifying and addressing the needs of orphans, but also for domestic and international NGOs working on child welfare issues to register, raise funds, and operate. While some of these NGOs have been able to negotiate mutually beneficial arrangements with state agencies such as state orphanages, or quasi-state organizations and GONGOs such as the China Charity Foundation, others operate more or less independently of the state, seeking ways to remain viable and effective while maintaining their autonomy in a restrictive and ambiguous legal and political environment.

Chapter 4, by Hong Zhang and Marsha Smith, looks at the response by the state and NGOs to migrant labor issues in the Pearl River Delta area. Focusing on three case studies, they show how migrant labor NGOs, which emerged as early as the mid-1990s, play a valuable role in providing a wide range of services, including legal aid and advocacy, to a group of workers who were experiencing widespread abuses and problems in the workplace, yet lacked representation in official labor unions. In this sense, NGOs filled a void created by marketizing forces and a retreating state. Zhang and Smith show how recent international and domestic trends have created a more welcoming environment for migrant labor NGOs. Internationally, globalization has opened up new sources of international assistance, and domestically, Hu Jintao's administration has issued new laws to protect the legal rights of migrant workers. At the local level, state agencies recognize the need to address the needs of migrant workers, and have shown a willingness to work with NGOs to provide needed services. But the local state has also clamped down on the activities of NGOs when they move from providing specific services to advocating for more expansive legal rights for migrant workers. Zhang and Smith conclude that migrant labor NGOs are in a precarious situation, given the political sensitivity of their work and legal and financial constraints that raise questions about their capacity and sustainability in the long term. Because of their political sensitivity, many of these NGOs are either registered as businesses, or unregistered, and many have a difficult time finding qualified professionals and academics who can assist them. And while they have attracted considerable funding and help from international organizations and businesses, their heavy dependence on international funds raises questions about their long-term sustainability.

The final chapter in the non-crisis section, Chapter 5 by Timothy Hildebrandt and Jennifer L. Turner, examines the response by the state and NGOs to environmental problems. They note that environmental NGOs (ENGOs) are among the most active and assertive in the NGO community. Compared with many other NGO sectors, they have been given greater political space by the central government, which has made environmental protection a national priority and has welcomed the environmental assistance of other governments, international organizations, and both international and domestic NGOs. ENGOs have used that space to deliver a range of social services that child welfare and migrant labor NGOs can only dream about. These include monitoring the environment through partnerships with local government, communities, and other NGOs; participating in national and local debates over legal and policy changes; partnering with businesses on environmental initiatives; and working with the media and other NGOs to publicize environmental problems. One of the more dramatic and public examples was the formation in 2005 of the Green River Network, consisting of a number of ENGOs, which worked with the media to publicize the problems associated with the Nu River dam project.

But, as with other NGOs examined in this volume, ENGO cooperation with the state has definite limits, particularly at the local level. As Hildebrandt and Turner illustrate, ENGOs face problems with registration, monitoring, and harassment from the state when NGO efforts encroach on local state interests such as economic development. These constraints are apparent even in provinces known for being more open to ENGOs, such as Yunnan. In this political environment, informal ties with the government are still regarded by many NGOs as more important than being legally registered. In addition to these obstacles, ENGOs cite other common challenges encountered by other NGOs, such as funding and capacity building. Like many of the NGOs discussed in this volume, ENGOs rely heavily on international funding, owing to the lack of a philanthropic culture, and government policies restricting fundraising by non-governmental organizations. Hildebrandt and Turner argue that this dependence on international funding is largely negative because ENGOs have now reached the stage where they need to build capacity to sustain themselves in the long run. While project-based funding provided start-up funds for many ENGOs, it has not served their mission of building a sustainable organization.

The crisis section starts with André Laliberté's discussion of Buddhist philanthropic organizations (Chapter 6). While many of these organizations are domestic, Laliberté also explores cooperative relations between domestic and non-mainland organizations. He does so with a focus on the Taiwan-based Tzu Chi foundation, a Buddhist organization that was first encouraged by both China's domestic and central government officials to provide social services support in response to the 1991 Yangtze River flood crisis.

Laliberté notes that with the permission of the avowedly secular communist state, Buddhist organizations have steadily increased their social service provision roles. However, these organizations remain highly constrained by the state and enjoy little political space in which to agitate for greater autonomy to provide services. Laliberté notes that, recognizing their own limited capacity and the constraints of the state, these organizations are not striving to achieve greater autonomy to drive change.

Laliberté distinguishes between constrained freedoms at the central government level and relative autonomy at the local government level. He concludes that while local autonomy is growing, owing to shared interests between local governments and Buddhist associations, there is as yet no evidence of Buddhist organizations taking advantage to increase their social service provision role vis-à-vis the state.

Jonathan Schwartz also explores the impact of crises on state–civil society social service provision. Focusing on the 2003 SARS crisis, Schwartz opens by noting that the state was unprepared to respond to a nationwide infectious disease outbreak. In response to SARS, the state both invested tremendous resources in strengthening its public health emergency response capacity and drew on non-state actors for additional assistance. Among those actors participating in SARS prevention and control were traditional NGOs (which provided limited assistance) as well as residence committees (RCs).

Schwartz suggests that while RCs are not traditional NGOs, neither can they be considered wholly government entities. He explores the nature and role of RCs in combination with the state, arguing that the RCs were key contributors to China's effective SARS response, reflecting a growing recognition by the state of the need for cooperation between state and non-state actors in social service provision.

Joan Kaufman's contribution (Chapter 8) is the last of the crisis-related chapters. She explores the role played by civil society organizations in providing social services in the face of the HIV/AIDS crisis. This chapter views a combination of the SARS outbreak and the rapid spread of HIV/AIDS as constituting a health care crisis that has forced the state to identify new solutions to a growing challenge after 2003. Recognizing its lack of capacity to respond to HIV/AIDS, the government at both central and local levels has turned to a variety of civil society organizations – including GONGOs, domestic and international NGOs – for assistance.

Kaufman argues that the state recognizes that because of the stigma attached to HIV/AIDS, NGOs have greater success in reaching out to and assisting infected people. As with Laliberté's discussion of Buddhist organizations, Kaufman notes the difference in the relationship between the state and social organizations at the central level and at the local level of government. Where Laliberté argues that Buddhist organizations have greater autonomy of action at the local level, Kaufman notes that greater autonomy is mostly supported by the central government level, though with increasingly pragmatic local governments expanding the political space available to these social service organizations.

In the concluding chapter, we synthesize the lessons that may be derived from these chapters, focusing in particular on the themes and questions raised in this introductory chapter. We also explore additional motifs that run through these chapters and deserve emphasis, ending with a discussion of what this volume says about the future of state–society relations in China.

Notes

1 In China, the terms "NGOs," "CSOs," and "non-profit organizations (NPOs)" are often used interchangeably. We follow the same convention but have chosen to use the term "NGO" throughout the book to be consistent.

2 See Wexler *et al.* (2006: 9–10) for a discussion of the fine line between "social service delivery" and "advocacy" in China.
3 For a discussion, see McCormick *et al.* (1992: 187–8).
4 This definition corresponds closely to international and Chinese definitions of NGOs. Ma observes that international definitions of NGOs have been influential in China since the World Conference for Women in Beijing in 1995 and have been increasingly accepted among Chinese NGO leaders and scholars. They have influenced the official Chinese definition of SOs and non-profit organizations (NPOs).
5 However, since the mid-1990s, staff members of all mass organizations have no longer had civil servant status, which is now reserved for employees of government agencies (Ma 2004: 100).
6 Ma (2004) refers to CNEUs as non-governmental, non-commercial enterprises (NGNCEs).
7 One reason many NGOs register as businesses is that they cannot find a governmental unit or GONGO to sponsor them.
8 Dittmer and Hurst (2002/2003) suggest that civil society is typically defined in an unrealistic liberal fashion that is more relevant to US realities than to those of Asia. In observing US society, De Tocqueville described civil organizations as central to establishing a democracy. By contrast, Habermas views democracy as *preceding*, and necessary to, the establishing of civil society.
9 Ma (2004: 96, 101) uses the case study of one of China's best-known NGOs, the China Youth Development Foundation (CYDF), to make this point. The CYDF, also known as the Hope Project, was originally a spin-off of a mass organization, the Chinese Communist Youth League (CCYL), yet was able to use its connections within the CCYL to benefit the NGO's influence and effectiveness.
10 According to Fewsmith (2001), to ascend to the WTO China was required to accept a range of conditions that forced open its domestic markets to international competition. The near- to middle-term likelihood of increased social inequality (both within and among regions) and job losses, closed factories, and failed farms, resulting in social unrest, was anticipated, and efforts were made to prepare Chinese society in advance.
11 In cases such as the Henan AIDS scandal, local governments were accused of stifling or repressing social organizations in ways that contravened central regulations. See the Human Rights Watch report (Davis 2005).

References

"Blurred Law May Be Better Than None" (2004) *China Development Brief* (10 June). Online, available at: www.chinadevelopmentbrief.org (accessed 28 July 2008).

Brooks, T. and Frolic, M. (eds.) (1997) *Civil Society in China*, New York: M. E. Sharpe.

Cooper, C. (2006) "'This Is Our Way In': The Civil Society of Environmental NGOs in Southwest China," *Government and Opposition* 41 (1): 109–36.

Croll, E. (1999) "Social Welfare Reform: Trends and Tensions," *China Quarterly* 159: 684–99.

Davis, S. (2005) "Restrictions on AIDS Activists in China," *Human Rights Watch* 17 (5): 1–57.

Dickson, B. (2003) *Red Capitalists in China: The Party, Private Entrepreneurs, and the Prospects*, New York: Cambridge University Press.

Ding, Y. (2000) "The Conceptual Evolution of Democracy in Intellectual Circles' Rethinking of State and Society," in S. Zhao (ed.) *China and Democracy*, London: Routledge.

Di Palma, G. (1991) "Liberalization and Democratization in the Soviet Union and Eastern Europe," *World Politics*, 44 (1): 49–60.

Dittmer, L. and Hurst, W. (2002/2003) "Analysis in Limbo: Contemporary Chinese Politics amid the Maturation of Reform," *Issues and Studies* 38 (4)/39 (1): 11–48.

Fewsmith, J. (2001) "The Political and Social Implications of China's Ascension to the WTO," *China Quarterly* 167: 573–91.

Fidler, D. (2003) "SARS: Political Pathology of the First Post-Westphalian Pathogen," *Journal of Law, Medicine and Ethics* 31 (4): 485–505.

Foster, K. W. (2002) "Embedded within the Bureaucracy: Business Associations in Yantai," *China Journal* 47: 41–65.

Gallagher, M. E. (2004) "China: The Limits of Civil Society in a Late Leninist State," in M. Alagappa (ed.) *Civil Society and Political Change in Asia*, Stanford, CA: Stanford University Press.

Gellner, E. (1994) *Conditions of Liberty*, London: Hamish Hamilton. Online, available at: www.ids.ac.uk/ids/civsoc/final/china/chi1.html (accessed 20 February 2004).

Goertz, G. and Diehl, P. (2000) *War and Peace in International Rivalry*, Ann Arbor: University of Michigan Press.

Gu, E. and Zhang, J. (2006) "Health Care Regime Change in Urban China: Unmanaged Marketization and Reluctant Privatization," *Pacific Affairs* 79 (1): 49–71.

Howell, J. (2004) "New Directions in Civil Society: Organizing around Marginalized Interests," in J. Howell (ed.) *Governance in China*, Lanham, MD: Rowman & Littlefield.

Kennedy, S. (2005) *The Business of Lobbying in China*, Cambridge, MA: Harvard University Press.

Krasner, S. (1985) *Structural Conflict*, Berkeley: University of California Press.

Lardy, N. (2002/2003) "Evaluating Economic Indicators in Post-WTO China," *Issues and Studies* 38 (4)/39 (1): 249–68.

Lindenberg, M. (1990) "World Economic Cycles and Central American Political Instability," *World Politics* 42 (3): 397–421.

Ma, Q. (2004) *Non-governmental Organizations in Contemporary China: Paving the Way to Civil Society?* London: Routledge.

McCormick, B. L., Su, S., and Xiao, X. (1992) "The 1989 Democracy Movement: A Review of the Prospects for Civil Society in China," *Pacific Affairs* 65 (2) (Summer): 182–202.

McFaul, M. (2002) "The Fourth Wave of Democracy and Dictatorship: Noncooperative Transitions in the Post-communist World," *World Politics* 54 (January): 212–44.

Meng, Y. (2002) "New Roles of NPOs and Partnership with Government and Business," NGO Research Center, Tsinghua University (Zhongguo NGO Wubai Jia – *500 NGOS in China*), United Nations Centre for Regional Development.

Misztal, B. A. (2001) "Civil Society: A Signifier of Plurality and Sense of Wholeness," in *The Blackwell Companion to Social Theory*, Oxford: Blackwell.

Pearson, M. (1997) *China's New Business Elite: The Political Consequences of Economic Reform*, Berkeley: University of California Press.

Saich, T. (2000) "Negotiating the State: The Development of Social Organizations in China," *China Quarterly* 161: 123–41.

Schwartz, J. (2004) "Environmental NGOs in China: Roles and Limits," *Pacific Affairs* 77 (1): 28–48.

Shigetomi, S. (2002) "The State and NGOs: Issues and Analytical Framework," in S. Shigetomi (ed.) *The State and NGOs: Perspective from Asia*, Singapore: Institute of Southeast Asian Studies.

Solinger, D. (2005) "Path Dependency Reexamined: Chinese Welfare Policy in the Transition to Unemployment," *Comparative Politics* 38 (1): 83–101.

Stern, E. K. (1999) *Crisis Decision Making: A Cognitive-Institutional Approach*, Stockholm: Stockholm University Press.

Strecker-Downs, E. and Saunders, P. C. (1998/1999) "Legitimacy and the Limits of Nationalism: China and the Diaoyu Islands," *International Security* 23 (3): 5–8.

Tong, Y. (1994) "State, Society and Political Change in China and Hungary," *Comparative Politics* 26 (3): 333–53.

—— (2005) "Environmental Movements in Transitional Societies: A Comparative Study of Taiwan and China," *Comparative Politics* 37 (2): 167–88.

Turner, J. (2004) "Small Government, Big and Green Society," *Harvard Asia Quarterly* 8 (2).

Wang, M. (2002) "NGOs in China," in NGO Research Center, Tsinghua University (ed.) *Zhongguo NGOs Wubai Jia* [500 NGOs in China], United Nations Centre for Regional Development.

Wang, M. and Gu, L. (2000) "Zhongguo NGO Gaikuang" [The General Situation of NGOs in China], in M. Wang (ed.) *Zhongguo NGO Yanjiu-yi ge'an weizhu* [Research on China's NGOs: With a Focus on Case Studies], United Nations Centre for Regional Development.

Wang, S. and Sun, B. (2002) "Zhongguo Minjian Zuzhi Fazhan Gaikuang" [Introduction to the Development of Civil Organizations], in K. Yu *et al.* (eds.) *Zhongguo Gongmin Shehuide Xingqi Yu Zhilide Dianqian* [The Emergence of Civil Society and Its Significance to Governance in Reform China], Beijing: Social Science Documents Press.

Wank, D. (1995) "Civil Society in Communist China: Private Business and Political Alliance," in J. A. Hall (ed.) *Civil Society: Theory, History, Comparison*, Cambridge: Polity Press.

Wexler, R., Ying, Y., and Young, N. (2006) "NGO advocacy in China: A Special Report from China Development Brief," *China Development Brief*. Online, available at www.chinadevelopmentbrief.org (accessed 23 November 2007).

White, G. (1996) "The Dynamics of Civil Society in Post-Mao China," in B. Hook (ed.) *The Individual and the State in China*, Oxford: Clarendon Press.

White, G., Howell, J., and Shang, X. (1996) *In Search of Civil Society: Market Reform and Social Change in Contemporary China*, Oxford: Clarendon Press.

Wiktorowicz, Q. (2000) "Civil Society as Social Control: State Power in Jordan," *Comparative Politics* 33 (1): 43–61.

Wong, L. (1994) "Privatization of Social Welfare in Post-Mao China," *Asian Survey* 34 (4): 307–25.

Yu, K. (2003) *The Emerging of Chinese Civil Society and Its Significance to Governance in Rural China* (China Center for Comparative Politics and Economics of the Translation Bureau).

Zhao, X. (2000) "Guanyu Beijing Huabao NGO de Diaocha Fenxi" [An analysis of environmental NGOs in Beijing], in M. Wang (ed.) *Zhongguo NGO Yanjiu* [Research on China's NGOs], United Nations Centre for Regional Development Research Report Series, 38.

Zhong, K. (2007) "Crisis Management in China," *China Security* (Winter): 90–109.

2 Beyond corporatism and civil society

Three modes of state–NGO interaction in China

Shawn Shieh

Introduction

The Tiananmen Square protests of 1989, and the subsequent "velvet revolutions" in the former Soviet Union and Eastern Europe, touched off a lively debate among China scholars about the potential for civil society in China. Since then, much has happened to dampen the initial euphoria about China's emerging civil society. Reaping the benefits of a rapidly growing economy, the Chinese state has grown stronger and moved to co-opt emerging social interests such as private entrepreneurs and business and professional associations. The state has also clamped down on what it views as more independent and threatening forms of association, such as the Democracy Party in 1998 and Falun Gong in 1999. At the same time, social organizations of all kinds – what we choose in this volume to call NGOs – continue to proliferate like ivy around the sprawling trellis of the state bureaucracy. Some of these NGOs have been co-opted by the state, some have been closed down or banned, but many continue to operate in that political space between cooptation and repression. This chapter explores the different ways in which the state and NGOs have interacted over the past few decades, and what these interactions tell us about the prospects for civil society in China.

The aim of this chapter is to sketch out an alternative framework to the corporatist and civil society frameworks that have been dominant in the literature. This framework views the state–NGO relationship through three important modes of interaction: regulation, negotiation, and societalization. The chapter starts by discussing the uses and shortcomings of existing frameworks, and the advantages of focusing on modes of interaction as an alternative framework for understanding state–society relations in China. It then looks at how these modes capture important patterns of interaction taking place between the Chinese state and society, and how these patterns have changed over the reform period, drawing from case studies of NGOs both in this volume and elsewhere. The conclusion discusses what this analysis can tell us about the evolution of state–society relations in China.

Modes of state–society interaction: an alternative framework

Much of the discussion of state–NGO relations in China has been viewed through theoretical frameworks such as corporatism and civil society, or variations thereof such as Margaret Pearson's (1997) "socialist corporatism," Ru and Ortolano's (2008) "agency corporatism," Baogang He's (1997) "semi-civil society," or Michael Frolic's (1997) "state-led civil society."[1] Yet despite these efforts, we believe state–NGO relations in China are becoming too complex and dynamic to be captured by any one of these frameworks. As the chapters in this volume and other case studies show, state–NGO relationships do not fit into any single pattern; they assume different forms and dynamics across sectors and regions. Another problem with these frameworks is that they tend to focus on one particular mode of interaction, to the neglect of other modes.[2] State corporatism, for example, emphasizes the mode of control, coordination, and regulation by a domineering state over compliant social actors, while societal corporatism focuses on the mode of negotiation between state and social actors that are relatively equal in power. The civil society approach, on the other hand, emphasizes the efforts of social actors in confronting and expanding their autonomy relative to the state.

We believe that a more dynamic, interactive, and multidimensional framework of state–NGO relations would examine all of these modes: regulation, negotiation, and what we call societalization. Regulation refers to formal state initiatives and mechanisms designed to control and manage social organizations involved in the provision of social services. Negotiation refers to consensual, and generally more informal, interactions between state and social actors in the provision of services. These interactions may be over areas of conflict or cooperation and may be initiated by either the state or social actor, but involve the active, voluntary participation of both sides. Finally, societalization refers to a mode whereby NGOs provide social services through initiatives in which the state is not a partner. The state may recognize and tolerate these initiatives, but is not directly involved in this mode. In contrast to the other two modes, societalization signifies greater distance from the state. It also signifies greater ownership and moral autonomy on the part of NGOs over their initiatives, though not necessarily institutional autonomy. As we explain below, institutional autonomy is less a function of distance from the state, and more a function of having the resources and influence to resist state interference. For Chinese NGOs, resources and influence often come about not because they are removed from the state, but because they enjoy close ties with the state.

A few caveats are in order about this framework. These modes are analytical lenses meant to capture important differences in state–society interactions. In reality, though, many NGOs engage in multiple modes to varying degrees. For example, some NGOs may work closely with government agencies in carrying out social service programs. Other NGOs may negotiate with a public institution such as a university for office space, but undertake most of their activities without any help from the state and its affiliated units. Still other NGOs may have little or no support from units of the state. To put it another way, these modes should not be seen as mutually exclusive; indeed, a central assumption of our framework is that they should be viewed as overlapping and interrelated. There is no clear-cut boundary between these modes since they are meant to capture the state–NGO interaction over a period of time. Some forms of societalization may at some later stage involve negotiation with state agencies or lead to regulation. This dynamic occurs in cases where NGOs that worked under the radar become so successful or assertive that they begin to draw the attention of local officials.[3] Conversely, negotiation may lead later to societalization. Also, NGOs often engage in more than one mode, for example negotiating with local government agencies while at the same time pursuing societalization strategies such as networking with other NGOs and international foundations that enhance the NGO's outreach and capacity.

Regulation: state control and management over NGOs

The Chinese state's efforts to regulate NGOs involved in social service provision has taken different forms during the reform period. In her study of NGOs in China, Qiusha Ma (2004: 62–3) divides post-1978 policy toward social organizations (SOs) into two stages. In the first stage, from 1978 to 1989, the government relaxed its policy by allowing associations to form outside of the state system. During this period, the creation of new SOs went largely unregulated, as any government bureau or SO could approve new organizations and place them under its supervision (Ma 2004: 62).

This state of affairs changed in 1989 around the time of the Tiananmen Square protests. During that year, the Division of Social Organizations was created in the Ministry of Civil Affairs (MOCA) to supervise NGO activities, and various regulations concerning NGO management began to be issued. During this second stage, from 1989 to the present, the government put in place a more comprehensive system for regulating NGOs. A special meeting of the Politburo Standing Committee in 1996 to discuss strengthening NGO management resulted in a series of revised regulations that came into effect in 1998. These included the Regulations for Registration and Management of Social Organizations (*shehui tuanti guanli tiaoli*) and Temporary Regulations for Registration and Management of Civil, Non-enterprise Units (CNEUs) (*minban feiqiye danwei dengji guanli zanxing tiaoli*). In 2004, the Regulations on the Management of Foundations (*jijinhui guanli tiaoli*) came into effect.[4] As is discussed in Chapter 1, SOs, CNEUs, and foundations all belong in the NGO category.

These regulations on paper contain many elements consistent with the state corporatist framework. For example, the regulations for SOs and CNEUs just mentioned call for a monopoly of representation in any one sector and geographical area by stating that SOs can be denied approval if "in the same administrative area, there is already a social organization active in the same or similar area of work."[5] These regulations also ban the establishment of regional chapters, although the SO regulations allow branch chapters as long as they are in the same administrative area.[6] The regulations also require that national SOs register with the national MOCA while local SOs register with the civil affairs bureau in that area. As Saich (2000: 132) explains, this stipulation makes it difficult for SOs to enroll members from different areas and thus develop national or regional representation.

In addition, as we discuss in more detail below, both SOs and CNEUs must find a professional supervising unit that is willing to sponsor and supervise their activities.

In addition to formal laws and regulations, the Chinese state also regulates NGOs through its formidable bureaucratic apparatus. This apparatus is divided into four main categories: Party–government agencies (*dangzheng jiguan*), public institutions (*shiye danwei*), social organizations (*shehui tuanti*),[7] and state-owned enterprises (*guoying qiye*). The Party–government agencies form the first tier of the Party-state bureaucracy and are the organizations with the power to carry out and enforce laws and regulations. Social organizations and public institutions make up an extensive network of second-tier organizations created by the Party-state to function as "transmission belts" linking the state and society. During the Maoist period, social organizations such as the people's organizations, and mass organizations such as village/neighborhood committees, were developed to encourage popular participation along Party-sanctioned lines, while public institutions (*shiye danwei*) were created to provide public services to society in the areas of education, science and technology, culture, health, and other areas (World Bank 2005).

During the reform period, many NGOs were created or sponsored by these bureaucratic organizations, which became responsible for their supervision. These government-organized NGOs (GONGOs) have an interesting dual character. On the one hand, one can see them as proto-forms of civil society, with greater autonomy from the state than the Maoist-era SOs.[8] On the other, they can be seen as another addition to the bureaucratic structure, serving as part of the state's regulatory apparatus.[9] As we shall see, these GONGOs can and do play a role in supervising other NGOs. The same can be said for other organizations that take on a hybrid character, for example mass organizations such as neighborhood committees, community organizations (*shequ*), and village committees. These belong to the above category of social organizations that were part of the state, but during the 1990s certain reforms gave them more autonomy and ability to represent the interests of their members.[10]

The 1998 regulations for registering SOs and CNEUs discussed on p. 24 formalized the supervisory role of these bureaucratic and quasi-bureaucratic organizations by requiring any NGO that wanted to register with the MOCA to be sponsored by a professional supervising unit (*yewu zhuguan danwei*) in the same field and within the same locality. The supervising unit will generally come from one of the four categories of bureaucratic organizations. However, it can also be a GONGO that is authorized or entrusted to be a supervising unit (Ge 2003). Thus, the supervising agency of a women's legal aid NGO in Beijing might be the Beijing Women's Federation, which is a Party-created mass organization, or a GONGO created by the Women's Federation.

This registration requirement means that every registered NGO actually comes under what the Chinese call the "dual supervision" of the MOCA and a professional supervising unit. Under this arrangement, the supervising unit assumes responsibility for the NGO's behavior. The rationale for such a requirement is that the MOCA would not be able to supervise all of these registered NGOs, and thus "dual supervision" enables the supervising unit to play that role.[11]

The regulatory structure I have described of course applies only to those NGOs that choose to register legally as SOs or CNEUs. In reality, a growing number of NGOs are choosing not to register with the MOCA. In general, these NGOs are not as tightly regulated as their MOCA-registered counterparts, although the degree of regulation for this population of NGOs varies, as Figure 1.1 shows.

On the more regulated end, one finds a growing number of NGOs that are registered as secondary (*ciji* or *erji*) organizations "affiliated with" (*guakao*) a bureaucratic or quasi-bureaucratic organization. This organization provides the NGO with office space, personnel, funds, and legitimacy (Ru and Ortolano 2008: 50). Well-known NGOs such as the Beijing University Women's Legal Aid Center (affiliated with Beijing University's law department) and the Center for Legal Aid to Pollution Victims (affiliated with the University of Politics and Law) operate under this arrangement. These "affiliated" NGOs do not come under MOCA supervision or regulations, but they are subject to informal regulation from their "affiliated" organization, which may intervene in the selection of NGO leaders and staff.[12]

Somewhat less regulated are the many NGOs that register as businesses with the Industrial and Commercial Bureau. A 2005 source cites a rough estimate of 100,000–200,000 NGOs registered as businesses.[13] Many NGOs choose to register as a business to avoid the regulatory hassles of registering as a legal SO or CNEU. NGOs that register as businesses do not have to find a professional supervising unit, nor do they have to worry about whether their area of interest overlaps with that of an existing NGO. The main regulatory drawback to registering as a business is that the NGO has to pay taxes.

At the least regulated end, one finds NGOs that are neither affiliated with the bureaucracy nor registered as businesses. It is unclear just how many of these unregistered NGOs there are in China. Wang Ming of Tsinghua's NGO Research Center provides what he calls a "conservative estimate" of between 2.5 and 2.7 million. Of this number, around 150,000 are NGOs registered as businesses; another 400,000 are urban community organizations (*shequ neide minjian zuzhi*). But the majority, around 1.7 million strong, are grassroots NGOs in rural areas (Wang 2007: 99).

Regulation can also take the form of more extralegal and repressive measures such as the use of Party cells, shutting down NGOs, or declaring them illegal. Saich (2000: 132–3) discusses some of these measures, including an internal Party circular calling for the establishment or strengthening of Party cells in all SOs. Other NGOs have been declared illegal because of the nature of their activities. After the 1989 Regulations for SOs came out, the MOCA investigated and reorganized SOs, merging a number of SOs with similar objectives, and shutting down many other "illegal" NGOs. Chapters 4 and 5 both give examples of NGOs and activists who were punished by local authorities for their activities.

This examination of the NGO regulatory system shows that it has become more comprehensive and systematic over time, particularly since the late 1990s.

The question is, how effective has this regulatory system been? If the intent of such a system is to set a high bar for NGOs to be legally registered, create an environment that makes it difficult for NGOs to operate without political interference and raise funds, and give preferential treatment to NGOs with close ties with the state, then the regulatory system has been effective. However, if the intent has been to regulate the growth of NGOs and their activities and bring newer, more independent NGOs into the unified regulatory system presided over by the MOCA, then the system has been less than effective. The regulatory system, and particularly the "dual supervision" rule, has been more a source of frustration for grassroots NGOs than it has been a deterrent. Many have chosen not to register with the MOCA because they either do not want to be restricted by a supervising unit or cannot find a supervising unit willing to take on that responsibility (Ma 2004: 65; Saich 2000: 130; Ru and Ortolano 2008). Organizations rejected by a unit that is seen as the authoritative professional unit for their field find it difficult to get another sponsor. These obstacles have led NGOs to find other strategies for setting up shop.

Why has this corporatist-type effort not succeeded? One reason is lack of resources; the MOCA just does not have the staff needed to supervise these NGOs. Another has to do with the fragmented nature of the authoritarian state. Much of the supervisory responsibility over NGOs has fallen to a bewildering variety of bureaucratic and quasi-bureaucratic organizations at different levels of government with their own interests and agendas.[14] Lieberthal's (1992) earlier insights into the nature of China's "fragmented authoritarian" system are still relevant in describing the NGO regulatory system. This is a system in which administrative resources and mechanisms and personal ties play a greater role than laws in shaping the negotiating environment. It is a system that on the one hand allows a great deal of flexibility in terms of how policies and laws are implemented, but on the other hand can be arbitrary and capricious. In other words, behavior in this system is guided more by administrative rank and control over resources, and the fear of state reprisal, than by rules.

While China's reforms have made progress toward establishing the rule of law, the legal and regulatory system governing NGOs is still very rudimentary, contradictory, and not well understood or enforced. More importantly, this fragmented authoritarian structure has allowed NGOs to fill the political space within the interstices of the Chinese bureaucratic apparatus, hemmed in on all sides by the bureaucracy but watched carefully by no one particular state agency. Within this bureaucratic structure occur the other modes of state–society interaction, to which we now turn our attention.

Negotiation: embedded autonomy within a fragmented authoritarian state

The discussion of the regulatory mode in the previous section makes it clear that any interactions between the state and NGO occur in an environment in which the state is by far the stronger party, and where the legal position of NGOs is tenuous and can be overruled by administrative fiat. In other words, these interactions occur in what is largely a state corporatist arrangement. Nevertheless, the regulatory mode does not capture much of the actual negotiations that go on between Party or state agencies and NGOs as the latter jockey for survival, resources, and influence. This section looks at why and when negotiations take place, strategies that NGOs use in negotiations, and conditions that shape an NGO's ability to negotiate.

Negotiation between the state and NGOs has become an important mode as NGOs have blossomed and sought various strategies for gaining a foothold and greater influence in society. Over time, and particularly in the past decade, NGOs have been able to carve out greater autonomy from the state while also maintaining ties with various party organizations and state agencies. This balancing act is similar to Peter Evans' (1995) concept of "embedded autonomy," a term that describes how a developmental state's autonomy was a result not only of its ability to remain independent of powerful business interests, but also of its ability to stay connected with the business community.[15]

Why do negotiations occur and what to do they occur over?

Negotiations between the state and NGOs occur for a variety of reasons and at different stages of an NGO's existence. Negotiations happen because the state cannot completely impose its will on NGOs and must allow NGOs some latitude in their operations to provide social services that the state is either unwilling or unable to provide. The state needs NGOs, just as NGOs need the state. Examples of this symbiotic relationship at the local level can be found in many of the chapters in this volume. Chapter 8, for example, reveals that the growth of the AIDS epidemic in China led centers for disease control in some localities to form partnerships with NGOs to address the epidemic. Chapter 7 also provides some examples of collaboration between NGOs and the Chinese government in addressing SARS. At the central level, Chinese leaders also recognize the need for state–NGO cooperation. At the most recent Party Congress, the seventeenth, Hu Jintao's report mentioned several times the important role of non-governmental organizations in providing services in the education and health sectors. This shared enterprise gives NGOs room to maneuver and negotiate with the state to stay relevant and increase their influence. Not surprisingly, negotiations between NGOs and the state occur in a range of areas: NGO efforts to get an administrative sponsor or affiliation; obtaining resources to strengthen their capacity to deliver services or engage in advocacy; increasing their autonomy and influence; and influencing policy.

One important area of negotiation occurs when the NGO is being established and seeks a state sponsor. As we have discussed, getting a supervising unit that will agree to be responsible for that NGO can be difficult, and NGOs engage in negotiations with various agencies or institutions over their willingness to serve as a supervising unit.[16]

Negotiations also take place if NGOs decide not to register with the MOCA and instead look to affiliate with a state agency or institution, or a legally registered SO, as a secondary organization. The well-known Beijing University Women's Legal Aid Center was established in 1995 under this arrangement. Initially, the center was associated with a law office in Beijing, but because of objections from the Beijing City Legal Commission was forced to change its affiliation. After about six months of negotiation, the center was able to find a new sponsor in the Beijing University Law Institute, a public institution under the Ministry of Education, and became a secondary organization within that institute (Wang 2000: 196).

Another important area of negotiation occurs over resources that provide NGOs with a measure of autonomy and influence. Many NGOs in China face shortages of funds, personnel, and office space and their ability to acquire resources can depend on negotiations with units of the state. Negotiations occur and depend heavily either on Party or state organizations or on international organizations. He (2007) cites a Tsinghua University survey that highlights this dependence. The survey shows that about 47 percent of SOs received office space from their supervising units, and about 50 percent of their revenue came from government funding and subsidies. During the 1990s, funding and other forms of support were critical in starting up some well-known NGOs. Rural Women Knowing All (RWKA), a Beijing-based NGO devoted to helping rural women, was started with an initial investment of 60,000 yuan by the Women's Federation, which also assigned one of the editors of its publication *China Women News* to run the organization. That editor, Xie Lihua, is credited with keeping the RWKA alive and finding new sources of funding from non-governmental sources during its initial years (Qian and Young 2006; Wang 2000: 222–3). Chapters 3 and 4 also show child welfare and migrant labor NGOs obtaining resources and support from a wide range of state and state-affiliated agencies, including mass organizations such as the All-China Federation of Labor Unions, public institutions such as universities, and GONGOs such as the China Charity Foundation.

Another important resource that the state, in particular national organizations or agencies, can provide is a network that crosses geographical boundaries. This network is important for NGOs intent on expanding their influence, given the restrictions on NGOs setting up branch organizations in other localities. RWKA, for example, has utilized the national network of the Women's Federation to carry out its literacy and microfinance projects in the countryside (Wang 2000: 229–32). Similarly, Chapter 8 shows how AIDS NGOs in China have been able to expand their access to funds and coordinate with other NGOs through the China Association for STD and AIDS, a GONGO, which occupies a privileged position because of its close ties with the Ministry of Health and its access to a network of national affiliates.

Negotiations also occur in other areas where NGOs and the state work together. Some NGOs have been able to work with local governments, which rely on those NGOs to implement international projects and gain access to international donor funds (Howell 2004: 159). A China Development Brief survey of Chinese NGOs (Wexler *et al.* 2006: 34) noted that many grassroots NGOs had significant experience of cooperation with local governments. Two had reached agreements to operate fairly large-scale social service facilities. In one case, the government provided substantial resources. In another, the NGO obtained substantial international funding for poverty relief and development projects, and the local government was helping with implementation. Similarly, Chapters 4 and 8 discuss collaboration between, on the one hand, local government centers for disease control and, on the other, migrant labor and HIV/AIDS NGOs to work on projects funded by international agencies and governments.

There is also evidence of NGOs negotiating with their supervising agency to adopt a more flexible, hands-off position in managing the NGO. There are cases of NGOs getting around various regulatory hurdles with the help of their supervising agencies. The agency may provide this help because it has its own interest in expanding the influence of that NGO. White *et al.* (1996: 137) relate the example of how the Shenyang government interpreted the 1989 SO regulations creatively by allowing the Shenyang Pharmacy Association to have members in eleven provinces. Studies of the well-known China Youth Development Foundation (also commonly known as Project Hope) show that the foundation's ability to raise funds and attract publicity was to a significant extent due to the creativity and hands-off attitude of its supervising organization, the Communist Youth League (Lu 2007: 177–84).

Finally, negotiations occur over policy. A number of NGOs involved in the social welfare area seek not only to provide services, but also to advocate for their constituents and push for favorable policies on their constituents' behalf.[17] Studies of trade and professional NGOs have shown how they are able to influence local and even national decisions, normally through their supervising or sponsoring state institution (Kennedy 2005). The same can be said of social service NGOs, particularly large national NGOs such as the China Family Planning Association, a GONGO set up by the State Family Planning Commission that has influenced the government's approach to family planning (Saich 2004: 191–2). There are also numerous accounts of grassroots NGOs, such Friends of Nature and other environmental NGOs, influencing policy through both formal and informal channels (Zhao 2000; Saich 2004: 191–2; Cooper 2006). Chapter 5 shows how a coalition of NGOs was able to change legislation regarding dam projects in Yunnan. Chapter 4 discusses a petition drive launched by several migrant labor NGOs calling for revision of labor legislation in Shenzhen. This case offers an interesting example of how even NGOs in politically sensitive areas such as labor rights are becoming more assertive in influencing legislation.

Conditions shaping negotiations

A number of conditions shape an NGO's ability to negotiate and expand its autonomy and influence. One of the most important conditions is having institutional and/or personal ties with the state. NGOs with institutional ties with Party or state organizations tend to exercise more leverage when it comes to asking for cooperation from the state, or influencing policy. Thus, GONGOs are generally seen as having greater access to the state because they are creations of the state. The problem with GONGOs is that they tend to face greater restrictions by the state. In many cases, GONGOs have several "mothers-in-law": a professional supervising unit, and an affiliated unit (*guakao danwei*) that provides the GONGO with office space, staff, and funds.

More independent NGOs can still maintain ties to the state by having a leader with status and ties to the state. The importance of the NGO's founder or leader is seen by many scholars as critical to an NGO's effectiveness.[18] The NGO's heavy reliance on its founder or leader also suggests a low level of institutionalization for NGOs during this stage of reform. As Ru and Ortolano (2008: 64–5) note, having such a leader gives grassroots NGOs greater autonomy, influence, and legitimacy. Normally, NGOs suffer from one or the other. They may have greater autonomy but little legitimacy and few ties and influence with the state. Or they may be closely tied to the state through their supervising or affiliated agency but have little autonomy. A strong and well-connected leader allows NGOs to remain at arm's length from the state while still keeping access to the state.

Clearly, NGOs such as RWKA and the China Youth Development Foundation (the Hope Project) enjoy an advantage in having leaders who have worked in the party or government apparatus and who therefore enjoy access to resources and legitimacy that grassroots NGOs do not have. Yet there are also various strategies that grassroots NGOs can use to increase their influence with the state. Many NGOs, for example, devote considerable time and energy to improving their relations with their supervising agency or with local government officials. Kwong (2004: 1084–5) discusses migrant schools that avoided being closed down because they cultivated ties with local government offices and officials, going so far as to wine and dine them and offer them gifts. Other NGOs maintain good relations by having prominent academics or political figures such as a representative of the local People's Congress on their board of directors (Howell 2004: 157). Similarly, Amity International, a Christian-based NGO that forms partnerships with local governments on various projects, also has a number of serving or retired government officials on its board of directors, including a member of the national Chinese People's Political Consultative Conference (CPPCC; Bentley 2004). The China Development Brief report also cites the migrant schools that the researchers interviewed as placing

> more emphasis on cultivating relationships with local government and local government leaders. One of them stressed that they frequently invite officials to visit the school as this helps to let the officials know how things are going while also serving to motivate the schoolteachers
>
> (Wexler *et al.* 2006: 93–4)

Another factor shaping negotiations is the attitude of the supervising agency, and other actors within the state bureaucracy, toward NGO activities. There are many examples of how some agencies and local governments are more flexible and supportive in their implementation of NGO policy than others. One study comparing civil society in the two Chinese cities of Shenyang and Nantong noted that Shenyang was more flexible and creative than Nantong in permitting the registration of local trade and professional associations (White *et al.* 1996: 138–9). Several chapters in this volume, such as Chapter 8, note that provinces such as Yunnan and Sichuan have been more supportive of NGO participation than other provinces such as Henan. Chapter 5 notes that environmental NGOs, and more recently HIV/AIDS NGOs, have received more support in Yunnan and from particular sectors of the bureaucracy such as the Ministry of Environmental Protection. Chapter 4 suggests that local governments in the Pearl River Delta appear to be quite tolerant of migrant labor NGOs, recognizing that these NGOs fill an important gap in mitigating worker discontent, or at least steering that discontent through legal channels. Similarly, Chapter 6 shows that opportunities for the development of Buddhist charities are quite extensive at the local level, and that some local governments adopt a more liberal attitude than others toward such charities.

As long as NGOs face a restrictive and unclear regulatory environment in which they are subject to interference from state agencies, negotiation will continue to be an important mode for state–NGO interactions. The fact that there are so many areas in which negotiations occur is itself a sign of the state's growing tolerance of, and willingness to work with, NGOs. There is at this point an uneasy partnership between the state and the NGO community. Yet while this negotiated relationship may be necessary in the current environment, it does not represent a healthy long-term arrangement for NGOs. The reason is that these negotiations occur in an unpredictable environment in which the state is the stronger party and can change the rules at any time. NGOs, as we have seen, face a wide range of attitudes on the part of local governments and their agencies. To survive, they must negotiate arrangements that are not institutionalized and depend heavily on clientelistic connections between NGO leaders and state officials.

Societalization: the emergence of a more autonomous civil society?

The most interesting, yet least visible, mode may be societalization because of the possibilities it affords for the emergence of a more autonomous and assertive civil society in China. As was mentioned earlier, societalization differs from negotiation in referring to a mode of interaction whereby NGOs create space and autonomy through initiatives in which the state is not a partner. Societalization, then, is the clearest indicator we have of a more autonomous civil society in China. However, societalization should not be seen as separate from negotiation, which, as we have seen, can be another way for an NGO to achieve greater autonomy. Societalization can also be seen as a way to enhance an NGO's influence and leverage in negotiations with the state at some point in the future. A quote by the founder of the RWKA suggests that NGOs do in fact view societalization instrumentally. In other words, they see societalization not just as a way to achieve greater autonomy for its own sake, but also as a means to other ends such as exercising some influence, however small or indirect, over the regulatory system.

> In China, you do things not because there is a legal channel to do them; you occupy the space before the government claims it, and the legal mechanisms all happen after the fact.... Use the space you have – don't wait for policies and laws because you have to create new ways of doing things.
>
> (Bentley 2004)

The reality is that many NGOs engage in both modes, improving their relations with local government through negotiations in some areas, but also exploring strategies intended to enhance their independence from the state. Each mode reinforces the other.

One extensively studied case is that of the CYDF. The CYDF has been successful in developing a separate, and increasingly autonomous, identity from its supervising agency, the Communist Youth League, by publicizing its work in the media and developing a nationwide mechanism for raising funds. Yet the CYDF's ability to carry out these activities, some of which were not approved and even went against regulations, was made possible because of institutional ties negotiated between the CYDF and the Youth League.[19] To use the language of our framework, negotiation made it possible for the CYDF to pursue societalization and put distance between itself and the Youth League.

Not surprisingly, some of the conditions discussed earlier that enhance NGO leverage in negotiations can also be seen as conditions for enhancing greater societalization: leadership, networking, funding from international sources, and use of the media. Indeed, engaging in these dual modes is a good example of the "embedded autonomy" that many NGOs seek.[20] On the one hand, they desire more ties with the state because those ties enhance their ability to provide services and engage in advocacy; on the other, they are wary of becoming too dependent on the state, and susceptible to the interference and other political troubles that such dependence brings. Thus, when we talk about greater autonomy as a goal of many NGOs in China, we need to add that these NGOs are often in pursuit of "embedded autonomy."

Societalization strategies

Over the years, NGOs in China have adopted a number of ingenious methods for creating space and autonomy, ranging from working around regulatory hurdles to expanding their network, membership, and sources of funding. We have already seen that NGOs get around the MOCA's restrictive registration regulations by attaching themselves to a part of the state apparatus without registering, or negotiating with its supervising agency to set up branch organizations in other localities (Ru and Ortolano 2008: 55). In each of these cases, the state acts as a partner in helping that NGO gain a foothold.

But NGOs can also get around these regulations without the help of the state, and have been very creative in doing so. They can simply register as a business, or affiliate with legally registered NGOs and even with businesses. Howell (2004: 151) gives an example of the Yunnan Reproductive Health Association, which is affiliated to the Yunnan Women's Theoretical Research Association, which is in turn affiliated with the Yunnan Women's Federation. A *China Development Brief* article cites an example of an environmental NGO that is affiliated to a nominally state-owned enterprise established by the Beijing branch of a national mass organization (Qian and Young 2005). Chapter 5 also mentions environmental NGOs that have engaged in networking and establishing branch offices in violation of MOCA regulations.

NGOs can also enhance their autonomy by forming ties with others in the NGO community. Naturally, the Chinese government is concerned about the growth of social networks and has made efforts to discourage them, such as by stipulating in various regulations that SOs and civil, non-commercial units cannot establish branches in other localities. Yet in spite of these regulations, one important trend in recent years has been the growth of informal ties and networks within the NGO community. There seem to be at least two types of networks operating in China. One type is an informal network of individuals concerned about a common issue such as the local MSM (men who have sex with men) groups, which, as discussed in Chapter 8 on HIV/AIDS, are used by GONGOs and local governments to reach out to the local MSM community. These types of volunteer networks are seen by NGO scholars as one of the more independent forms of grassroots organizations in China. Other examples include the Participatory Rural Appraisal (PRA) Network in Guizhou, which consists of individuals concerned about development and the environment in southwest China (Cooper 2006: 123); the China AIDS Network, a national network of professionals engaged in HIV/AIDS work; environmental volunteer networks; and the many virtual networks that have emerged on the internet.

The other type of network consists of linkages between NGOs. There are now a number of international NGOs and Chinese GONGOs and NGOs whose mission is to promote such linkages and build the capacity of the Chinese NGO community. These include China Development Brief, the Ford Foundation, the Asia Foundation, the China Association for NGO Cooperation (CANGO), and Tsinghua's NPO Center (www.npo.com). At the local level, there is now growing evidence of networking among grassroots NGOs, with the internet being a powerful tool facilitating networking. Chapter 4 mentions networking among migrant labor groups to address labor legislation, and Chapter 8 discusses the role of the China Association for STDs and AIDS in building a network of NGOs, including grassroots and unregistered, and NGOs such as AIZHI Action, which networks and shares information with other AIDS NGOs via listservs. But perhaps the most striking example of networking, discussed in Chapter 5, is the coalition of environmental NGOs that came together to oppose the Nujiang dam project in 2003. That remarkable effort eventually resulted in the project being suspended by the central government.

Networking also helps NGOs gain autonomy in another important way: by broadening and diversifying their sources of funding, in particular international funding, which has been critical to promoting societalization in China. A number of influential grassroots NGOs, as well as GONGOs, would not have become established without international funding. The Beijing Women's Legal Aid Center, the Center for Legal Aid to Pollution Victims (CLAPV), and the Rural Development Association (RDA) are just some of the better-known NGOs (Wang 2000, 2001). The same can be said for many migrant labor and AIDs NGOs that work in sensitive areas and receive little support from the state, as Chapter 4 and other sources show (Huang 2007). International funding has been important in building NGO capacity because it exposes NGOs to international requirements regarding non-profit management, and can come with training for NGO staff to ensure that the funds are managed and used effectively. One trend in the past few years has been GONGOs shedding their government label by becoming dependent on international funding, rather than support from the government. One example from Chapter 8 is the China Association for STDs and AIDS, which stopped receiving government funding in 1998. The state in turn has encouraged GONGOs to move in this direction as part of the broader effort to streamline the bureaucracy and move toward a system of "small government, large society" (*xiao zhengfu, da shehui*).

Funding in the form of project mechanisms is another way for activists and NGOs to expand their legitimacy and autonomy. A number of grassroots NGOs such as Global Village, the Rural Development Association in Sichuan, and Sanchuan Development Association in Qinghai have been successful in using project funding to expand their operations and influence.[21] A national-level example is the United Nation's Global Fund mechanism for combating AIDS, which is discussed in Chapter 8. This path to greater autonomy, however, also has its perils because eventually project funding runs out and the NGO must look for new sources of funding. The more successful cases suggest that pursuit of international funding is best carried out in tandem with strengthening ties with state agencies and other NGOs, which can be important partners in project implementation. In other words, a combination of societalization and negotiation with the state is necessary. An NGO's ability to implement a project successfully in turn increases its chances of getting more international funding down the road. As Chapters 4 and 8 show, NGOs that rely almost solely on project grants, yet get little support from the state, are in a more precarious position.

Societalization can also come about by NGOs broadening their membership base, assuming those members are not associated with the state. Studies of Chinese trade associations and chambers of commerce, which rely more on their members for fees and influence than do social welfare NGOs, suggest that NGOs that are member driven and rely on member fees for funding are less beholden to government and more attentive to member concerns and needs. White *et al.* (1996: 141) use the example of the Shenyang Construction Association, which had strong ties with the local construction bureau but also was drawn to serve the needs of its members, which consisted mostly of collectives. A clearer example of association autonomy driven by membership needs is the Wenzhou Chamber of Commerce, which represents Wenzhou-based private businesses around the country. Ma (2004: 159ff.) shows how these chambers actively advocate for their members' interests and enjoy a fair amount of autonomy in their leadership and organizational structure. The China Development Brief survey of Chinese NGOs also suggests that GONGOs and professional and trade associations are moving toward greater autonomy in coastal areas where the private economy is larger, and associations can reach out to members for funding rather than depend on the state (Wexler *et al.* 2006: 123). Outside of trade associations and chambers of commerce, however, societalization driven by expanding membership is a nascent phenomenon, particularly among social welfare NGOs. NGOs in these areas have much lower membership rates and, because their members tend to be volunteers or activists rather than enterprises, do not rely much on member fees for funding.

Finally, China's media, which have become increasingly commercialized, have begun to play an important role in increasing NGO influence. Grassroots NGOs such as Global Village have worked with the media to put on talk shows and other public relations events that have strengthened the NGOs' visibility, reputation, and influence. It is true that such media events occur with the consent of the state. NGOs such as Global Village could not use the media the way they have done if the state did not legitimize environmental protection as a pressing national issue. Still, the consequence has been to empower grassroots NGOs. Deng Guosheng (2001), a professor at Tsinghua's NGO Research Center, uses the case of the RDA, which started out as a small rural development NGO in Sichuan, to show how extensive media coverage of the RDA strengthened its organizational resources and network and enabled it to better resist government interference. The example of Beijing Sun Village, an organization that cares for children of the incarcerated, discussed in Chapter 3, is another good example of an NGO that gained greater visibility and influence through favorable media coverage. But again the most prominent example is the campaign against the Nujiang dam project. As Chapter 5 details, the media played a key role in helping the coalition of environmental NGOs by publicizing their message to a national audience.

Over the past decade, societalization has become a more visible mode on several levels. First, as has been discussed, the number of unregistered NGOs has grown rapidly over the past decade. These unregistered NGOs are an important indicator of societalization because many of them emerged without help from the state. Second, other indicators of societalization have become more prominent, such as the growth of NGO networks and the role of the internet in promoting such networks, the growth of funding from private sources, in particular overseas sources, and the growing commercialization of the media. The emergence of more autonomous and assertive NGOs in sectors deemed important by the government, such as environmental protection (see Chapter 5) and, more recently, HIV/AIDS (see Chapter 8), is another indication of how far societalization has progressed. Furthermore, societalization is taking place in areas such as migrant labor rights and HIV/AIDS that are politically more sensitive. In these areas, NGOs are pushing the state-defined limits on what services can and should be provided. In some cases, such as Zhang Zhiru's migrant labor organization (see Chapter 4) and Wan Yanhai's AIZHI Action (see Chapter 8), these efforts to push the envelope have resulted in the state closing down these organizations. According to a recent article on migrant labor NGOs in Guangdong, most of these NGOs that emerged after 2000 are either unregistered or registered as businesses (Huang 2007). Almost all of them depend on international funding and receive no support from the state, yet they are openly tolerated by local governments and even work together with local government bureaus to resolve migrant labor issues. There are also signs of growing ties and cooperation among these NGOs, such as the coalition of environmental NGOs that came together to oppose the Nujiang dam project in 2003. More recently, in 2006, a coalition of migrant labor NGOs in Guangdong came together to propose amending the laws on labor arbitration fees, putting together a petition with 10,000 signatures and contacting People's Congress representatives (Huang 2007).

Conclusion

The goal of this chapter was to offer a framework for assessing state–NGO relations that moves beyond the standard corporatist and civil society approaches to highlight the dynamic, multifaceted, and interactive nature of the state–NGO relationship in contemporary China.

What we find is a situation in which the regulatory mode has been inadequate in keeping pace with changes in the NGO community, and has even encouraged NGOs to engage in negotiation and societalization to stay relevant and effective. While the regulation of NGOs has become more systematic and comprehensive over time, it remains fairly rudimentary and overly restrictive. The regulatory system relies heavily on an understaffed and underfunded MOCA, and supervising agencies, to oversee an increasingly large number of social organizations, civil non-enterprise units, and foundations. Moreover, the system has not kept pace with the rapid expansion of NGOs and has produced some unintended consequences. Instead of restricting the growth and activities of NGOs, it has merely encouraged many NGOs to evade the regulatory apparatus and operate in a largely unregulated and unsupervised environment. Resembling the underground economy, where businesses were neither legal nor blatantly illegal, these NGOs form a large underground NGO sector.

The problems with the regulatory system have made the other two modes – negotiation and societalization – increasingly important. Of these two modes, negotiation is the more important. This chapter has only touched the surface of the complex negotiations that take place between NGOs and state agencies and other state-affiliated institutions such as mass organizations, public institutions, and GONGOs. It has shown the many areas in which negotiations occur. These negotiations offer NGOs a way to maneuver, survive, and provide services in a restrictive regulatory and political environment. Indeed, there is substantial evidence that such ties with the state can strengthen NGOs' influence, and autonomy from state interference. At the same time, the negotiation mode has its own set of problems stemming from an environment in which the state is the stronger party, and attitudes among local governments and supervising agencies toward

NGOs vary widely. Negotiations also rely heavily on clientelistic relationships and can end up with the NGO being overly dependent on the state. In the future, these problems will create pressures on the state for better regulation, and on NGOs to expand their autonomy and capacity in order to wean themselves from being overly dependent on the state.

Finally, societalization has become an increasingly important mode, although it appears to be more evident in certain sectors such as child welfare, HIV/AIDS, and migrant labor rights than in areas such as Buddhist charities, which are more tightly regulated, as Chapter 6 discusses. This trend toward societalization is important for several reasons. First, it shows the inadequacy of the regulatory system. Many of the NGOs that are registered as businesses or are unregistered have few ties with the state. They are truly independent, and their numbers seem to be growing. Second, it shows that there are now channels through which NGOs and other social organizations and networks can work to be less dependent on the state. Third, it shows the emergence of a civil society in which values, interests and goals can be independently articulated without interference from the state. The globalization of the NGO community, the influx of foreign donors, the growth of networks among NGOs, the commercialization of the media, and the internet are all factors that make societalization possible.

Whether societalization is a path to greater autonomy and, more importantly, greater influence for NGOs, though, is open to debate. To date, NGOs with no ties to the state tend to be small, more vulnerable to state interference, and constrained by a lack of funding, personnel, and other resources, which makes it difficult for them to deliver services. These problems explain why many NGOs as well as other non-state actors in China continue to see negotiation as an attractive mode, and why negotiation and societalization should be seen as interrelated modes, rather than mutually exclusive. Keyser's example of Beijing Sun Village is a case in point. Sun Village started off as an relatively autonomous CNEU, but as it became better known, in part because of media coverage, it decided to affiliate with the China Charity Foundation's Relief Aid Department for Special Children. This affiliation with the China Charity Foundation (CCF), a GONGO, enabled Beijing Sun Village to receive funds raised locally through the CCF. Societalization in this case became a way for Sun Village to negotiate an arrangement with a GONGO that gave it access to other sources of funds. In the process, Sun Village lost some of the autonomy that it enjoyed as a grassroots service provider in determining how these funds can be used.

To sum up, the majority of NGOs in China see their future as being not in opposition to, but in collaboration with, the state. In this sense, they make up that "non-critical" part of civil society that is too dependent on the goodwill and resources of the state to challenge it openly.[22]

Notes

1 For corporatist approaches, see Pearson (1994), Unger and Chan (1996), chapter 6 in White *et al.* (1996), and Ru and Ortolano (2008). For civil society approaches, see White *et al.* (1996), Frolic (1997), He (1997), and Cooper (2006).

2 Saich (2000) and Gallagher (2004) have made similar points about the limitations of these frameworks.
3 See, for example, the discussion in Chapter 4 of the interesting case of Zhang Zhiru's migrant worker organization, which was closed down after Zhang tried to organize a petition drive to call for legislation to better protect migrant worker rights.
4 The Chinese- and English-language versions of these regulations can be found in *China's NPO Network* at www.npo.org or www.chinanpo.org, and on *China Development Brief*'s website at www.chinadevelopmentbrief.org.
5 Article 13 of the SO regulations, and Article 11 of the CNEU regulations.
6 Article 19 of the SO regulations, and Article 13 of the CNEU regulations.
7 As we discuss in Chapter 1, the term "social organizations" is somewhat confusing because it is used to apply to mass organizations that existed before 1978, and newer SOs that were established during the reform era. Unlike these newer SOs, which come under the 1998 Regulation for Registration and Management of Social Organizations, mass organizations are legal entities governed by separate laws and do not need to register with the MOCA.
8 For cases of how GONGOs have created political space for influencing policy, see the discussion of the China Family Planning Association in Saich (2000: 136–7), and Ma's (2004: 98ff.) discussion of the Women's Federation.
9 See Foster (2002) for this view.
10 See Chapter 7 for an extensive discussion of residence and village committees and their role in the SARS crisis. On community organizations (*shequ*), see Derleth and Koldyk (2004).
11 According to Saich (2000: 130–1), there was discussion during the drafting of these regulations about doing away with the requirement for a supervisory unit. However, powerful central leaders felt that removing this requirement would weaken control over NGOs. Saich confirms that the intention behind these regulations was in fact to control and restrict NGOs and their growth.
12 Interview with Wang Ming, director of the NGO Research Center, Tsinghua University, 14 April 2008. White *et al.* (1996: 113) note that these secondary associations are only required to deposit a file with the MOCA. For examples of interference by these supervising agencies, see Ru and Ortolano (2008: 56), He (2007), Ge (2003), and the case studies of the Women's Legal Aid Center and the Center for Legal Aid to Pollution Victims in Wang Ming (2000).
13 This number is provided by Wang Ming of Tsinghua's NGO Research Center and cited in a *China Development Brief* article by Qian and Young (2005).
14 White *et al.* (1996: 139) call this "departmental corporatism," while Ru and Ortolano (2008: 45) use the term "agency corporatism."
15 I borrow this insight from Saich (2000: 139), who cites Kevin O'Brien's insight that co-opted groups, by becoming embedded in the system, can gain greater legitimacy and effectiveness.
16 The survey of NGOs by Wexler *et al.* (2006) suggests that some small grassroots NGOs do spend considerable amount of time and energy trying to find a government sponsor in order to register.
17 Although Chapters 3 and 6 are a reminder that in some areas, organizations such as orphanages and Buddhist charities have shown little interest in advocacy work.
18 The importance of the NGO's founder or leader is underlined by the *China Development Brief* survey by Wexler *et al.* (2006) and the many case studies of NGOs provided by Wang (2000, 2001). Also see Ma (2004), who looks at the role of intellectuals as leaders of NGOs in chapter 4 of her book, and Saich's case study of Friends of Nature (2004: 191–2).
19 See the extensive discussion of this case in Lu (2007).
20 This desire is expressed by a number of NGOs surveyed in the *China Development Brief* survey by Wexler *et al.* (2006).

21 See the case studies of these NGOs by Wang (2000). An even more forceful case that international funding can enhance NGO autonomy is made in the case study of Sanchuan Development Association (SDA) by Zhang and Baum (2004).
22 For a discussion of the distinction between critical and non-critical civil society, see Tong (1994).

References

Bentley, J. (2004) "Survival Strategies for Civil Society Organizations in China," *International Journal of Not-for-Profit Law*, 6 (January). Online, available at: www.icnl.org/knowledge/ijnl/vol6iss2/art_1.htm (accessed 21 April 2007).

China's NPO Network. Online, available at: www.npo.org.cn or www.chinanpo.org (accessed 30 April 2007).

Cooper, C. M. (2006) "'This Is Our Way In': The Civil Society of Environmental NGOs in South-West China," *Government and Opposition* 41 (1): 109–36.

Deng, G. (2001) "Yilong xian xiangcun fazhan xiehui" [Yilong County Township and Village Development Association], in M. Wang (ed.) *Zhongguo NGO Yanjiu* [Research on China's NGOs], United Nations Centre for Regional Development Report Series No. 43, Nagoya, Japan: UNCRD.

Derleth, J. and Koldyk, D. (2004) "The Shequ Experiment: Grassroots Political Reform in Urban China," *Journal of Contemporary China* 13 (41): 747–77.

Evans, P. (1995) *Embedded Autonomy: States and Industrial Transformation*, Princeton, NJ: Princeton University Press.

Foster, K. W. (2002) "Embedded within State Agencies: Business Associations in Yantai," *China Journal* 47 (January): 41–65.

Frolic, M. (1997) "State-Led Civil Society," in T. Brooks and M. Frolic (eds.) *Civil Society in China*, New York: M. E. Sharpe.

Gallagher, M. E. (2004) "China: The Limits of Civil Society in a Late Leninist State," in M. Alagappa (ed.) *Civil Society and Political Change in Asia*, Stanford, CA: Stanford University Press.

Ge, Y. (2003) "Feiyingli zuzhi fazhande falu huanjing" [The Legal Environment of NPO Development], in L. Xie (ed.) *NGOs in China*, Shanghai: Shanghai Academy of Social Science Press. Online, available at: www.npo.org.cn (accessed 13 November 2007).

He, B. (1997) *The Democratic Implications of Civil Society in China*, New York: St. Martin's Press.

He, Z. (2007) "Institutional Barriers to the Development of Civil Society in China" [Zhongguo gongmin shehui zuzhi fazhande zhiduxing zhang'ai fenxi], University of Nottingham China Policy Institute Discussion Paper 15. Online, Chinese version available at: www.npo.org.cn (accessed 13 November 2007).

Howell, J. (2004) "New Directions in Civil Society: Organizing around Marginal Interests," in J. Howell (ed.) *Governance in China*, Lanham, MD: Rowman & Littlefield.

Huang, A. (2007) "Workers' 'self-help' efforts under globalization," *South Wind Window* [Nanfeng Chuang] (15 November). Online, available at: www.clntranslations.org/article/27/labor-ngos-in-guangdong-province (accessed 9 January 2008).

Kennedy, S. (2005) *The Business of Lobbying in China*, Cambridge, MA: Harvard University Press.

Kwong, J. (2004) "Educating Migrant Children: Negotiations between the State and Civil Society," *China Quarterly* 180 (December): 1073–88.

Lieberthal, K. (1992) "Introduction: The 'Fragmented Authoritarianism' Model and Its Limitations," in K. Lieberthal and D. Lampton (eds.) *Bureaucracy, Politics, and Decision Making in Post-Mao China*, Berkeley: University of California Press.

Lu, Y. (2007) "The Autonomy of Chinese NGOs: A New Perspective," *China: An International Journal* 5 (2): 173–203.

Ma, Q. (2004) *Non-governmental Organizations in Contemporary China*, London: Routledge.

Pearson, M. (1994) "The Janus Face of Business Associations in China: Socialist Corporatism in Foreign Enterprises," *Australian Journal of Chinese Affairs* 31 (January): 25–46.

—— (1997) *China's New Business Elite: The Political Consequences of Economic Reform*, Berkeley: University of California Press.

Qian, T. and Young, N. (2005) "Rule on Names Starts to Close Door to NGO 'Businesses,'" *China Development Brief* (15 April). Online, available at: www.chinadevelopmentbrief.com (accessed 11 November 2007).

—— (2006) "Profile: Veteran Fighter for 'Ugly Duckling' That Serves Rural Women," *China Development Brief* (3 April). Online, available at: www.chinadevelopmentbrief.com (accessed 23 October 2007).

Ru, J. and Ortolano, L. (2008) "Corporatist Control of Environmental Non-governmental Organizations: A State Perspective," in R. L. Edmonds and P. Ho (eds.) *China's Embedded Activism: Opportunities and Constraints of a Social Movement*, London: Routledge.

Saich, T. (2000) "Negotiating the State: The Development of Social Organizations in China," *China Quarterly* 161: 124–41.

—— (2004) *Governance and Politics of China*, 2nd edn., Basingstoke, UK: Palgrave Macmillan.

Tong, Y. (1994) "State, Society and Political Change in China and Hungary," *Comparative Politics* 26 (3): 333–53.

Unger, J. and Chan, A. (1996) "Corporatism in China: A Developmental State in an East Asian Context," in B. L. McCormick and J. Unger (eds.) *China after Socialism: In the Footsteps of Eastern Europe or East Asia?* Armonk, NY: M. E. Sharpe.

Wang, M. (ed.) (2000) *Zhongguo NGO Yanjiu* [Research on China's NGOs], United Nations Centre for Regional Development Report Series No. 38.

—— (2001) *Zhongguo NGO Yanjiu* [Research on China's NGOs], United Nations Centre for Regional Development Report Series No. 43.

—— (2007) "The Development and Present Situation of NGOs in China," in Special Issue on NGOs and Social Transition in China, *Social Sciences in China* 28 (Summer): 96–104.

Wexler, R., Ying, Y., and Young, N. (2006) "NGO Advocacy in China: A Special Report from *China Development Brief*," *China Development Brief*. Online, available at: www.chinadevelopmentbrief.org (accessed 23 November 2007).

White, G., Howell, J., and Shang, X. (1996) *In Search of Civil Society: Market Reform and Social Change in Contemporary China*, Oxford: Clarendon Press.

World Bank (2005) *China: Deepening Public Service Unit Reform to Improve Service Delivery*," Report No. 32341-CHA, Washington, DC: World Bank.

Zhang, X. and Baum, R. (2004). "Report from the Field: Civil Society and the Anatomy of a Rural NGO," *China Journal* 52 (July): 98–107.

Zhao, X. (2000) "Guanyu Beijing huabao NGOde diaocha fenxi" [An Analysis of Environmental NGOs in Beijing], in M. Wang (ed.) *Zhongguo NGO Yanjiu* [Research on China's NGOs], United Nations Centre for Regional Development Research Report Series No. 38, Nagoya, Japan: UNCRD.

Part II

Social welfare responses in non-crisis situations

3 The role of the state and NGOs in caring for at-risk children

The case of orphan care

Catherine H. Keyser[1]

Introduction

As urban and rural arrangements for social welfare under state socialism have collapsed in China's lurch toward capitalism, a patchwork of arrangements has begun to emerge to address the most fragile part of the Chinese population: abandoned, orphaned, disabled, and/or homeless children. Welfare provision and protection by the state is limited but a wide variety of state, quasi-state, non-state, and internationally funded efforts are stepping into the breach to address the problems of China's at-risk children. This chapter briefly surveys the landscape of organizations working on behalf of one group of at-risk children: orphans. It is not an exhaustive list of these organizations. Rather, using examples I survey the various ways the state and the NGO community interact (or not) against the background of an ambiguous legal and policy environment for NGOs. Indeed, the ambiguousness of the policy environment and the limited nature of welfare provision have partially engendered the growth of social organizing on behalf of at-risk children in general, and orphans in particular. Further, this survey also serves to highlight the dynamic and overlapping modes of state–society interaction as outlined by Shieh in Chapter 2. These modes – regulation, negotiation, and societalization – are evident when we look at the arena of welfare provision for orphans as reviewed in the conclusion to this chapter.

I argue that active non-state or quasi-official organizations, led by international efforts, are not only addressing the gaps in child welfare left by a retreating (and sometimes simply absent) state, but are doing so by developing relationships at the local level, much as with other areas such as poverty relief, worker rights, and HIV/AIDs awareness. There are two simple reasons for this. The first is that there is no central-level coordination mechanism in place to facilitate a relationship between NGOs and the locality. The second reason is the high degree of localization of welfare issues, both historically and in light of the socialization of welfare in the transition period. Further, the overarching but vague legal framework, the decentralization of policy and management, and the absence of a single coordinating agency to address children's welfare issues create both challenges and opportunities for the development of NGOs. The opportunities for growth grew from the failure of orphan care in China in the mid-1990s, and the rapid growth of children on the streets (K. Gao 2001). The obstacles to further coordination and growth remain the structural and legal framework of the political system, as will be explained. After placing the discussion in the context of the general change in state provision of welfare, I define at-risk children and review the historical and legal framework for child welfare issues. I then turn to a survey of the different kinds of organizations engaged in work with orphans and foster care to make the argument. In the conclusion, I return to the question of modes of interaction between the state and the NGO community engaged in orphan care. Most names and places of activity are not included, in order to protect the groups and organizations operating in various locations.

The socialization of welfare

As theorists of development have long argued, social stability is a key variable in development, and as we know from other transition experiences, the success of political and economic transition is closely tied to social stability. The literature on economic transition and on the problems of political transition in China is vast. As the transition literature generally suggests, the state delegates to market-like forces, semi-official organizations, and local government the responsibility for certain policy areas such as social welfare. Studies of what the retreat of the state means for social welfare and the emergence of NGOs look at areas such as social security, health care, labor issues, poverty alleviation, urban housing issues, and vulnerable groups such as women, children, people with disabilities, and those affected by HIV/AIDS. But of the many social issues to emerge in the past decade, the one concerning the most fragile part of the population – abandoned, homeless, and/or abused children – has received less attention. Part of the reason is that the nature of child abandonment itself has changed, and is also a function of birth control policies and the scaling back of welfare provision for old age. Kay Johnson (1996, 1998) has done important foundational work on the question of why people would choose to abandon children in the first place, and what the logic is concerning why and when a family chooses not to keep a child. However, this research, done in the 1980s and 1990s, looks mainly at the abandonment of baby girls as a result of the one-child policy. The dynamics by the early years of the twenty-first century had changed somewhat as the success of the birth control plan (or the ability to hide children) resulted in somewhat fewer healthy girls being abandoned, while at the same time more children are being abandoned because there is something wrong with them, or there is fear that there might be. As the incidence of birth defects rises, so does abandonment, as is further discussed in the next section. The provision of social welfare for this group, however, has been little studied.

Child welfare is unusual in that unlike some areas of social welfare that can be understood at least partially in market terms, the area of child welfare and protection cannot be privatized in the same way that, say, pension reform or health care can be privatized. Serving the vulnerable child involves a more complex arrangement between state and non-state actors, in part because they themselves cannot participate in the acquisition of welfare, but also because welfare for an orphan, for example, involves multiple agencies. In China, there is no child welfare and protection agency in which questions concerning child protection and welfare can be addressed across disciplines – say, medical and educational issues. Moreover, orphans are kept behind closed doors – and the general public cannot see the problem in the way that unemployment, pollution, or villages of HIV-positive people can be seen. In short, the child is not able to participate in the same way as, say, a worker with an advocacy framework as discussed in Chapter 4. Indeed, the growth of international non-governmental organizations (INGOs) for child welfare, and the continued effort on the part of non-state actors such as Catholic-run orphanages in particular, are due in part either to an absence by the state altogether, or to the very limited role the state is playing with regard to increasingly complex child welfare issues, or orphaned and abandoned children.

After outlining who at-risk children are, I then review the historical and legal framework for child welfare in China. Following the review, I survey state and non-state activity in the area of orphan care.

At-risk children

Children at risk may plausibly include all children who are financially or physically disadvantaged. All abandoned, orphaned, or neglected children (either because of family disruption or parental incarceration), the "left behind" children and/or abused children who are in non-family care either because they are living on the streets or are in state or non-state institutions, or special needs children are children at risk for a host of physical, social-emotional, and/or cognitive problems. Setting aside the question of education for reasons of space (and not because it is less important), what does the population of orphaned, homeless street children and children with special needs look like in China today? The statistics are not clear for each group of at-risk children, especially since many of the children live in rural areas.[2]

There are roughly 370 million children in China, of whom some estimates say roughly 573,000 are without parents because they are orphaned or abandoned (sometimes because they are disabled), or because one or more of their parents are incarcerated. The government's 2005 Child Development report stated that there were 54,000 disabled orphans in the state's care. An internal Ministry of Civil Affairs report from 2005 places the number at about 66,000 being cared for in 274 social welfare institutes (which by the time of a speech to a Chinese Social Work Association held in April 2008 had climbed to 78,000 children in nearly 500 welfare institutes, 300 of which are Child Welfare Institutes). In 2005, Shang and colleagues provided a conservative rough estimate of the number of rural orphans at around 400,000 (Shang 2005: 124). These are orphans who live with relatives or others in villages. Further, HIV/AIDS has created a new category of orphan. Careyouth.com (the website for AIDSORPHAN, a clearinghouse for information on and help for the care of children orphaned by AIDS) states that at present there are between 70,000 and 80,000 children orphaned by AIDS and that by 2010 there will be between 138,000 and 260,000 AIDS orphans.[3] A retired Ministry of Civil Affairs cadre who has worked on children's issues for many years puts the current total number of orphans closer to 1 million if one takes into account all of the above plus all the unregistered children; that is, children who do not go through the state-run orphanage system and are living in non-state orphanages and other facilities such as the Beijing Sun Villages, discussed on p. 58 (Int. 14B, Beijing, 29 March 2007). Accurate figures for street children, acknowledged as a growing problem in China, range anywhere from the official 150,000 to estimates of nearly 600,000.[4] Counting this population is difficult, as the children are at times transient and can turn up at more than one shelter. The point is that the number of children living on the streets is significant, and by all accounts growing as the social effects of the "left behind" children of parents who have migrated to the cities to work, growing economic strains on the rural poor, and the rise of children being lured to the cities to "work" result in children leaving their home and living on the streets. In sum, accurate total numbers are not, at present, well documented.

Sadly, another growing population of children is those born with birth defects. According to the *China Daily*, citing a report from the national population and family planning commission, the number of children born with birth defects has grown by 40 percent since 2001, with about one million affected children being born each year, according to official records (Hu 2007). This report, however, would not include those children not born in hospitals (because the birth parents could not afford a hospital birth) who then are abandoned when found to have birth defects. The report argued that, while there can be no certainty, scientific research suggests that increased pollution is linked to an increased incidence of birth defects. Shanxi Province, China's center for coal production, is reported to have the highest incidence of birth defects. In the rural areas or among the urban poor, these children are frequently abandoned because the cost of necessary surgery or long-term care is too much for a family to bear. Those families who do keep the children face significant medical and educational challenges. Not only is the educational system not equipped to address the needs of these children, but there is no legally mandated special education alternative, only the legal provision that they ought to be educated. In this area, their rights are intertwined with the rights of disabled people in general (Wang 2005: 212–13). At the local level, it is not at all certain they will be able to obtain satisfactory education. Families are largely on their own in finding help in caring for and/or educating their children with special needs (such as cerebral palsy, Down's syndrome, autism). In all of the areas reviewed above, one can find an array of official, quasi-official, and non-official organizations working with each group of children. How many is not clearly known. The now closed *China Development Brief* made an extensive attempt to list domestic NGOs in China (China Development Brief 2001). Indeed, part of the argument I make is that the various structural and legal challenges faced by many of these organizations discourage them from making themselves widely known. To understand the rise of organizations, it is important first to ask how child welfare was provided in the communist and transition periods.

Child welfare provision under communism and challenges in transition

How were children of the kinds described in the previous section taken care of before reform, and what are the challenges faced by the government now? In the very brief review to follow, one of the organizing themes of the book – namely, changes and continuities in the state's role in welfare provision – is underscored. In this case, we find the contradictory message that the state continues to have full legal responsibility for orphan care, while at the same time asserting that care for children is the responsibility of society. Only a child abandoned and registered within the state framework is eligible for all the welfare benefits afforded orphans. Any child not registered through a state-run child welfare institute (CWI; called an orphanage in English) is simply not counted, as I have indicated. This framework constrains NGO activity with regard to orphans on the one hand, while the very scale of the problem has created openings for groups to organize to care for these at-risk children, on the other.

China is often categorized as a late-Leninist political system in transition economically, socially, and – to a lesser degree – politically. This simply means that the political structure remains little changed while the economic and social structures are changing rapidly. As is detailed in the introductory chapter, a defining characteristic of communism as a political-economic framework is the assumption that social welfare is provided as a function of the economic unit. In the urban areas, this meant that social welfare in all of its manifestations, including those concerning children, would be the purview of either the state-owned enterprises (SOEs) or the collectively owned enterprises. Childrearing and child welfare have historically been the purview of the family, and children's rights did not exist except in relation to the family, which itself was cared for under the work unit welfare scheme. Social welfare provision in rural China was provided through traditional forms of kinship and village community arrangements. During the early communist period, rural social welfare was addressed as part of collective or commune arrangements. Disabled children who made it out of infancy remained the responsibility of the family. Orphaned children (that is children without parents or relatives) were cared for within the village or locality, as they had been in the pre-communist period. Children in Catholic orphanages and other non-traditional institutions either remained there or were housed with local families in fostering arrangements.

There did exist, however, state efforts to provide housing for abandoned and orphaned children. For example, one early way of addressing the "orphan problem" was to move the children from populated parts of the country to less populated areas. For example, children from the Hangzhou area were sent to live with families in Mongolia in 1950. At that time, Hangzhou had too many orphans and not enough families able to care for them, and Mongolia had families with few children. They were raised there by Mongolian families in a kind of fostering arrangement (interview 14B, March 2007). Shang and Wu (2003b) have detailed another arrangement in northern Shanxi Province, where the local state entity fostered the children out as best it could since there was no CWI. But early in the Maoist period, the focus for child welfare, as in other areas, shifted toward an ideological framework that promoted the collective over the individual. It was argued that orphaned children would be better cared for in state-run institutions (Lu *et al.* 2005: chapters 4 and 5; Shang 2003b). Thus, from early in the communist period the state asserted its right to be the sole provider of welfare for orphans.

There are two places the state may house orphans. One is a general social welfare institute (SWI) (*shehui fuliyuan*), where elderly people, disabled people, and orphans are housed together. The other is a child welfare institute (CWI) (*ertong fuliyuan*). Both are state entities under the Ministry of Civil Affairs. Thus, except in remote rural areas, orphans and disabled people were cared for by the state in local institutions. Further, there was not, and still is not, one single agency charged with child welfare and protection. Finally, the pre-reform period was characterized by fixed populations through the *hukou* (registration) system, which keeps welfare issues geographically and bureaucratically distinct. The *hukou* system remains in place and, as will be discussed, is an important conditioning factor in the development of NGOs involvement in orphan care.

In the transition era, the state began to outline its role and legal responsibility for children. The Law on the Protection of Minors (LPM; *zhongguo renmin gongheguo weicheng nian baohu fa*) was promulgated in 1992 and then amended on 26 December 2006. In between these two dates, however, migration from the rural areas to the cities surged to new levels, the numbers of children living on the streets rose steadily, and the number of children being born with birth defects increased. Also during this period, an outcry arose over the revelation of very poor conditions in China's orphanages, as captured in the British-produced documentary *The Dying Rooms*. These fourteen years saw the issue of child welfare become increasingly complex. The law outlines the rights of children to be cared for and protected, as well as asserting that it is the responsibility of the state and society to provide this care and protection. Under discussion since 2004, the revised law was supposed to clarify further exactly what role the state has in child welfare and protection. Tong Lihua, a well-known child rights lawyer, notes that the final draft of the new law included 300 articles covering all areas of child rights and welfare and explicitly outlines the central government's fiscal and regulatory responsibility to all categories of children. But in the process of negotiation, the law was whittled down to just 72 articles. The main reason, Tong suggests, is that child welfare issues, in the absence of one overarching agency to deal with social security and no central-level organization to address issues of child protection, required the involvement of many bureaucratic entities. These include the Supreme People's Protectorate, the Public Security Bureau, and the Ministries of Education, Health, and Civil Affairs, "all of whom have their own concerns about what they are willing to commit to legally because of their own financial constraints; it's a very complicated process" (interview with Tong Lihua, January 2007).

State fiscal constraints, bureaucratic positioning, center–locality differences, and the absence of national-level institutions for child protection are all reflected in the new law. Most important for understanding the constraints faced by both domestic and international NGOs working with at-risk children, however, is a gap in the law: it fails to provide a legal mechanism for non-state entities to contract to care for children, yet is vague regarding what the state is committed to providing. The law says only that the state may legally care for orphans (in an SWI or CWI), but also asserts that the whole of society is responsible for caring for and protecting children, without clearly outlining what that care and protection includes or does not include. While noting that all children have a right to education, for example, it stops short of guaranteeing education for special needs children, or allowing non-state organizations to legally step in to help as independently registered NGOs. But private schools run as businesses (for example, vocational or training schools) are legally permitted. The law is vague in clarifying the role of the state, while admonishing "society" to take responsibility, but is silent on what the legal framework would look like. Workers in the area of children's rights and protection are disappointed with the vagueness of the law in terms of spelling out the state's responsibility for child welfare and protection. Further, the LPM supersedes all local child welfare laws, but, as with many other policy and legal issues, local-level implementation is not guaranteed. Indeed, one of the projects Tong's center (a semi-official NGO itself) is undertaking is to utilize local bar associations to help in monitoring local adoption of the new law over the next two to three years. The bar associations (considered professional associations, as is outlined in Chapter 1) are also active in promoting the rights of children and advocating for better protection for children. But their work does not extend directly to the orphan population.

The non-state involvement in orphan care is dominated by non-official orphanages and international groups, and frequently the non-official orphanages get funding from abroad. The story in orphan care is similar to what Kaufman, working on HIV/AIDs, and Laliberté, working on Buddhist charities, describe in relation to the growth of NGO activity. That is, the involvement of foreigners spurs local social groups (NGO, associations, and the like) either to become more active or to continue in a fiscally uncertain environment (see Chapters 8 and 6 respectively). In short, the involvement of foreigners creates somewhat of a demonstration effect for local NGOs as well as being a source of funding for these groups.

The failure of orphan care and the state response

The implementation of the one-child policy resulted in the now well-known escalation of child (largely female) abandonment, placing greater pressure on local areas to care for the increase in abandoned children throughout the 1980s and early 1990s. Increased abandonment occurred at the same time as local governments faced increased financial burdens in relation to orphans.[5] Awareness of the situation grew alongside a small increase in international adoption in China, as well as greater international attention to the plight of orphans in the post-communist world in places such as Romania and Russia. Thus, the stage was set for the moment that ushered in greater involvement of non-state actors in the form of INGOs to participate in orphan care. As in the case of HIV/AIDS, the catalyst for change came with the airing of a documentary on the problem. *The Dying Rooms*, produced by Channel 4 in Great Britain in 1995, with a follow-up, *Return to the Dying Rooms*, in 1996, looked inside Chinese orphanages in search of the rumored rooms where abandoned baby girls were left to die if they became ill. Filmed with undercover cameras by journalists posing as charity workers, the film provided a visual for connecting the reality of the controversial one-child policy and the increase in abandoned girls and disabled boys. Then there was the Chinese doctor who also filmed, under cover, the conditions in state CWIs. The state's initial response, predictable in its denial and a tightening of control, soon gave way to enhanced cooperation with INGOs and international adoption agencies. As one Chinese NGO worker at the time put it:

> [O]n the one hand, it [the film] forced the government to pay attention and to provide money to address the situation; on the other hand, it stopped all international efforts for a while over a loss of face, but also then led to the adoption agencies being able to bring in the charity to better care for these children.
>
> (Interview 13, Beijing, March 2007)

This controversy led to two related changes in orphan care. The first is the growth of non-state actors', and in particular INGOs', involvement with orphan care, and the second is the growth of foster care as an alternative to institutional care. After reviewing the role of INGOs and non-state welfare institutes, I review non-governmental involvement in foster care. Foster care as an alternative model for a parentless child provides an interesting arena for illuminating one of the underlying assumptions of this book: the growth of social space in China. Foster care is the area in which we find international and domestic organizations at work as well as the development of civic-mindedness in the form of foster families. But first, how are INGOs helping to fill the welfare vacuum where it concerns orphans? And what strategies do they use to operate in an unclear legal and policy framework?

International non-governmental organizations and orphan care

The term "international non-governmental organization" is used in an expansive way. I include not just formally established large groups, but also any group that is established and funded by foreigners. This can range from small businesses or privately backed homes caring for as few as 20 orphans, or entities as large as, say, Half the Sky's programming, which involves several thousand children. Large INGOs such as Save the Children, UNICEF, SOS Children's Villages, Half the Sky Foundation, and Plan International, to name just a few, work under the umbrella of a central government agency such as the Civil Affairs Ministry, or work directly with a research institute to pursue projects. Organizations also work with what are characterized as government-organized non-governmental organizations (GONGOs), which are sometimes sponsored by mass organizations (*qunzong zuzhi*). These include, to name just a few, the All-China Youth Federation and the China Youth Development Foundation, both sponsored by the Youth League; the Spring Bud program under the China Children and Teenagers Fund under the Women's Federation; and the China Charities Federation. These organizations introduce themselves as non-governmental, which essentially means they must be largely self-supporting, and have some leeway in developing relationships with various domestic and international donors. But they are government owned in that organizationally they are sponsored by what are classically known as the "big eight" mass organizations within the Party-state organization (see the discussion in Chapter 1 by Shieh and Schwartz). Further, the Social Work Association (SWA) (*Zhongguo shehui gongzuo xiehui*), housed as a division under the Ministry of Civil Affairs, is a semi-official professional organization. It is the most active in promoting the needs of orphans.

Most INGOs (which are also called charity organizations or foundations) register under one of several business categories with the labor bureau. Several are registered in Hong Kong as charities but operate as business subsidiaries on the mainland. Others have registered as wholly owned foreign subsidiaries. Some operate under an individual's name for signing contracts and renting space, etc., and thus are completely unregistered. A significant number of groups (though not all) are faith-based organizations. They are largely Protestant Christian, with a smaller number of Roman Catholic organizations, all of which receive funding from overseas. Proselytizing is illegal in China, and, if they are thought to be doing so, they can be and have been shut down. They cannot, and most do not, attempt to raise money in the country. The registration issue, even for well-established organizations, remains a problem, and staff members are faced with having to sign contracts and other official documents under an individual's name rather than the foundation or organization's name. This creates challenges for foreign staff because they are essentially bearing the risk for the organization. All of these groups work directly with local CWI, or with non-official, non-registered orphanages such as the private Catholic orphanages to be discussed on p. 56.

The controversy

The final scene in *The Dying Rooms* is shot at a CWI just outside of Shanghai, where the last child profiled, a little girl in one of the "rooms," dies three days after the journalists' visit. The comment is made that the CWI lies just thirty minutes from a five-star hotel. Shortly thereafter, Shanghai CWI took the lead in promoting foster care as a way to improve care for orphans. It began to deal directly with INGOs, which followed with money, training, and support. The CWIs or SWIs had more children than they had the money or staff to care for adequately. Localities needed money and access to training and the provision of alternative care for orphans, and the INGOs had it to provide. The relationship developed as local CWIs heard about foreign groups and would contact them regarding children needing surgery or who were fragile. Some groups worked with many different CWIs around the country, while some focused on working only with one or two and had an enduring relationship.

The initial state–INGO relationship blossomed, beginning with governmental cooperation between Care for Children, a British charity started with seed money from the British government (which was facing severely strained relations with China as a result of *The Dying Rooms*) and the Shanghai CWI.[6] After two years of negotiation, a pilot project was started in Shanghai, and then projects were developed in Chengdu. Care for Children's focus was on promoting foster care by training CWI staff on how to train people to become foster families. It provided training in nearly all of China's provinces. In China, Care for Children was registered under the Ministry of Civil Affairs' Social Workers Association as an NGO with tax-free status, following the regulation that any money Care for Children raised in China must be spent in China. Care for Children was one of some thirty-four organizations able to register during a six-month period in 2004 when the ministry was able to be the supervisory body as well as the point of registration for INGOs and charity groups. The opening for registration soon closed as bureaucratic debate over what should be the registering and overseeing government unit heated up.[7] Since then, all other groups have remained unregistered.

Half the Sky Foundation, begun in 1998 by Jenny Bowen, an adoptive mother, also has close government ties. This is an interesting example of a foreign group that has gone from working with localities to working on a large-scale project backed by the central government. It works in partnership with the Ministry of Civil Affairs (MOCA) in the context of the new Blue Sky plan (*lantian jihua*). The goal is to locate Half the Sky projects in various local CWIs where the Blue Sky capital investment projects are taking place in an effort to enhance the social, emotional, cognitive, and motor development of orphans.[8] At the semi-governmental end of the spectrum, the SWA is emerging as a participant in facilitating a closer relationship between the state and INGOs. The SWA is coming into its own as the field of social work grows, and as the top layers of retired civil affairs cadres who have moved into the organization begin to fully retire. (A joke about the SWA says that it used to be called the "national association of retired civil affairs cadres" because it lacked any activist orientation and is in fact staffed by a large number of retired officials.) Further, it has become the supervisory agency for both Care for Children and Half the Sky.

The range of activity for INGOs includes building care units within CWIs, even to the extent of placing their own staff in them as a supplement to regular staff. For example, organizations can be given a floor in a CWI to set up their own foster care facilities. In one case, part of the arrangement was for the charity group to fully renovate the space as part of the agreement, and then move in. In cases I have investigated, the foreign groups are given autonomy to run their floors according to their own regulations (a lower child to caregiver ratio, for example). Other groups take the children away to be cared for in their own facilities under agreement with the CWI. These groups develop legally binding contracts with local CWIs to take the orphans, many of whom are disabled, and get them surgeries or provide them with foster care while they are awaiting adoption. Oftentimes supporting the INGO–local CWI relationship is the Chinese Center for Adoption Affairs (CCAA), whose own focus is on getting orphans healthy and adopted. The CCAA was established as an agency within the MOCA in 1996 to handle the adoption process and to oversee the care of children in welfare institutes. For example, "The Tomorrow Plan," a fund set up to make money available to welfare institutes to provide surgeries for cleft lip and palate, is managed by the CCAA.

There are also a smattering of groups that work with the local CWI to provide financial assistance or other support. These range from large foundations to individual clubs that support a specific CWI, or the CWIs in a specific province,[9] to small homes caring for a few children. But even the local approach can have challenges if local government agencies are not in agreement. For example, a group working with several CWIs in a western province has had a hard time continuing to bring in doctors and staff to help the orphans with which it works. The group is known in Beijing and supported among social work professionals at the central level, but because of security concerns on the part of the local public security bureau, the foster care center continues to encounter problems.

Another INGO, Children's Hope Welfare Foundation, was established as an offshoot of Children's Hope International Adoption Agency. Children's Hope runs four programs: medical aid, foster care, educational aid, and a donation program. In a rather unusual move, the foundation was able to register itself as a division of the SWA beginning in 2001, but it still remains in the legal limbo other charities are in because it cannot register as an NGO. Nonetheless, the foundation is active itself in promoting closer INGO and/or domestic NGO and government relations. Acquisition of NGO status would expand these organizations' abilities to reach out to Chinese organizations, work with local governments more easily, and further engage Chinese citizens.

The bulk of foreign charity organizations in China, however, work on a smaller scale and work directly with local CWIs. Of this group, China Care is one of the largest. This foundation cares for some 300 children at any given time in four provinces. China Care's specialty is saving babies, whether through providing proper care for premature infants, or by complicated heart surgery. Once well, the children (nearly one-half) are placed in foster homes to await adoption or, if because of disability they are not adoptable, to be cared for and given treatment or special schooling to enhance their quality of life. In addition, China Care, like Care for Children, Half the Sky, and other INGOs, funds foster families through local CWIs with which it works. China Care is also unique because its foster families are recruited and trained by China Care staff, but sign the care agreements directly with the CWI, as well as signing an agreement with China Care. In an ambiguous legal environment, China Care's approach seeks to legally protect both the CWI and China Care in the provision of foster homes for orphans.

Chinese NGOs and "orphan" care

Chinese NGOs and other charity organizations face the same registration restrictions, and sometimes even greater scrutiny, as the INGOs working in child welfare. I put the term "orphan" in quotation marks because this area of social service provision includes children not legally deemed orphans, but who nonetheless have no parents. This spectrum of activity runs from organizations with a strong religious identification that prevents them from having any interaction with the government to those that work closely and openly with the government. Ironically, the inability to register gives all of these groups some level of decision-making autonomy and functional flexibility since they do not work with state CWIs and thus are outside the official welfare system. Finally, it is in this arena that we find most of the estimated 250,000 or more unregistered children.

Many of the domestic social organizations caring for unregistered children are faith based. One example is the Catholic convents, which range from those that shun interaction with the government to those that would like help from the government but cannot get it for political and financial reasons. Many of these convents were connected to the Roman Catholic Church as it was spread to the rural areas by missionaries, starting in the late eighteenth century. Many were closed down, or cut their official ties with Rome to become part of the Patriotic Catholic Association. The Cultural Revolution years saw most cease to take children, who then started returning in large numbers in the 1990s. Making an official count of Catholic or other private orphanages is extremely difficult, mainly because they survive by functioning quietly, a key theme in domestic NGOs in general. Shang *et al.* (2005) profiled one such Catholic-run orphanage, "Bright Children's Home," where, in an interesting twist on the otherwise usually limited government connection, the local officials and the home live in an openly acknowledged non-legal arrangement that is allowed to exist because the local government needs the nuns to care for the children, and there otherwise is no legal framework for making the children's home legal. There are "private" Protestant-run orphanages that avoid any contact with the state on religious grounds and raise funds abroad to provide any welfare services the children require. The only Buddhist monk-run orphanage I have come across was closed down in an agreement with the local CWI because it could not raise enough money to provide welfare for the children in its care.

Abandoned children are brought to these faith-based orphanages by those who believe the care will be better than at the state-run welfare organizations. This may or may not always be the case, however. In one Catholic-run orphanage, the children were only marginally better off than those in some state CWIs I visited, because of the serious financial limitations the sisters faced, and the inability to access state help for the children. Unlike Bright Children's Home, the orphanage concerned is not acknowledged by the local government. As the head sister said,

> They don't want to help us, because then they would have to acknowledge us. They don't have much money, and if they were to work with us, they would have to acknowledge our existence as well as give our children help.
>
> (Interview, Sister H., 11 December 2007)

By help she means free access to schools and medical care.

Another kind of orphanage arrangement is the "private orphanage" that can be certified by the government, and whose children mostly have *hukous* (residency permits). These may not be called "welfare homes" (*fuliyuan*), and not only do they not receive state funding, but they are required to pay a 3 percent "management fee" to the local government, which is charged with overseeing the operation of the orphanage. A private individual or group of individuals can raise funds to support the orphanage, but the money must be raised overseas. One such example is found in the rugged western area of China that I call "grassland home." It was founded by a devout Buddhist Chinese national married to a foreign national. Close relations with the local government were established, and after the money had been raised and the local government "negotiated" with, the orphanage was built. The area where the orphanage was built is very poor and the parental disability rate is high. Very few families can take on extra children, so the children whose parents cannot care for them end up begging on the streets. Further, the number of abandoned and orphaned children has continued to creep up in the past few years. Funding remains a challenge since the government will provide no funds and the group must rely on expatriates and multinational businesses working in China.

A key issue in social service provision for these children, as already mentioned, concerns the *hukou*. Without it, children are not eligible for welfare services. The assignment of a *hukou* requires the local Public Security Bureau to issue a certification of abandonment (or proof of being an orphan), after which the local social welfare institute (or child welfare institute) proceeds to wait the required three-month period of "looking for the parents." After a set period, a local *hukou* for the child is obtained. In short, there must be an official record of abandonment in a given locality and an attempted search for the parents since abandoning a child is illegal in China. However, the legal record is also a function of the overarching birth planning policies. The concern noted in many places, and in conversations with officials, is that people will attempt to use abandonment as a way to hide over-plan births. The idea is that they might try to hide an over-plan birth by claiming the child is not theirs but was found abandoned and then attempt to register the child. The issues of finding and attempting to register children who have not gone through the CWI system was variously discussed in local newspapers in the late 1990s and early 2000s (Keyser 2001). Thus, all children taken in by Catholic or other non-governmental orphanages remain unaccounted for in the system.

Other organizations with good government relations are the Sun Villages, spread over several provinces, with the "model" village being in Beijing. They were started by Zhang Sujin, a former prison warden who was troubled by the children who lived outside the gates of the prison because they had nowhere to go. The Sun Villages provide housing and care to children whose parents have either been executed or been given long prison sentences. It has five locations across China. These children are not considered orphans under Chinese law, a status that would entitle them to welfare benefits such as schooling and medical care. Begun in Shaanxi in the mid-1990s, the Sun Village was then established in Beijing in 2000 as a research institute. It was then picked up by the China Charity Federation, which is under the MOCA, and in 2003 became an education center. It is listed as an NGO and thus can receive no government funding, but by attaching it to one of the four approved charity organizations the government can help the organization raise money domestically, and can help promote it in the press and on Chinese television.[10] Sun Village's existence vividly highlights gaps in child welfare policy. It is also an example of how a societal response to a problem, namely Zhang Sujin's caring for these children, then transposed into a negotiated relationship with the state, coming under the China Charity Federation in order to receive more press coverage, and funds to continue to expand as the need expands.

When parents are arrested for a crime and prosecuted, they return to their native place to serve their sentence. However, no such provisions for returning a child exist, so the children stay in the city where the crime was committed. If the parent is executed, it is likely that neither the surviving parent nor the extended family members will be found, or, if they are found, that they will not want to care for the child. The child thus becomes virtually an orphan, though not recognized as such under the law.[11] For example, on a visit I made to one of the Sun Villages I came across a little Uighur boy about 18 months old whose parents had been arrested for theft and then found to be under the legal age to have a child (they were both teenagers). I was told that they would be returned to Xinjiang, but at that time it was probable that the boy would have to remain in Beijing since no family in Xinjiang could be found to take him, nor was there a government agency responsible for escorting him back home, for working with the family, or for "fostering" him out to a local family in his own community. He will remain in legal limbo, likely growing up in what amounts to an orphanage, well run and caring but an orphanage nonetheless.

Foster care as social service provision

Foster care as a policy initiative complements the promotion of the socialization of welfare push launched in 2000, and the idea of "small government, big society," which is that society will help take care of the children as an act of civic-mindedness. As awareness of orphans grew among the general population, public space for discussing and debating the "problem" of orphans also grew. Newspapers started carrying stories about society's responsibility to care for orphans, stories about the idea of fostering non-biological children, exposés on the joys of this kind of social action, as well as discussion about the legal and policy contradictions where it concerns the birth planning policies and domestic adoption policies. Widespread publicity also helped localities with the problem that all foster care systems around the world face: the recruitment of good foster homes.[12] Foster care itself, as a policy initiative, sought to reduce the cost of caring for orphans (since it costs less to house them with a family than in an institution), provide them a home life, and engage society in caring for its members. Thus, foster care in the reform period has undergone a change as compared with that in the pre-reform era in both the scope and the practice of social involvement where it concerns orphans.

The example of foster care illuminates the gaps in orphan care. Foster care also represents a change in the state's relationship to society in that it pays one group of people to care for another group of people. The controversy surrounding orphan care led to alternative ways of thinking about how to care for orphans, and to the effort to engage society in caring for these children by providing a monetary benefit to citizen foster families. While the specifics for foster care vary among CWIs and localities, the basics are as follows. Foster care involves recruiting families to care for non-biological children for a monthly fee, currently running from 300 to as high as RMB 900 per child, based on level of disability. Poorer localities have lower fostering fees, while cities and wealthier regions pay higher rates. In nearly every case of foreign-dominated fostering, the fees paid are higher than those paid by the orphanage, but the expectations are also usually higher as well. It involves some amount of training, and monthly (or in some cases more frequent) visits by staff from the CWI or contracted organization. There are now several "models" of foster care throughout China supervised by both INGOs and state-run CWIs. Some involve foster parents moving to live within the CWI compound, or to live together in CWI-owned apartments. Other arrangements are based on recruiting local families to become foster families in the same village. Finally, while levels of income and education vary, a non-scientific survey of reports, investigations, and my own visits with roughly 50 families suggests that many foster families are in the lower middle to low income bracket. Many are rural families. In urban areas, there is likely better organization, and some urban areas have even started foster family associations. These social groups help to promote the idea of volunteerism and civic engagement.

One well-known example of state-sponsored organizing around foster care is found in the Tianjin CWI. Having received much help and significant foreign involvement early on from international charities, businesses, and the International Committee for the Care of Orphans (ICCO – a volunteer organization of spouses living in Beijing and Tianjin), the orphanage has become a "model" CWI and developed an extensive foster care center. The "Jinghai Fostering Base" brings families to live together, and foster parents are organized into small groups of ten families that support one another, share information, and work to recruit new families. The foster care families also have a newsletter. They hold awareness activities and are visible in the community. This and other efforts to organize foster families promote civic engagement and civic-mindedness. This is exactly what a retreating state needs society to do.

Another example is found in the "Angel Moms," an unregistered Chinese NGO. This group promotes foster care and education among the poor. Its motto is "the more mothers involved, the more children saved." It recruits foster families to care for children needing or recovering from surgery. Most are orphans. But it also seeks to raise awareness of children falling through the cracks in social welfare provision, and has been active in promoting the cause of children. For example, it petitioned the government to address the problem of kidnapping and child trafficking. The petition was signed by 6,000 mothers across China whose children had been kidnapped. Though not allowed to present its petition to the Communist Party Congress held in 2007, the group nevertheless tried.

Local governments, officially saddled with much welfare provision, also benefits from society-based efforts and on occasion, as in the case of Bright Children's Home, exist in a mutually beneficial environment. An example that captures this potentially positive relationship is found in the example of "Joy Children's Foster Care Center" in "G" province. This group began as an effort by local expatriate Christians, who took in orphans and fostered them. Over time, their local Chinese Christian counterparts joined them, and as a group eventually took over Joy Children's Center. The Chinese Christians in turn developed good relations with the local government and local CWI.[13] The negotiations over time have resulted in close relations between the group and the government. So solid is the relationship that the local orphanage pays for two medical personnel to staff the foster care center but itself does not run the center, or fund it. The foster care center recruits and trains the families, and manages the running of the center and the monitoring of the children. The local group raises funds to support the foster care center, while the CWI pays the foster family fees. Started by foreigners and then indigenized, this is an example of a society-based organization (and a religious one at that) cultivating a relationship with the government for the purpose of welfare provision, in this case to orphans.

Conclusion

One could argue that all orphans in state care are basically being provided for by the state. This is not incorrect, and there are examples of extremely well-run CWIs that do a good job not just keeping the children alive, but nurturing them despite tight financial circumstances. Indeed, one of the goals of Half the Sky's program under the Blue Sky policy is to help the fifty-three CWIs with which it will work to improve care. Others, having benefited from foreign involvement, are doing a better job at raising the standard of care of orphans. But unfortunately there are too many CWIs that are failing China's orphans, especially as financial pressures on the localities have increased, along with the abandonment of not just healthy infants, but infants who have some level of disability and thus are likely to require more funding to care for them. Added to the official number are the hundreds of thousands of children who are not provided for in the system at all, either because they have no registration or because they are not documented "orphans." This is where the state is not providing welfare and where, as the survey in this chapter demonstrates, one finds non-governmental groups stepping in to provide welfare services. These groups, as outlined in Chapter 2, all strain under regulation from the state, and engage in negotiation either to provide services where the state does not, or to work to build on the limited services that do exist. Further, as surveyed in this chapter, many of these groups look for strategies to increase their autonomy from the state, or for ways to maintain the autonomy they have from the start.

A significant constraint woven through many, if not all, of these organizations is the limitations on registering as NGOs, or outright inability to do so. They exist in legal limbo. The limitation placed on who may raise money further constrains development of domestic charities and domestic NGOs. Most do not want to allow themselves to be absorbed by a supervisory unit because they will be able neither to help unregistered orphanages nor to decide how to spend their money. Indeed, as one local activist told me,

> there is deep suspicion (in general) about giving to state-controlled charity foundations, so most of the money has to come from abroad. We cannot seriously raise money in China because the government feels that any money raised is theirs to decide how to distribute.
>
> (Interview M, 23 April 2007)

Another constraint in the case of orphans is the large number of children who are not registered and thus rely solely on the kindness of others to acquire basic social services. The domestic non-governmental, non-registered groups that care for these children are further at the mercy of the local government to either assist them or allow others (oftentimes foreign groups) to provide welfare for their charges. The unregistered children problem is bubbling to the surface of policy discussion, but the solution will require a level of center–local coordination across multiple agencies that may or may not be possible given the current political and economic structure. However, this is not to say that in the fluid and dynamic changes under way in China there is no way to resolve the problem, at least some of the time. And here we glimpse some of the opportunities created by the ambiguous environment. The following example highlights what, in the restrictive and ambiguous political/legal environment, can take place on behalf of orphans. In one province, a foreign group with good ties to a local CWI managed to persuade the sisters of a convent in a nearby county within the same province to stop taking any more children, and then absorbed those children into an ongoing project. With extensive political connections, the group was then able to persuade the CWI to "claim" at least some of these children and create a record of abandonment so that it could begin the process of getting them registered (that is, getting *hukous*), which then makes the children eligible for welfare services and, potentially, adoption. It is a win–win situation. The children are registered, the CWI will get any income from adoptions but does not have to absorb the cost of their care (which is covered by the group the CWI was working with), and the children get access to welfare provision.[14]

In sum, political, bureaucratic, and financial constraints hamper the legalization of both INGOs and domestic NGOs as full players in welfare provision for orphans. The political constraint is tension over how, and under what circumstances, INGOs can be registered, which involves competing bureaucratic claims and raises the question of who will monitor the money. While these are constraints, the very vagueness in the law on the protection of children as well as the ability to operate at the local level has also created opportunities. Another way to think about it is captured in Gao Bingzhong's work (2001) on the rise of social organizations. He describes negotiation and socialization as the horizontal organizing of society away from the vertical organizing under conditions of tight state control or, to use language adopted in this book, societalization under conditions of tight regulation. In this case, the tight state regulation is the legal and political framework for who may care for an abandoned or orphaned child in China on the one hand, and the unclear legal status of foreign and domestic NGO organizations on the other. The horizontal organizing is the negotiated relationship between all manner of NGOs and charity groups and local CWIs. It is also the activity of unregistered society-run orphanages that exist outside of the legal framework altogether – what this volume dubs the societalization of welfare provision. The social space has grown in this ambiguous environment, and all the players continue to find ways to "weave and flow and inch forward," like Beijing traffic.

Notes

1 Research for this chapter was supported by a Fulbright Research Scholarship Grant. The author wishes to thank the editors for their insightful comments.

2 Indeed, Plan International, together with the Social Development Institute of Beijing Normal University and the Ministry of Civil Affairs, is currently conducting a multi-year project to research the numbers of "invisible" children, raise awareness about them, and then advocate on their behalf.

3 Its web address with statistics is www.careyouth.com/guerx/about%20us/aboutus.html.

4 See "Country Report on Child Development in China, 2003–2004." English version posted on www.china.org.cn/english/2005/May/130426.htm. See also Shang *et al.* (2005). *China Daily On-line* cited the deputy director of the social welfare office under the Ministry of Civil Affairs as estimating that there are "at least 150,000 homeless children wandering the country's cities." See "Xinhua" (updated 7 March 2005), "China Strives for Providing Help for Street Children" at www.chinadaily.com.cn (accessed 20 July 2005). See also Murphy (2004) and Zuo *et al.* (2006).

5 Quoting an internal report and an interview with an Anhui Bureau of Civil Affairs cadre, Zhong (2006) notes that the money available for supporting orphans sometimes amounts to little more than 10 percent of the total amount needed for orphan support.

6 Information on Care for Children comes from interviews with Robert Glover, executive director of Care for Children in Beijing, in 2006 and 2007.

7 The issue centered on whether or not the Ministry of Civil Affairs was the appropriate place for registering private foundations as well as being the supervisory agent. The State

Council did not like it and worried about corruption, channeling of funds, tax evasion, and the potential for cronyism and fraud. It argued that there must be an "oversight" unit. Or, as Robert Glover put it, "there were concerns over gate-keeping." The result is that the list of "*zhuguan*" *danwei* is much shorter and regulated. Further, as Nick Young put it, "the civil affairs bureaucracy went into freeze mode and were somewhat disempowered." Young was invited to consult on the law, and Glover was the director of Care for Children, one of the thirty-four organizations able to register during the brief window of 2004. The process of granting registered status is ongoing, and supposedly in March 2008 some eleven foundations of the many that have applied were given registered NGO status, though the full list as of June 2008 has yet to be made public.

8 The Blue Sky plan, announced in 2007, seeks to provide social welfare centers where they do not exist, as well as to expand facilities in various sites across China. The idea is to create full-service child welfare centers that can reach beyond orphan care to provide medical care, rehabilitation, education, and training for needy children in localities. The plan was greeted with mixed reviews at the 2007 orphanage directors' meeting because it seems to undermine the goal of foster care, and puts the money not into training or care for the children, but into buildings.

9 For details on this situation, see "New Diaspora, New Ways of Giving Back" published on www.chinadevelopmentbrief.com. One of the organizations, Half the Sky Foundation, was featured in Li (2005). It can be accessed online at www.bjreview.com.cn. International schools in Beijing and other major cities conducted drives organized by Our Chinese Daughters Foundation, Half the Sky, and other groups created through clubs such as Families with Children from China (FCC). Further, other local charity organizations raise money and goods for poor children and orphans.

10 Zhang herself is well connected within the public security apparatus, and has parlayed that into coverage from the state for the purpose of promoting her cause. The villages have been featured on Chinese television, and received coverage in both the Chinese- and English-language press in China. It is featured in the corporate social responsibility page for Microsoft, for example. Further, like the Huiling School for the Mentally Challenged, Beijing Sun Village hosts tour groups that visit on "beneficent" trips to get a taste for social organizing. At Huiling, the students put on a short show of traditional Chinese "rap" music for the visitors.

11 The reason this would be has to do with the surviving spouse's desire to *gai jia* (change homes) – in other words, remarry. Also, as Ms Zhang, head of the center, explained to me, there is a stigma attached to the child of someone executed or imprisoned for life: "it's the idea that their parents are bad, so they are probably bad too." Often, the family will not want to take care of the child, who ends up being bounced from home to home and suffers abuse. The child then will often run away and live on the streets.

12 The early years saw confusion and concern as the awareness of the orphan situation and the need for foster families came up against the birth planning policies, the domestic adoption law, as well as local ordinances for collective distribution of welfare benefits. Moreover, local interpretations of existing laws and policy further created fodder for newspaper discussions and legal opinions about the legal status of these children and of the legal framework itself. See Keyser (2001).

13 To protect the center, its staff, and its relationship with local government, a fictitious name is used.

14 All identifying references have been withheld because it is illegal for CWIs (working with other government agencies) to "create" a record of abandonment. But recall the description by Shang and Wu (2005) of the local government–Catholic orphanage relationship, where if it was possible for a child to be adopted, the local government would help facilitate the "necessary" paperwork for the child to be able to be adopted. Outside the scope of this chapter, but no less interesting, are the political and financial dynamics of CWIs and adoption.

Bibliography

Chang, Y. (2000) *Zai likai fumu de rizili: zhongguo shoujiazuifan zinu ertongcun jishi* [A Day in the Life Separated from Parents: A Record of China's Children of the Incarcerated at Children's Sun Village], Beijing: Weilai Press.

Chen, H. H. (2003) "Paradigm Shifts in Social Welfare Policy Making in China: Struggling between Economic Efficiency and Social Equity," in C. J. Finer (ed.) *Social Policy Reform in China*, Burlington, VT: Ashgate Publishing.

China Development Brief (2001) *250 Chinese NGOs: Civil Society in the Making*, Beijing: China Development Brief.

Davis, D. (1989) "Chinese Social Welfare: Policy and Outcomes," *China Quarterly* 119 (September): 577–97.

Ding, D. (1998) "Corporatism and Civil Society in China: An Overview of the Debate in Recent Years," *China Information* 12 (4): 45–6.

Ding, H. (2006) "Jiuzhu liulang ertong, tamen xiang dang zhuanye" [Their Relative Expertise in Housing Street Children], *Xinhua Daily Broadcast* No. 007 (10 June).

Ding, K. (2003) "The Crucial Role of Local Governments in Setting Up a Social Safety Net," *China Perspectives* 48 (July–August): 37–49.

Full Text of Beijing Declaration on Commitments for Children (2001) *Xinhua* in English 16 May; in FBIS-CHI-2001-0516.

Gao, B. (2001) "The Rise of Associations in China and the Question of Their Legitimacy," *Social Sciences in China* 1 (Spring): 73–87.

Gao, K. (2001) "Charity Groups Foresee a Boom," China Internet Information Center. Online, available at: www.china.org.cn (14 March; accessed 21 July 2007).

Howell, J. and Pearce, J. (2001) *Civil Society and Development: A Critical Explanation*, Boulder, CO: Lynne Rienner.

Hu, Y. (2007) "Baby Born with Birth Defects Every 30 Seconds," *China Daily* (30 October): 3.

Huang, W. (1992) "Minors Protected under the Law," *Beijing Review* (22–28 June): 19–23.

Huang, Y. (2004) "Bringing the State Back In: The Political Economy of Public Health in Rural China," *Journal of Contemporary China* 13 (39): 367–90.

Johnson, K. (1996) "The Politics of the Revival of Infant Abandonment in China, with Special Reference to Hunan," *Population and Development Review* 22 (1): 77–98.

—— (1998) "Infant Abandonment and Adoption in China," *Population and Development Review* 24 (3): 469–510.

Keyser, C. (2001) "Protecting, Fostering, Adopting: The Search for Coherent Policies towards China's Children," paper presented at the 2001 Association of Asian Studies Annual Meeting, Chicago, Illinois.

Li, L. (2005) "Holding Up Half the Sky," *Beijing Review* (25 May).

Li, W. (2000) "Luliyuan daomai erzi? Aixin ye suyao diya?" *Beijing Qingnian Bao* (29 November): 1.

Lu, S. Z., Wei, Z. P., and Hu, W. (2005) *An Introduction to China's Child Welfare Policy* [Zhongguo ertong zhengce: gailun], Beijing: Social Sciences Academy Press.

Magnier, M. (2006) "Child-Theft Racket Growing in China: Thousands Are Abducted for Profit Each Year", *Los Angeles Times* (1 January): A1.

Murphy, D. (2004) "The Lost Generation," *Far Eastern Economic Review* (19 February): 48–50.

Palmer, M. (1989) "Civil Adoption in Contemporary Chinese Law: A Contract to Care," *Modern Asian Studies* 23 (2): 373–410.

Pei, M. (1992) "Societal Takeover in China and the USSR," *Journal of Democracy* 3 (January): 108–17.

Peng, Bo (2003) "The Policy Process in Contemporary China: Mechanisms of Politics and Government," in C. J. Finer (ed.) *Social Policy Reform in China*, Aldershot, UK: Ashgate Press.

Qiao, D. P. and Chan, Y. C. (2005) "Child Abuse in China: A Yet-to-Be Acknowledged 'Social Problem' in the Chinese Mainland," *Child and Family Social Work* 10: 21–7.

Saich, A. (2000) "Negotiating the State: The Development of Social Organizations in China," *China Quarterly* 161 (March): 124–41.

Saywell, T. (2000) "Nowhere to Run," *Far Eastern Economic Review* (8 June): 78–80.

Shang, X. Y. and Wu, X. M. (2003a) "The Changing Role of the State in Child Protection: The Case of Nanchang," *Social Service Review* 77 (4): 523–40.

—— (2003b) "Protecting Children under Financial Constraints: 'Foster Mother Villages' in Datong," *Journal of Social Policy* 32(4): 549–70.

Shang, X., Wu, X., and Wu, Y. (2005) "Welfare Provision for Vulnerable Children: The Missing Role of the State," *China Quarterly* 181 (March): 122–36.

Shevchenko, A. (2004) "Bringing the Party Back In: The CCP and the Trajectory of Market Transition in China," *Communist and Post-communist Studies* 37: 161–85.

Short, S. E., Zhai, F., Xu, S., and Yang, M. (2001) "China's One-Child Policy and the Care of Children: An Analysis of Qualitative and Quantitative Data," *Social Forces* 79 (March): 913–43.

Tong, Y. (1997) *Transitions from State Socialism*, Lanham, MD: Rowman & Littlefield.

Wan, Y. H. (2006) "Liulang ertong jiuzhu shou kun falu mangqu" [The Law Is Not Clear in Aiding Street Urchins], *Gansu Jinji Ribao* (4 August): 2.

Wang, X. M. (2005) *Ertong Quanli Lun* [On Children's Rights], Beijing: Social Sciences Academic Press.

Xin, R. Z. (2000) "Knowledge on Self-Protection Is Far Removed from Children," *Renmin Ribao* (9 November): 2.

Xu, S. (2000) "Qiying nengfou xiangshou tongdeng daiyu?" [Should an Abandoned Child Receive Equal Treatment?], *Huaxi Dushibao* (10 October): 2.

Zhong, J. (2006) "573,000 Orphans in China", *Circle* (a monthly magazine for Chinese Children Adoption International) 52 (March/April): 6. Online, available at: www.chinesechildren.org/Newsletter%5CWindow%20to%20China/WTC_03_2006.pdf (accessed 10 January 2008).

"Zhongguo Renmin Gongheguo Weicheng Nian Baohu Fa" (People's Republic of China Law on the Protection of Minors) 1992. (An English version of the law is available online from the Chinese government-sponsored website Human Rights China: www.humanrights-china.org.)

Zhou, X. (2004) *The State and Life Chances in Urban China*, Cambridge: Cambridge University Press.

Zuo, Y., Zhou, X., Shi, X., and He, J. (2006) "Ting zhu liulang ertong de jiaobu" (Steps to Halt Children Living on the Streets), *Guangyuan Ribao* (16 August): 5.

4 Navigating a space for labor activism

Labor NGOs in the Pearl River Delta of south China

Hong Zhang and Marsha Smith

Introduction

China's market reform has dramatically altered the relationship between the state and society in the provision of public goods and social services. The development of China's market economy is facilitated to a large extent by the creation and unleashing of an entirely new labor force in the manufacturing and service sectors: rural migrant labor in urban China.

It has been estimated that around 150–200 million rural migrant workers are now working in cities (*People's Daily* 2006; Shan 2007). A survey conducted in 2003 by China Enterprise Confederation found that peasant workers comprised 57.6 percent of the labor force in the industrial sector, with 68 percent in processing or manufacturing industries and about 80 percent in the construction industry (Zhongxinshe 2004). However, despite the great contribution made by rural migrant workers to China's economic growth and urban boom in the past two decades, there is yet no central policy to integrate them into urban life and the social service provision system. Migrant workers remain on the margins of society and are excluded from benefiting from the prosperity and economic development that their labor has created (Solinger 1999; Wang 2005). The plight of migrant workers highlights the pitfalls of China's uneven market reform and an urban-biased social policy and household registration system (the *hukou*) that divides the Chinese population into urban and rural, with differential entitlements to state welfare and social service provision (Wang 2005: 148–9).

The marginalization of migrant workers occurs alongside two other important developments in China's state–society relationship: one is the withdrawal of the state as the sole provider of social services, and the other is the rise of social actors such as non-governmental organizations (NGOs) seeking to fill the gap. As Saich notes about the state's withdrawal,

> continued rapid economic growth is vital to party survival but this will entail further layoffs, downsizing of the government bureaucracy, and the shedding of more government functions on behalf of society or the likelihood of social instability and unrest will increase. Pluralism of service delivery is now a fact of life with voluntary organizations supplementing the

> state in providing basic services and with private institutions in health and education expanding.
>
> (Saich 2006: 288)

On the rise of new social actors, Jude Howell notes that from the 1980s to the early 1990s, the development of civil society was marked by the rapid "proliferation of business, trade, professional, and academic organizations"; and this development trend reflected "both the changing nature of the economy and the Party/state's recognition of the need to liberalize spaces for association to facilitate the development of the market" (2004: 145). However, Howell finds that from the mid-1990s on, "a new phase of civil society" began to develop, with "the rapid growth of associations concerned with providing services on behalf of and/or representing the interests of groups marginalized in the reform process" (p. 145). Concerned about the interests of those marginalized in China's market reform, this new "stratum of associations" tackles "the problems of marginalization, poverty, and equity," and "confronts head-on some of the social consequences of rapid economic change" (p. 150). Howell (2004) further points out that these new societal groups and organizations have circumvented restrictive registration requirements in providing services and help to marginalized and vulnerable groups such as people with HIV/AIDs, disabled people, elderly people, children, women, and migrant workers.

In assessing civil society in China as a late-Leninist state, Mary Gallagher (2004) argues that we need to distinguish two types of civil society that are at work in reshaping state–society relations in reform-era China: "official civil society" and "unofficial civil society." By "official civil society," Gallagher emphasizes the continuous tight state control over social organizations "through four major mechanisms": "the legal and administrative regulations that govern them," "their restricted financial autonomy," "the practice of 'double-posting' government or party cadres to leadership positions within social organizations," and the "ideology of the CCP" (p. 424). Gallagher uses the All-China Federation of Trade Unions (ACFTU) and business associations as two case studies of how the state regulates and exerts control over both labor and private capital through incorporation and co-optation. However, Gallagher also points out that despite "China's repressive political environment, much change is happening outside official civil society." In particular, she cites migrant workers – "the floating population" – and unorthodox religious practitioners as "unofficial civil society" groups and sees their growth as "directly related to the state's unwillingness to deploy corporatist organizational tactics to capture, co-opt, and control new kinds of resistance and civil action" (p. 436).

In this chapter, we follow up both Howell's and Gallagher's leads in discussing some new trends of civil society development in China by focusing on the recent rise of labor NGOs for migrant workers in the industrial hub of the Pearl River Delta (PRD) area in Guangdong Province of south China. In line with Howell's and Gallagher's arguments, we will show how migrant labor NGOs have emerged to provide services and advocate on behalf of groups marginalized in the reform process, and how migrant labor NGOs have carved out a space for their activism and responded to their marginalization as the state refuses to grant them organizational legitimacy.

Although China's market reform has been accompanied by the retrenchment of the Party-state from certain social and economic spheres and a dramatic increase in social organizations, the Party-state has not relinquished its Leninist style of control in its regulation of the social organization sector. The current regulatory framework requires that every NGO must be registered as a "social organization" (SO), a "civil, non-enterprise unit" (CNEU), or a "foundation" (see Chapters 1 and 2). Moverover, it must go through a dual registration process that requires it first to get a corresponding government institution as its supervisory agency before it can become registered with the Ministry of Civil Affairs or local bureaus of civil affairs. The requirement of a government supervisory agency – which is aptly dubbed "the mother-in-law" (*popo*) in Chinese – not only superimposes the state power on an NGO but also makes it difficult for a grassroots NGO to find a government institution to agree to serve as its supervisory agency, because this government agency can be held accountable should any political problem occur in an NGO it supervises (Ma 2005: 65). Another important controlling feature in the current regulatory framework can be seen in the policy that no similar organizations can coexist at the various administrative levels. This stipulation clearly aims at state monopoly on representation, as it "ensures the mass organizations such as the All-China Women's Federation and the All-China Federation of Trade Unions enjoy monopoly representation and cannot be challenged by independent groups seeking to represent the interests of women and workers" (Saich 2006: 290).

This strict top-down regulation on permissible social organizations is still effective in preventing potential grassroots organizations from being formed and is frequently used by government agencies at various levels to prevent any attempt to set up social organizations they deem suspicious and a threat to their monopoly control. The failed attempt in 2004 by Zhang Zhiru, a migrant worker from Hunan Province, to register and set up an association for migrant workers in Shenzhen is a case in point. In 2004, Zhang and several fellow migrant workers attempted to organize migrant workers and establish a "Shenzhen Migrant Workers' Association" (*Shenzhen wailaigong xiehui*). He first went to the Shenzhen Municipal Federation of Trade Unions (SMFTU) to ask for sponsorship, but was told that he could not establish a separate organization for migrant workers because China already had the official ACFTU to represent workers. Zhang then wrote a letter to Shenzhen's mayor for support and the mayor redirected him to the Shenzhen bureau of civil affairs. When Zhang went there, the civil affairs officials told him that there was no way they could approve his request: "Whoever does so will get fired" (Long 2007).

Under such onerous restrictions, how have NGOs for migrant workers come to exist and operate in the PRD area of south China where rural migrants have formed a major part of the workforce? This chapter tries to answer that question by focusing on three labor NGOs in the area: the Chinese Working Women Network (CWWN) in Shenzhen, the Panyu Migrant Worker Documentation

Center (MWDC) in Guangzhou, and the Institute of Contemporary Observation (ICO) in Shenzhen.[1] We address the following questions: How did these NGOs come into being? What services do they provide for migrant workers? How are they funded? What difficulties and constraints currently face these NGOs? What are the factors that have enabled these organizations to carve out a space for their activist work in a Party-state that is so wary of any organization outside its control? Where is this new labor movement heading? As funding for labor NGOs in the PRD area comes almost exclusively from abroad, this chapter will also look into the role international support has played in facilitating labor activism from the bottom up in the PRD area. This is an area where foreign direct investment and multinationals are highly concentrated in export-oriented industries, and where rural migrants form the major labor force in this era of globalization.

Social exclusion, migrant workers' self-organizing, and labor NGOs in the Pearl River Delta area

Since China's market reform in the early 1980s, Guangdong Province has witnessed an annual double-digit GDP growth rate of 13.7 percent (Song 2006). As one of the earliest experiments in the market economy, Guangdong is home to three of the first five special economic zones (Shenzhen, Zhuhai, and Shantou) set up in 1980 to attract foreign investment and develop export-oriented industries. The actualized foreign direct investment (FDI) in Guangdong shot up from US$919 million in 1985 to US$10.01 billion in 2004. During the same period, the total export sales also jumped from US$10.14 billion to US$191.6 billion. The large flow of FDI into Guangdong Province has led to the mushrooming of tens of thousands of foreign-invested enterprises (FIEs) and privately owned firms in the province.

One major factor that has attracted foreign multinationals, their subcontractors, and other private enterprises to set up factories in Guangdong Province, and the PRD area in particular, is the large inflow of cheap labor supplied by millions of farmers turned migrant workers. According to a national survey conducted in 2002 on cross-provincial migration, Guangdong was the largest recipient, attracting a whopping 46.7 percent of China's total cross-provincial migration, followed by Zhejiang and Jiangsu Provinces with a distant 9.8 percent and 5.3 percent respectively (MOLSS 2006: 75). And 86 percent of these migrant workers were concentrated in the PRD area, with 55 percent working in the labor-intensive manufacturing sector and 42 percent in tertiary industry (GBLSS 2006: 433)

However, while their labor has created the so-called "Shenzhen Speed" and transformed the area from an agricultural backwater just two decades ago into an economic boom area, migrant workers themselves remain marginalized and are excluded from benefiting from the economic development and the new wealth because of their non-resident status. They have no access to basic social welfare, which is granted only to local *hukou* residents. Worse still, as a marginal social group, migrant workers are frequently subject to predatory labor practices that violate their basic labor rights (Chan 2001; Chan and Zhu 2003). Now that economic growth has become China's new mantra, local governments are much more eager to adopt a pro-management stance and ensure a "business-friendly" environment to attract investment than to protect the labor rights of migrant workers.

China's one-party political system continues to forbid any independent workers' unions and labor organizations, and the top-down All-China Federation of Unions (ACFTU) is the only official union allowed to represent workers' interests. However, there are severe limitations hindering migrant workers from joining the ACFTU and its official local branches. First, migrant workers are employed predominantly in foreign-invested enterprises (FIEs) and private firms, where few official trade unions even exist. Second, as a legacy of China's socialist economy, the ACFTU is still a government bureaucracy and serves the traditional "transmission belt" function of supporting the Party and state's priorities. As Feng Chen points out, the ACFTU's

> institutional embedding in the Party-state sets the limits for the union's operational autonomy. It is preordained that the organization's priority is to serve the state's goals rather than labor interests, and that its actions cannot be at odds with the state's preferences.
>
> (2004: 30)

Moreover, despite the recent efforts by the ACFTU and its local branches to urge migrant workers to join official trade unions, only 21 million rural migrant workers had joined a trade union by the end of 2005, representing only 13.8 percent of the union labor (Zhao 2006). Migrant workers are still very skeptical about whether they can seek real help and protection from the ACFTU when they encounter abuses and problems in the workplace.

Given the lack of independent labor unions and organizations, rights-conscious activists and migrant workers began to organize in the PRD area during the mid-1990s. Described as forming a "migrant labor self-salvation movement" (*laogong zijiu yundong*), these new groups began to advocate labor rights protection and provide legal aid and education about workplace safety to migrant workers (Chen *et al.* 2005; Huang 2007). Because of the difficulty of legally registering as an NGO, and of the political sensitivity of labor organizing, it is not clear just how many such organizations exist in the PRD. One labor activist estimated that there were roughly fifty or so labor NGOs in the PRD area, but the majority of them are not registered (Long 2007). In the following, we discuss and analyze three migrant labor NGOs in the PRD.

*Case study 1: the Chinese Working Women Network (CWWN) (***Nugong Guanhuai***)*

The Chinese Working Women Network (CWWN) was formed by a group of academics in Hong Kong in 1996 with the mission of "promoting betterment for the lives of Chinese migrant women workers and developing feminist awareness of workers' empowerment."[2] Dr. Pun, now an associate professor of anthropology at Hong Kong's University of Science and Technology, established the CWWN and served as its first president.[3] The CWWN is a "membership-based NGO" registered in Hong Kong. Its current five executive committee members are all from Hong Kong and serve as volunteers. Three project coordinators from Hong Kong are hired to collaborate with a team of ten mainland staff to implement various programs in China.[4] Initially the CWWN received enthusiastic support from and had a partnership relationship with the ACFTU in the Nanshan District of Shenzhen from 1996 to the early 2000s. The Nanshan District ACFTU even provided the office for the CWWN. But since 2004, the Nanshan District ACFTU branch has begun to distance itself from the CWWN.[5] In 2006, the CWWN lost its office in Nanshan and was relocated to Bao'an District, a large labor-intensive export-oriented manufacturing zone where millions of young female migrants work. Describing the CWWN's initiatives as "community-based labor organizing," Pun and Chan (2004) discuss four types of service offered by the CWWN for female migrant workers in the PRD: the Center for Women Workers, the Mobile Health Express Service, the Women Workers' Cooperative (the Co-op), and the Occupational and Health Education Center.

The Center for Women Workers

Established in 1996, the Center for Women Workers "provides migrant women workers a cultural and physical space to build up their collectivity apart from their factory shop floor and dormitory." The center offers "labor rights education, protections against workplace sexual discrimination, sexual health education as well as training for returning migrants" (Pun and Chan 2004: 11). Through such interactive programs such as poetry reading and writing, singing and dancing, drama and role-play, and movie sharing, the center has tailored its services to meet the needs of female migrants, while also helping them to "express themselves and articulate their collective identity as migrant workers" and developing their leadership skills. The center also reaches out to workers in factory dormitories to form dormitory support networks, since many workers have little free time to visit the center.

The Mobile Health Express Service

The CWWN set up the Mobile Health Express Service in 2000 by converting a bus donated by Reebok, Inc. into a mobile health station. The bus carries books, magazines, a television set, video and broadcasting equipment, and some simple diagnostic health check-up tools. It also contains a counseling room where organizers and migrant workers can speak privately. According to Pun and Chan, the Mobile Health Express received local government support and was "the first project" for which the CWWN worked with the Guangdong Prevention and Treatment Center for Occupational Diseases (Pun and Chan 2004: 11).

The Women Workers' Cooperative (the Co-op)

The CWWN has also helped women workers to seek alternative economic activities through a collective and cooperative form. In 2002, a group of women migrant workers in Nanshan District of Shenzhen decided to leave factory work and, with help from the CWWN, set up a cooperative, which runs a shop selling daily necessities, books, and magazines for migrant workers. According to Pun and Chan (2004), the Co-op "commits to self determination among women workers on a collective basis. It is an alternate model of economic practice and adheres firmly to principles of mutual cooperation and social equality and emphasizes participation and democratization."

The Occupational Health Education Center

Established in 2002, the CWWN's Occupational Health Education Center (OHEC) is another joint project with the Guangdong Prevention and Treatment Center for Occupational Diseases, and has close working relations with Sun Yat-sen University and Shenzhen University. OHEC staff "offer hotline consultation services, produce education kits, provide information occupational health risk assessment, and organize participatory training workshops for workers at the plant level" (Pun and Chan 2004). From 2003 onward, the CWWN has made regular visits to hospitals to see injured workers, and facilitated the formation of the Concerned Group for Chinese Injured Workers for occupational and safety education and legal knowledge about work injury compensation. Also in 2003, the CWWN set up a specialized legal education unit for migrant workers to provide them with legal knowledge concerning matters such as labor rights, work-injury compensation, and social insurance.

The CWWN operates through volunteer help. It carries out projects with funding from a number of international organizations such as Social Accountability International (SAI), Hong Kong Oxfam, and the Asia Foundation, and from corporations such as Reebok, to conduct factory training and auditing programs.[6] Through its various projects and initiatives, the CWWN provides a vital service to young female migrant workers in Shenzhen's export industries. According to Dr. Pun, local government officials were initially supportive of the CWWN's work for female migrant workers. Such government agencies as Shenzhen Nanshan District ACFTU and Guangdong Prevention and Treatment Center for Occupational Diseases even assisted the CWWN and undertook joint projects with it. But since 2004, local government officials have become more cautious and less enthusiastic.[7] One reason could be that once the CWWN became more visible and active in advocating rights protection for female migrant workers, local government officials came to see it as a potential political threat.

*Case study 2: the Panyu Migrant Worker Documentary Center (MWDC) (***Panyu Dagongzu Wenshu Chuli Fuwubu***)*

The Panyu Migrant Worker Documentary Center (MWDC) was established and registered as a self-employed entity (*geti gongshanghu*) with the Bureau of Industry and Commerce Administration in 1998. One of its original founders, Liao Xiaofeng, was a migrant worker from Sichuan province. In 1994, a fellow migrant worker from his hometown had two fingers cut by an electric saw, and his boss was willing to pay only 6,000 yuan (around US$725) for the work injury. Having served in the army before, Liao began to read books about labor law and decided to write an appeal to the Labor Dispute Mediation Committee on his fellow migrant worker's behalf. To their surprise, his appeal letter worked and his fellow migrant worker obtained an additional 6,000 yuan in compensation. Soon after, a female fellow worker came to him for help as she was denied compensation for her work-related injury. This time, Liao helped the worker collect 10,800 yuan. Encouraged by these two successes and inundated with similar requests, Liao decided to set up the MWDC in 1998 to provide a fee-based service for migrant workers in handling their labor dispute and compensation cases. Hailed as the very first self-initiated migrant labor organization, the MWDC initially received praise and support from the Chinese Communist Youth League, and Liao was called a "rights defense hero" by some mainstream media (Sun 2007). But from the very beginning, the MWDC lacked the funds to cover its rent, telephone and utility bills, investigation expenses, and even staff salaries. Just three months after the MWDC had been established, Liao left the organization abruptly and has not appeared in public since.

After Liao's departure in late 1998, cofounder Zeng Feiyang took over MWDC's work. Zeng had a law degree from South China Normal University in 1996. After a year working in Nanxiong Municipal Court in northern Guangdong, Zeng decided to give up his government position and join a law firm in Guangzhou, where he began to handle labor dispute cases and encounter firsthand experiences of migrant workers' legal issues in the PRD. In 1998, Zeng left the law firm to cofound the MWDC and has held the position of director since Liao left the MWDC in 1998. From 1998 to 2001, the MWDC continued to charge small fees for its legal aid services for migrant workers. In December 2000, Zeng was invited to attend a legal aid seminar in Beijing sponsored by Beijing University Women's Law Studies and Legal Aid Center. It was at this seminar that Zeng for the first time learned what an NGO was and how it functioned, and heard about the work of other NGOs in China. His own work for migrant workers in the PRD also caught the attention of some foreign donors that were cosponsors of this seminar. After receiving start-up funds in January 2002 from the Evangelischer Entwicklungsdienst (EED) Church Development Service, a German body, Zeng turned the MWDC into a not-for-profit organization providing legal aid services to migrant workers free of charge even though it is still registered as a self-employed business entity. Between 2002 and

2006, the MWDC received foreign funds from a wide range of international organizations.

The MWDC's programs for migrant workers include four major initiatives: the Legal Aid Counseling Center, the Cultural Development Center for Migrant Workers, the Occupational Safety and Health Support Network, and the Factory Auditing and Training Program.

The Legal Aid Counseling Center

Currently, the MWDC provides legal support for migrant workers in three ways: (1) legal counseling; (2) handling labor dispute cases on behalf of migrant workers; and (3) hosting monthly seminars on labor laws and rights protection for migrant workers. Much of the Legal Aid Center's work has focused on familiarizing migrant workers with the legal process for seeking compensation for workplace injuries and health hazards, and educating migrant workers about labor law and the legal procedures for redressing violations of that law. The MWDC has one full-time staff member in its Legal Aid Counseling Center and collaborates with law professors and law student interns from Sun Yat-sen University Law School and South China Normal University, and volunteer lawyers, in providing legal counseling and running legal seminars.

The Cultural Development Center for Migrant Workers

Established in 2003, the Cultural Development Center for Migrant Workers provides recreational activities and learning and socializing opportunities for migrant workers. The center also holds theme-centered activities every night.[8] Since its establishment in March 2003, the center not only has become a favorite place for local young migrant workers to socialize and relax, but also has established a venue where migrant workers can find a network of mutual support.

The Pearl River Delta Occupational Safety and Health Support Network

From 2000 on, MWDC staff began to pay hospital visits to injured migrant workers in the PRD area, documenting their injuries and compensation cases and offering legal counseling on workplace injuries. In March 2004, the MWDC established the Pearl River Delta Occupational Safety and Health Support Network. Under this new initiative, the MWDC published a periodical called *Occupational Safety and Health Briefs* (*OSH Briefs*). In collaborating with Sun Yat-sen University Law School's Clinical Legal Education and the CWWN (profiled earlier), the MWDC also published a *Handbook on the Rights of Workplace-Injured Workers* (*Rights Handbook*) and distributed the *OSH Briefs* and *Rights Handbook* to the workers during its staff's regular visits to injured workers in the hospitals. Besides making hospital visits, the MWDC also held free monthly seminars for migrant workers on occupational safety and health at its Cultural Development Center, given by experts from several colleges in the area on a voluntary basis.

The Factory Auditing and Training Program

In 2004 and 2005, the MWDC began to collaborate with several international audit organizations and NGOs to conduct factory inspections, and also training sessions for management and workers on the implementation of codes of conduct and labor standards. The main activities of the MWDC in this area include promoting corporate social responsibility initiatives, inspecting code of conduct implementation, collecting information on labor conditions, interviewing workers, and providing workshops on Chinese labor law and international labor standards.

As of 2006, the MWDC had five full-time staff members but it has developed a pool of 150 volunteers consisting mostly of migrant workers but also some university professors, college students, lawyers, and local residents. As a grassroots organization, the MWDC is mostly run by migrant workers turned activists. Zeng Feiyang, its director, is the only person who has a college degree. Zeng emphasized that the MWDC's ultimate goal is to raise workers' rights awareness and help them help themselves and each other in creating a better life and future for themselves.[9]

*Case study 3: the Shenzhen Institute of Contemporary Observation (ICO) (***Shenzhen Dangdai Shehui Guancha***)*

Founded and registered as a company in 2001, the ICO gained both domestic and international recognition as a labor rights NGO in China. Its founder, Liu Kaiming, had a Ph.D. degree in literature from Nanjing University and worked as a reporter for the *Shenzhen Legal Daily* from 1997 to 2001. As a reporter for the *Shenzhen Legal Daily*, Liu was able to interview government bureaucrats, factory managers, and migrant workers, and thus gained firsthand knowledge about the working and living conditions of migrant workers and their lack of access to support from the government and the legal system. In 2001, Liu decided to give up his reporter's position to set up the ICO. On its website, the ICO is described as "a civil society organization dedicated to labor development and corporate social responsibility."

Between 2001 and 2006, the ICO attracted diverse sources of domestic as well as international grant donors, including Shenzhen Telephone and Communication Bureau, Shenzhen Statistics Bureau, Oxfam Hong Kong, the Ford Foundation, and the World Bank. It also built an impressive list of multinational clients that included Burberry (UK), Nike, Inc., Reebok, Inc., Timberland, and Adidas AG. It offered supply-chain factory training and corporate social responsibility (CSR) consultation, and established partnerships with Tsinghua University, Beijing University, the University of California at Berkeley, and the University of Oslo.[10] With these resources and partnerships, the ICO launched a wide range of research projects and multilevel collaborative initiatives that aimed at "research, labor rights advocacy, social responsibility consultation, education and training, legal aid, [and] community service" for migrant workers. In the following, we sum up some of the ICO's major initiatives.

Worker empowerment and social service initiatives

From the very beginning, labor empowerment (*laogong fuquan*) has been "one of [the ICO's] key strategies" and is implemented through three initiatives: the Migrant Worker Legal Support Center, Establishment of Internal Complaint Mechanisms in Supply-Chain Factories, and Migrant Workers Community Education and Training. In 2002, with financial support from Oxfam Hong Kong, the ICO set up the Legal Center, which provides free legal counseling to migrant workers concerning labor disputes, work-injury compensation, and wage arrears. From 2002 to 2005, the ICO's Legal Center provided assistance to over 100,000 workers and helped workers recover 6 million yuan in monetary compensation.[11] Facilitated by Business for Social Responsibility (BSR),[12] five major multinational companies, including Nike, Reebok, and Adidas, agreed to allow the ICO to establish internal complaint mechanisms and distribute Guangdong Labor Law Briefs (*Guangdong laogong falu zhinan*) in fifteen of their supply-chain factories in Guangdong.

Corporate social responsibility consultation and factory training initiatives

Since 2003, the ICO has worked closely with international organizations, multinational corporations, and domestic companies to conduct factory training programs aimed at achieving a win–win situation of "finding the balance point between benefits of enterprises, employees and local community."[13] The ICO's CSR and Factory Training Initiatives are carried out via three projects: CSR Consultation and Training, International Labor Standard Advocacy Project, and Factory Training for Management and Workers. Since 2003, the ICO has provided CSR consultation on social responsibility auditing, investment assessment, and risk management training; monitored the supply-chain compliance practices; and made suggestions for transnational companies and investment groups. Under its International Labor Standards Advocacy Project, the ICO ran workshops for small and medium-sized enterprises in Guangdong, Zhejiang, Shanghai, Shandong, and Jiangsu to help them develop management systems in line with international labor standards.[14] Management training covered subjects ranging from professional ethics to conflict management, while training for workers focused on occupational safety and health, HIV/AIDS prevention, reproductive health, communication skills, and psychological adjustment, as well as the raising of awareness concerning workers' labor rights and helping workers to organize workers' committees through elections.

Navigating a space for labor activism in the PRD

The case studies we have discussed show that labor NGOs in the Pearl River Delta area have emerged as a new social force not only in providing crucial services to migrant workers, but also in labor rights advocacy in the area. But how far does the state's regulatory arm reach in controlling these emerging social organizations? What are the factors that have enabled these organizations to carve out a space for their activist work in a Party-state regime that is so wary of any organization outside the Party-state's control? What difficulties and constraints do these organizations currently face? And how does the rise of migrant labor NGOs in the PRD shed new light on our understanding of changing state and society relations in contemporary China?

None of the three NGOs discussed above is actually registered with the local bureau of civil affairs. The CWWN is registered in Hong Kong as a not-for-profit organization but has an office in Shenzhen, and both the MWDC and the ICO are registered with the local bureaus of industry and commerce, with MWDC as a self-employed entity (*getihu*) and ICO as a company. Saich points out that it used to be a popular evasion strategy for a social organization to register as a business under the relevant industrial and commercial bureaus because such registration required a minimal management structure and offered a high degree of autonomy. "However, the 1998 regulations closed off this method of registration as a commercial entity for social organizations" (Saich 2006: 293). But apparently these regulations are not strictly enforced, and registering as a business entity is the most common way if not the only way for migrant labor NGOs to operate if they are openly registered at all. The lax enforcement of the registration regulations is supported by one survey which found that out of sixteen migrant labor NGOs in the PRD area, nine were "registered," six were "unregistered," and one's registration status was not known. Of the nine registered NGOs, six were registered as "self-employed" business entities, two as "companies," and one as an "overseas" entity (Huang 2007).[15] The fact that Huang could track "unregistered" labor NGOs suggests that some migrant labor NGOs can operate openly even without any formal registration.

While scholars such as Saich (2006: 292) suggest that registering as a business is a conscious strategy that allows NGOs to negotiate more beneficial relations with the state, our interviews with labor activists suggest that migrant labor organizations register as business entities more out of necessity than through choice. In other words, they do not want to evade government controls but have little choice, because none of the corresponding government bodies is willing to serve as their supervising agency. These labor activists told us that affiliation with government agencies can actually enhance labor NGOs' capacity to serve migrant workers since government agencies have more resources and authority to deal with management. But apparently it is the government agencies that avoid serving as supervisory bodies to migrant labor organizations. One exception seems to be the initial "partnership" relationship between the CWWN and the Nanshan District ACFTU. But the CWWN was technically an "overseas" NGO, not a real home-grown labor NGO, and the Nanshan District ACFTU was supportive of the CWWN only in its service-oriented activities for female migrant workers. It withdrew its support in more recent years when it felt that the CWWN was organizing female workers for collective action. As for home-grown labor NGOs such as the MWDC and ICO, there is almost no interaction between them and local ACFTU branches.

On the other hand, by registering as businesses these labor NGOs do have the advantage of not having to go through the dual registration process with local civil affairs bureaus and can thus operate more independently of state control. However, this is not to suggest that as long as these labor NGOs can register as business entities, they are out of reach of government control and regulations. In fact, by making it impossible for labor NGOs to become legally registered NGOs the state also sets the parameters of what constitutes a legitimate NGO. By "forcing" migrant labor NGOs to register as business entities, the state can basically refuse to recognize them as legitimate social organizations. In this way, the state can condone some activities of these migrant labor organizations while keeping a close eye on and cracking down on others, using the pretense that these are not legitimate NGOs.

Here we can again use the sequel to Zhang Zhiru's botched "Association for Migrant Workers in Shenzhen" to show the calculated reach of the state. After Zhang failed to gain official permission to establish this migrant association in 2004, he did not give it up entirely but instead openly put up a sign for the association, claiming that the association was at "the preparation stage" (*choubei jieduan*). From 2004 to October 2006, no government officials came to harass Zhang or try to force him to take the sign down. However, during the Shenzhen's People's Congress Meeting in early October 2006, Zhang began to call upon several other labor NGOs in Shenzhen to jointly launch a 10,000-signature movement demanding that the Shenzhen's People's Congress revise certain legislation concerning labor mediation fees and better enforcement of migrant workers' rights. Soon after, Zhang's office was ransacked, his computer was confiscated, and his sign for the Association for Migrant Workers in Shenzhen was taken down (Long 2007). Later, Zhang was forced to denounce himself publicly by saying that he had "[set up] the association without getting the permission from Shenzhen Civil Affairs Bureau and using the association's name to start activities and make illegal profits" (Zhang 2006). This example shows that the government was tolerant only when Zhang's labor organizing action was localized and isolated. As soon as he attempted to make horizontal connections with other local labor NGOs to make a collective demand on behalf of migrant workers in Shenzhen, his actions were declared illegal and met with an immediate crackdown.

As for the activities of labor NGOs, we find that they mostly concentrate on providing legal advice, psychological counseling, education about labor law, occupational health and safety and skills training, and a social venue for recreational activities for migrant workers. In other words, as long as migrant labor NGOs focus on such service-oriented activities, the government seems to step back and even allow some unregistered NGOs to operate openly. This type of labor activism suggests that even though migrant labor NGOs in the PRD are allowed to operate as "business entities" and enjoy a certain degree of autonomy from the state, most have to adopt a self-regulated approach and stay away from sensitive issues such as calling for independent trade unions or mobilizing workers for strikes or other collective action.

Labor activism in the era of globalization: strategies and limitations

Even though limited and constrained by the state's determination to prevent any political opening that can galvanize labor discontent, migrant labor activism is stirring at the grassroots level and has gained momentum in more recent years due to new global and domestic forces.

Externally, as China's economy becomes further integrated with the global economy, the plight of migrant workers has caught international attention.[16] During the early 2000s, some international NGOs and foundations began to provide funds to initiate projects that aimed at providing legal knowledge concerning labor law and rights protection for migrant workers. International labor organizations have also begun to press China to enhance its labor rights protection in compliance with international standards. Working with the International Labour Organization (ILO), BSR, and SAI, the ICO designed and organized training sessions on international labor standards for factory managers and government officials. At about the same time, concerned about their corporate image, which has come under scrutiny by the global anti-sweatshop movement, Western multinational companies started to implement corporate codes of conduct in their supplier factories in China. These codes required factory managers to "have safer and cleaner shop floors and dormitories, comply with the codes or China's labor law in terms of wages and work hours, and establish better occupational and health programs" (Chan 2006: 194–5; Pun 2005b). By the early 2000s, some multinationals had begun to turn to local labor NGOs or international labor NGOs such as SAI (the United States) and Fair Wear Foundation (the Netherlands) to monitor and verify the implementation of corporate codes of conduct and labor standards and to conduct factory training sessions. In other words, both international attention to the poor working conditions of migrant workers and the concern of Western multinational companies about their corporate image provided some funding sources for migrant labor NGOs. As we have described, the projects in our three case studies were funded by international sources such as the Ford Foundation, Asia Foundation, Oxfam Hong Kong, SAI, the Fair Wear Foundation, and a number of multinational corporations. The recent sharp increase of migrant labor organizations is closely related to the money from international donors. Of the sixteen labor NGOs in the PRD documented by Huang, as many as eleven receive funding from international sources, while only five depend on internal membership fees. Also, in many cases, foreign funding was directly responsible for the initial setup of some of the labor NGOs (Huang 2006). Here we see another dimension of the impact of globalization and its linkage to the rise of grassroots labor activism in China's special economic zones, where foreign direct investment is highly concentrated and migrant workers make up the major labor force.

Domestically, several new developments since the early 2000s have created a more conducive environment for the rise of migrant labor activism. The new leadership under Hu Jintao and Wen Jiabao has begun to turn attention to the consequences of uneven development of the market reform by calling for the building of a "harmonious society" (*hexie shehui*). In 2003, the central government issued a number of important documents that specifically emphasized using the law to protect migrant workers' legal rights. In January 2003, the State Council issued "Successfully Managing the Employment of Rural Workers in the Cities and Their Access to Public Services," and in January 2004 it issued "The First Document."[17] As was pointed out by Froissart, "both documents call for the eradication of any kind of discriminative regulations or practices against migrant workers ... and also request equal access to employment, education, and public services" (2005: 32). In early August 2003, the ACFTU issued "Circular on Doing a Good Job in Protecting the Legal Rights of Rural Migrants Who Come to Cities to Work" (ACFTU 2003). This circular highlights four new priorities of the ACFTU and its local branches: protecting the legal rights of migrant workers, organizing migrant workers into trade unions in accordance with the law, coordinating with relevant departments to tackle the violations of migrant workers' legal rights, and strengthening the leadership to ensure enforcement of legal rights of migrant workers. Not incidentally, in October 2003 Premier Wen personally intervened and helped a migrant family retrieve a non-paid salary (Sun and Huang 2003). Since then, a nationwide campaign has been launched in China to resolve the longstanding problems of wage arrears of migrant workers.

Froissart's study in Sichuan shows that the provincial government was eager to follow the central government's call to pay attention to the protection of migrant workers' legal rights, and allocated four million yuan in 2003 to help set up legal training sessions. That year, 2.1 million migrants received training (Froissart 2005: 32). Owing to this new policy shift, "rights awareness among migrant workers improved greatly, as did their inclination to seek legal redress.... Training also helped migrant workers broaden their claims and to seek equal treatment with urban or more qualified workers" (Froissart 2005: 33). The government's new discourse on the rule of law and rights protection did generate a new opening for migrant workers to demand legal protection. In this sense, the central government's new legal discourse on rights protection has facilitated the rise of a rights-focused migrant labor activism in China.

While this study has been unable to collect field data to document whether and, if so, how local governments and ACFTU branches in the PRD area organized similar legal training sessions for migrant workers, migrant worker organizations have mushroomed in the PRD area since 2003 and have played an important role in organizing legal training for migrant workers. Among the sixteen labor NGOs documented by Huang, twelve were set up after 2002. These labor NGOs have been particularly active in raising rights awareness, giving legal advice, representing migrant workers in labor disputes, educating them about labor law, and providing training in occupational health and safety. According to Huang (2007), the reason the government currently tolerates these labor NGOs and even allows them a reasonably large space to operate in is that it thinks that "this can help these labor NGOs enhance their self-initiatives and avoid pushing these NGOs to become politicized organizations." In other words, the government allows these labor NGOs to exist because it can use them as a way to allow some letting off of steam and thus contain labor discontent. At the same time, our interviews suggest that another reason labor NGOs are tolerated is that they frame their work as promoting Chinese labor law. The government is thus careful in its handling of labor NGOs because they are simply following the government's call to protect the labor rights of migrant workers. As one labor activist told us,

> Shenzhen government officials are not very enthusiastic about our labor activism work because they are more concerned about making foreign investors and factory managers happy and maintaining an investment-friendly environment than enforcing the labor law to protect migrant workers' rights. But because most labor NGOs are promoting the rights protection of migrants in accordance with the Chinese labor law, the government officials find it difficult to intervene in our work and shut us down.
>
> (Hong Zhang field notes 2007)

Labor activists will often cite such official slogans as "building a harmonious society" and "defending the legal rights of workers" to describe their work, sometimes with the effect of putting government officials on the defensive and getting their support.

Froissart reported how this tactic was used by migrant workers and labor NGOs to end a Shenzhen factory strike successfully in favor of migrant workers. On 6 October 2004, more than 3,000 workers from Hai Yan Electronic Plant, a Hong Kong–Guangzhou joint-venture electronic component factory, went on strike, demanding legal minimum wages and overtime payment.[18] The strikers blocked the main highway linking Shenzhen to Hong Kong for four hours in an attempt to push the government into intervening. Even though the workers were ordered back to the factory, government officials from the municipal and district labor and social security bureaus held negotiations between workers' representatives and the factory managements. In the end, the managements agreed to raise the workers' salaries by 170 percent to meet the legal minimal wage, to increase the overtime payment, and to contribute to workers' social security. ICO staff participated in the negotiation process for the striking workers and reasoned with the local authorities, saying that "if workers had taken to the streets, it was not to create social disorder but to express legitimate claims." By framing the workers' strike in terms of the claiming of legitimate rights in accordance with Chinese labor law, the ICO successfully persuaded the police to release the two leaders of the demonstration, who had been held under arrest for two weeks. The labor authorities also imposed an unprecedented fine of two million yuan on the factory management (Froissart 2005: 35–6).

Here we can see that the government's new shift toward building a more harmonious society and its emphasis on the protection of migrant workers' legal rights has both informed and been utilized by migrant labor activists. However, while these NGOs have emerged as a new social force for migrant workers in the PRD area, they still face many constraints and obstacles that raise questions about their sustainability.

First, by making it impossible for migrant labor organizations to acquire legal status as legitimate social organizations, the government forces these NGOs onto shaky legal ground and to walk a fine line between what is permissible and what is not in their work on behalf of migrant workers. In her study of Chinese civil society organizations (CSOs), Bentley found that as long as CSOs can steer clear of action and rhetoric that may suggest a challenge to state authority, they have considerable room to maneuver. There is even evidence that

> most CSOs consider their relations with relevant government authorities relatively positive, characterized by cooperation rather than friction. In some cases government and party authorities are starting to recognize the value of CSOs in delivering services, serving as mediators between aggrieved parties, and representing the interests of their constituents through policy consultations and other means.
>
> (Bentley 2004)

This may be true for NGOs in areas such as environmental protection, health, education, and women's issues.[19] But as far as migrant labor NGOs are concerned, we have not seen much direct cooperation between government authorities and labor NGOs.

Second, most labor NGOs face severe financial constraints that limit their operation and expansion, and there is a direct link between their financial constraints and the current regulations and laws regarding registration of independent grassroots NGOs. Despite the fact that labor NGOs provide much-needed services for migrant workers, they have to register as commercial entities with the Bureau of Commerce and Industry. This registration status not only precludes labor NGOs from getting state funding, but also prohibits them from raising money from the public. Consequently, most labor NGOs depend heavily and even solely on foreign sources for funding, and this can itself hamper their capacity and development in at least three ways. One is that most foreign funds are project oriented; once the project is finished, the funding dries up. One clear example of this limitation can be seen in the fate of the ICO's publication of the China Labor Research and Support Network Forum (Forum). With funding from the Ford Foundation in 2003, ICO began to publish the bimonthly Forum, which dealt with labor rights protection, relevant government policies and regulations, workplace safety measures, international labor standards, and so on. Copies would be given free of charge to migrant workers who wanted them. But when funds dried up in 2005, the ICO was unable to continue publication. Another problem with this heavy dependence on foreign funding is that labor NGOs have to compete with each other for limited outside sources of funding, and this competition can sometimes lead to mistrust and lack of cooperation between them. A third problem is that the dependence on foreign funds also limits the type of services that labor NGOs can provide for migrant workers because they often have to accept conditions demanded by funding sources in order to secure funding. One labor activist in Guangzhou complained to Huang that foreign funding sources often set the rules about how projects should be carried out and that he felt helpless if he had to strictly "do things according to their ideas" (Huang 2007). Grassroots labor NGOs may identify more acute and needy areas to better serve migrant workers, but they must tailor their projects to meet the requirements of foreign funding sources, otherwise they cannot get funding.

Third, migrant labor NGOs are still marginalized socially because labor issues are politically sensitive. In our interviews with labor activist leaders, we were repeatedly told that for fear of government repression, many intellectuals and other professionals choose to work for NGOs in less sensitive areas such as environment protection, education, poverty relief, and public health. For this reason, in addition to lack of funding, labor NGOs find it hard to recruit and retain talented people. In the case of the CWWN, its management personnel were college professors in Hong Kong, but they did not supervise the day-to-day operation of the CWWN's work in Shenzhen, which was carried out mostly by its Chinese staff, who were migrant workers. As for the MWDC, with the exception of its executive director, Zeng Feiyang, who has a college degree, all the staff members were migrants-turned-activists. The ICO is a more research-oriented labor NGO and more than half of its staff have college degrees; Liu himself has a Ph.D. Even so, Liu told us that the ICO still experienced high staff turnover and it was difficult to maintain staff stability. In looking at social organizations that aim to help migrant workers integrate into urban society elsewhere, Gallagher finds that they all have one thing in common: "they are groups to protect migrants but not groups made of migrants" (2004: 437). She cited some organizations such as Rural Women Knowing All (national), the Migrant Women's Club (national), and the Center for the Protection of Migrant Workers' Rights (Shanghai).[20] But from our observation in the PRD area, it appears that migrants themselves have played a more active role in forming some labor NGOs. Among the three case studies we profile in this chapter, Zeng's MWDC is mostly made up of activists who are migrant workers themselves. Again among the sixteen labor NGOs in the PRD that Huang documented, at least eleven of them were founded by migrant workers themselves (Huang 2006). This may reflect a unique feature of labor activism in the economic boomtowns of the PRD area, where migrants form the major labor force, surpassing the registered local residents by a wide margin.

Clearly, while migrant workers have the potential to become an organized force, labor NGOs still need to attract support from the larger population in order to sustain their labor activism. One labor activist told us that migrants-turned-activists can be very effective in collecting information and connecting migrant workers, but for legal education and representation, experts and professionals are needed. Moreover, the task of managing an NGO, and making it sustainable and credible, often proves to be more difficult than just setting it up. In our interviews, many labor activists stated that they felt overwhelmed not only by the amount of work needed to help migrant workers in the region, but also by the amount of attention and energy needed to resolve internal conflicts and management issues within their organizations. The political, financial, and human resource constraints faced by most labor NGOs raise uncertainties as to how sustainable these labor NGOs are, both in their capacity to provide services for migrant workers and in their very survival as organizations.

Conclusion

China's market reform has triggered a massive rural-to-urban labor migration and led to the breakdown of the previous rigid rural–urban segregation under the command economy. But the huge exodus of rural migrant workers seeking urban employment in Chinese cities has also created a new underclass in the urban workforce. This is because rural migrants remain outside the state system of social service provision and protection, owing to the legacy of the household registration system, which continues to deny rural migrant workers urban residence status and its associated entitlements to welfare and social services. Moreover, rural migrants are subject to widespread labor rights abuses as factory managers take advantage of their semilegal status in Chinese cities.

However, as China's market reform deepens, new social space has opened up for non-state forces to play a role in filling in the welfare gap and especially in reaching out to the more vulnerable and disadvantaged groups. Our case studies on the rise of migrant labor NGOs in the PRD show that despite the state's refusal to allow migrant workers to organize through the state corporatist model, there are still other ways for migrant labor NGOs to register and operate. For the most part, these labor NGOs' work has been service oriented, providing legal advice, psychological counseling, and education about occupational health and safety, as well as a social venue for recreational activities for migrant workers. Funding for the labor NGOs under study comes almost exclusively from foreign donors, ranging from foundations, international NGOs, and human rights groups to multinationals. This points to a transnational linkage between China's integration with the global economy and China's migrant labor activism. With its membership of the World Trade Organization, China is also coming under more international scrutiny to determine whether it is complying with international business rules and labor standards. Since 2003, the new shift under the leadership of Hu Jintao and Wen Jiabao to the labor rights protection of workers and peasants has also played a key role in providing a permissible legal framework under which migrant labor NGOs could operate and push forward their agenda.

Even though their labor activism is still limited and mostly service oriented, focusing on legal advice, labor law and labor rights awareness, and information about occupational health and safety for migrant workers, their political implications are by no means less significant. As more and more migrant workers become increasingly rights-conscious, they will use the labor law and legal means to demand and defend their labor rights. As Ching Kwan Lee points out, "by echoing the official emphasis on providing 'education' and 'services' to migrant workers,... these grassroots labor organizations contribute to legal reform and raise social demands for legal justice" (2007: 250, 252).

Acknowledgment

The research trips for Hong Zhang were funded by Colby College Humanities Division Travel Grants. The author is grateful for this generous financial support.

Notes

1 The interview and field data for Chinese Working Women Network (CWWN) were collected by Marsha Smith, while the interview data and field visits for the Panyu Migrant Worker Documentation Center (MWDC) and Institute of Contemporary Observation (ICO) were collected by Hong Zhang.
2 See the CWWN website, www.cwwn.org/eng/main.html.
3 Dr. Pun did pioneering ethnographic work by embedding herself as an assembly worker in an electronic factory in Shenzhen in the mid-1990s and thus gained first-hand experience of the life and work of young female migrant workers in Shenzhen's export zone (Pun 2005a).
4 See the CWWN website, www.cwwn.org/eng/main.html.
5 Smith (field notes, August 2006).
6 Chan (2005) (interview, Pun, August 2006).
7 Smith (interview notes, August, 2006).
8 Hong Zhang (field notes, January 2006).
9 Hong Zhang (field notes, January 2007).
10 ICO Report on Activities, 2001–2005; ICO 2005 and 2006 Biannual Report; ICO Manual "Promoting Decent Work and Social Rights" (2006).
11 ICO 2001–5 Program Report, pp. 11–12.
12 BSR is a non-profit business association dedicated to "promot[ing] cross-sector collaboration in ways that contribute to the advancement of corporate social responsibility and business success." With its headquarters in San Francisco, BSR has two global offices, one in China and the other in Paris. See BSR's webpage at www.bsr.org/index.cfm.
13 ICO Brochure for Factory Training Initiative.
14 "Guoji Laogong Biaozhun: Quanqiuhua shidai de qiye hexin jingzhengli" [International Labor Standards: The Core Enterprise Competitiveness in the Era of Globalization], The Training Curriculum for International Labor Standards Advocacy Project, 2003, p. 3. Institute of Contemporary Observation Publication.
15 Huang's list of sixteen labor NGOs in the PRD area includes the three NGOs discussed in our case studies. In fact, the only registration status that indicates "overseas" is that of the CWWN.
16 Both international media and academic writings have exposed the poor working conditions and labor rights abuse in the economic boomtowns of the PRD. See Chan (2001), Eckholm (2001), Kahn (2003), and Pan (2002).
17 State Council Office, "Zuohao mongmin jincheng wuhongjiuye guanli he fuwu gongzuo [On Doing a Good Job in Providing Service and Management for Rural Migrants Who Seek Employment in Cities], 16 January 2003; "Yihao wenjian" (No. 1 Document), 1 January 2004.
18 In 2004, the legal minimum wage was 610 yuan a month. But the workers at Hai Yan Electronic Plant were paid 240 yuan monthly for a regular working day of twelve

hours. The legal overtime payment was 5.4 yuan an hour but the overtime payment at Hai Yan Electronic Plant was only 2 yuan.

19 Saich notes that NGOs working "in the field of education and environment have been permitted or have negotiated relatively freer space" (2006: 295). Howell makes a similar observation by saying that there is more tolerance in public debates on gender but less concerning HIV/AIDs and labor rights (2004: 161).

20 Gallagher also mentions the MWDC (Guangzhou) as a social association for migrant workers. But our fieldwork study of the MWDC in 2006 and 2007 made it clear that this organization is not only for migrant workers but also run by migrants-turned-activists.

References

ACFTU (2003) "Guanyu qieshi zuohao weihu jincheng wugong renyuan hefa quanyi gongzuo de tongzhi" [Circular on Doing a Good Job in Protecting the Legal Rights of Rural Migrants Who Come to Cities to Work], 4 August.

Bentley, J. G. (2004) "Survival Strategies for Civil Society Organizations in China," *International Journal of Not-for-Profit Law* 6 (2). Online, available at: www.icnl.org/knowledge/ijnl/vol6iss2/art_1.htm.

Chan, A. (2001) *China's Workers under Assault: Exploitation and Abuse in a Globalizing Economy*, Armonk, NY: M. E. Sharpe.

Chan, A. and Zhu, X. (2003) "Disciplinary Labor Regimes in Chinese Factories," *Critical Asian Studies* 35 (4): 559–84.

Chan, J. (2005) "The Chinese Working Women Network," in N. Ascoly and C. Finney (eds.) *Made by Women: Gender, the Global Garment Industry and the Movement for Women Workers' Rights*. Online, available at: www.cleanclothes.org/ftp/made_by_women.pdf (accessed 24 August 2007).

—— (2006) "Realities and Possibilities for Chinese Trade Unionism," in C. Phelan (ed.) *The Future of Organised Labour: Global Perspectives*, Oxford: Peter Lang.

Chen, G., He, L., and Dong, W. (2005) "Laogong zijiu suisheng NGOs, zhusanjiao mingong huang yifa zhidu chuanxin" [Labor Self-Salvation Gives Rise to NGOs: Labor Shortage in the PRD Has Led to Institutional Innovation], *Fenghuang Zhoukan* [Phoenix Weekly] 175 (6).

Chen, F. (2004) "Legal Mobilization by Trade Unions: The Case of Shanghai," *China Journal* 52 (July): 27–45.

Eckholm, E. (2001) "Workers' Rights Are Suffering in China as Manufacturing Goes Capitalist," *New York Times* (22 August).

Froissart, C. (2005) "The Rise of Social Movements among Migrant Workers," *China Perspectives* 61: 30–40.

Gallagher, M. (2004) "China: The Limits of Civil Society in a Late Leninist State," in M. Alagappa (ed.) *Civil Society and Political Change in Asia: Expanding and Contracting Democratic Space*, Palo Alto, CA: Stanford University Press.

GBLSS (Guangdong Bureau of Labor and Social Security) (2006) "Guangdongsheng jiaqiang nongmingong guanli he fuwu zhuyao zuofa" [Main Measures Taken by Guangdong Province in Strengthening Management of and Service for Rural Migrant Workers], Guangdong Research Team, pp. 432–46. *Zhongguo nongmingong diaoyan baogao* [Investigative Report on China's Peasant Workers], Guowuyuan yanjiushi ketizu [State Council Research Team], Beijing: Yanshi Publisher.

Howell, J. (2004) "New Directions in Civil Society: Organizing around Marginal Interests," in J. Howell (ed.) *Governance in China*, Lanham, MD: Rowan & Littlefield.

Huang, Y. (2006) "Wailaigong zuzhi yu kuaguo laogong tuanjie wangluo" [Migrant Worker NGOs and Transnational Labor Solidarity Network], *Kaifang Shidai* [Open Times] 186 (6). Online, available at: www.opentimes.cn/to/200606/89.htm (accessed 10 January 2008).

—— (2007) "Quanqiuhua beijing xia de laogong zijiu" [Workers' Self-Help Effort under Globalization], *Nanfengchuang* [South Wind Window], 19 November. Online, available at: www.nfcmag.com/ReadNews-12852.html (accessed 14 January 2008). An English translation of this article is available at China Labor News Translations (CLNT): www.clntranslations.org/article/27/labor-ngos-in-guangdong-province.

Kahn, J. (2003) "Chinese Factory Workers Tell of Trouble in Toyland," *New York Times* (9 December).

Lee, C. (2007) "Is Labor a Political Force in China?" in E. J. Perry and M. Goldman (eds.) *Grassroots Political Reform in Contemporary China*, Cambridge, MA: Harvard University Press.

Long, Z. (2007) "Huang Qingnan beikan shijian: laogong sijiu de jiannan shike" [The Incident of Huang Qingnan Being Brutalized: Workers' Self-Help Faces Tough Time], *Nanfang Doushibao* [Nanfang Daily]. Online, available at: www.nanfangdaily.com.cn/southnews/jwxy/200712160239.asp (accessed 10 January 2008).

Ma, Q. (2005) *Non-government Organizations in Contemporary China*, London: Routledge.

MOLSS (Ministry of Labor and Social Security) (2006) "Dangqian nongmingong liudong jiuye shuliang, jiegou yu tedian" [The Size, Composition, and Characteristics of Peasant Workers' Migration and Employment in Contemporary China], *Zhongguo nongmingong diaoyan baogao* [Investigative Report on China's Peasant Workers], Guowuyuan yanjiushi ketizu [State Council Research Team], Beijing: Yanshi Publisher.

Pan, P. (2002) "Work Till They Drop: Few Protections for China's New Laborers," *Washington Post* (13 May).

People's Daily (2006) "Improve the Welfare of 200 Million Migrant Workers." Online, available at: http://english.peopledaily.com.cn/200605/01/eng20060501_262543.html (accessed 29 July 2007).

Pun, N. (2005a) *Made in China: Women Factory Workers in a Global Workplace*, Durham, NC: Duke University Press.

—— (2005b) "Global Production, Company Code of Conduct, and Labor Conditions in China: A Case Study of Two Factories," *China Journal* 54: 101–13.

Pun, N. and Chan, J. (2004) "Community Based Labour Organizing," *International Union Rights* 11 (4). The CWWN's website also provides information on the four projects that it undertakes. See www.cwwn.org/eng/main.html.

Saich, A. (2006) "Negotiating the State: The Development of Social Organizations in China," in L. Dittmer and G. Liu (eds.) *China's Deep Reform*, Lanham, MD: Rowan & Littlefield.

Shan, J. (2007) "Migrant Population Swelling," *China Daily* (5 December). Online, available at: www.chinadaily.com.cn/cndy/2007-12/05/content_6298609.htm (accessed 29 January 2008).

Solinger, D. (1999) *Contesting Citizenship in Urban China: Peasant Migrants, the State, and the Logic of the Market*, Berkeley: University of California Press.

Song, D. (2006) "Guangdong GDP to Grow 14 Per Cent This Year," *China Daily* (19 December). Online, available at: www.chinadaily.com.cn/bizchina/2006-12/19/content_781379.htm (accessed 17 July 2007).

Sun, C. (2007) "Liao Xiaofeng, yi ge fufa yingxiong de chuzou" [Liao Xiaofeng: The Exit of a "Rights-Defense Hero"], *Nanfang Dushi Bao* [Southern Metropolitan Daily] (5 April).

Sun, J. and Huang, Y. (2003) "Wen Jiabao zoufang sanxia kuqu, zongli wei nongmin tao gongqian" [Wen Jiabao Visited Three Gorges Dam Areas and Premier Strove to Get Wage Arrears Back to Migrant Workers], *Xinhuanet*. Online, available at: http://news.sina.com.cn/c/2003-10-27/17221001834s.shtml (accessed 14 August 2007).

Wang, F. (2005) *Organizing through Division and Exclusion: China's Hukou System*, Stanford, CA: Stanford University Press.

Zhang, Z. (2006) "Guanyu tingzhi choubei shenzhenshi wailaigong xiehui de tongzhi" [Announcement on Discontinuing the Preparation Work for Establishing an Association for Migrant Workers in Shenzhen]. Online, available at: www.ngocn.org/?action-viewnews-itemid-2420 (accessed 28 January 2008).

Zhao, Y. (2006) "Gonghui shi women gongtong de jia: guanyu zuzhi nongmingong ruhui de shuping" [Trade Unions Are Our Common Home: On Organizing Peasant Workers into Trade Unions], *Gongren Ribao* [Workers' Daily], 26 June.

Zhongxinshe (2004) "Nongmingong zheng chengwei chanye gongren de zhuli" [Peasant Workers Have Now Emerged as the Main Labor Force in the Manufacturing Sector], Online, available at: www.china.com.cn/policy/zhuanti/yh/txt/2004-02/23/content_5503105.htm (accessed 23 July 2007).

5 Green activism?

Reassessing the role of environmental NGOs in China

Timothy Hildebrandt[1] *and Jennifer L. Turner*[2]

Introduction

In 1994, Friends of Nature (FON), an environmental group based in Beijing, became the first non-governmental organization (NGO) to legally register as a social organization, marking the beginning of green activism in China. More importantly, it represented a key moment in the birth of China's modern civil society, for FON's success in navigating the demanding registration regulations became a model for other activists across many sectors. Over the past fifteen years, the need for social organizations engaged in environmental work in China has increased, owing to growing environmental pressures and the associated economic and social costs. In response, the Chinese government has acknowledged the severity of environmental problems, passing ever more stringent pollution control laws and devoting financial and rhetorical support to improving environmental protection. The Chinese central government appears to understand its own limitations in addressing environmental problems and has made moves to open limited political space for environmental NGOs. Indeed, green groups are now frequently enlisted by some government agencies to act as "service providers" to address environmental concerns that the agencies are either unwilling or unable to implement.

The opening of political space for green activism has not led to the creation of domestic laws to help finance NGO work, which has meant that Chinese green groups are funded almost completely by international organizations and foreign governments. Green NGOs, like civil society groups in other sectors in China, have not had unlimited freedom to operate, yet despite constraints and dependence on international financing, Chinese environmental groups have grown in number and impact. These groups have boasted some real success and have moved into nearly every facet of environmental work, from environmental education to legal advocacy, often in partnership with international NGOs.

Because of their relatively long history, early success, and high visibility, environmental NGOs appear in both popular and academic literatures as China's vanguard of civil society. But have the past fifteen years been as kind to the environmental NGO sector as this characterization suggests? Will the sector be able to sustain itself as a service provider and civil society leader for another fifteen years? In this chapter, we draw on over a decade of work at the Woodrow Wilson Center's China Environment Forum to inventory and gather information on the green movement in China. We also draw on recent field research in Yunnan Province to explore the current capacity of Chinese environmental NGOs to achieve long-term sustainability for their organization and increase the impact of their social service provision, and the challenges they will face.

This chapter begins with a brief sketch of several acute environmental problems in China and the costs of degradation that have compelled the government to adopt more aggressive pollution control and natural resource protection policies, and to include green groups in its efforts to combat environmental problems. It continues with a summary of the different kinds of work in which environmental groups are engaged and then reassesses the state of environmental NGOs (ENGOs) in China by outlining several key issues that have proven problematic for the continued development of such groups: funding, registration, cooperation, and local government pressure due to China's political decentralization. Finally, to provide an understanding of the scale of the difficulties facing green groups in China, we offer the case of Yunnan, a province with high ecological biodiversity and a government that prioritizes environmental protection and welcomes many international green aid projects. Yunnan should be an ideal political environment for green NGO growth, and yet groups there continue to struggle to build sustainable organizations. Ultimately, this chapter suggests that local governments retain control and collaborate with NGOs only when they are useful.

China's environmental woes

Although no industrialized country is immune from serious pollution problems, the scale and speed of the environmental degradation in China have no parallel.[3] Over the past thirty years, China's transition to its new role as the world's manufacturing hub has brought millions of Chinese out of poverty – but at the cost of massive water, air, and soil pollution that threaten human and ecological health. Private cars in urban centers have become major polluters, but the biggest sources of air pollution are heavy industry, particularly construction, and coal-fired power plants – a new plant comes on line nearly every week. About 70 percent of China's energy comes from domestic coal, much of which is high in sulfur and mercury. Recent regulations require new plants to have scrubbers, but enforcement at the local level is weak and few existing power plants have been retrofitted with cleaner technology. The construction sector is a major source of particulates and other dirty emissions. China produces half the world's cement, and in the process its often antiquated and inefficient factories can release high levels of mercury and CO_2. China is responsible for approximately 14 percent of global CO_2 emissions, of which 6–8 percent can be attributed to its cement industry (Cho and Giannini-Spohn 2007).

China's pollution reaches far beyond its borders. Annual sandstorms caused by desertification in the country's northeast close schools and airports in South Korea and Japan, and Chinese sand has even been found in the Grand Canyon

(Futrell 2007). California and other West Coast states claim that particulates from Chinese coal-fired power plants are nullifying progress they have made under the Clean Air Act. A growing car culture and China's dependence on coal in a highly energy-inefficient industrial sector have driven a rapid rise in the country's CO_2 emissions. China's highly polluting energy sector made front-page news globally in 2007 when a study was released indicating that Chinese CO_2 emissions exceeded those of the United States – although per capita China's contribution to greenhouse gas emissions remains quite low. Most international climate change experts agree that China's response to these rising CO_2 emissions will be a key determinant of whether a post-Kyoto framework succeeds (Chandler 2008).

Water pollution is another serious threat, exacerbated in part by severe water shortages in many parts of the country – per capita water in northern China is one-tenth the world average per capita rate. One-third of China's waterways are categorized as Grade V – unsuitable for industry, much less agriculture or drinking (Otsuka and Turner 2006). On average, only 40 percent of municipal wastewater is treated, making it a leading source of this severe water pollution. All cities with populations above one million are required to have wastewater treatment plants, but municipal authorities have little incentive to operate them, given high energy costs and low fines for non-compliance. Water pollution is not merely an urban issue. More than 300 million rural Chinese – about a quarter of the country's population – lack access to clean drinking water, thanks to untreated industrial, municipal, and agricultural waste that flows directly into waterways (OECD 2007). Each year, water-related illnesses affect 190 million Chinese, mainly in rural areas.

The destruction of China's waterways by ill-conceived or poorly managed infrastructure projects – such as large water transfer projects and dams – is also seriously affecting river ecosystems. The new round of dam building in the southwest, which aims to triple hydropower capacity by 2020 in order to address the country's growing energy shortages, is a major concern. China is now home to 86,000 dams – 22,000 of which are large dams, accounting for 45 percent of large dams in the world. China's current dam building, which mainly focuses on 200-plus dams in the southwest, dwarfs the rest of the world's hydro schemes. Environmentalists worry that this construction will severely overexploit China's rivers and fragment river ecosystems within and outside the country, producing serious environmental and social harm (Birnbaum and Yu 2006).

Economic and social costs of environmental degradation

Government figures put the economic cost of pollution in China at $200 billion in 2005 alone, but the cost to the health of people and the environment, as well as social stability, is difficult to quantify. Estimates of premature deaths caused by air pollution range from 450,000 to 750,000 annually, and fatal illnesses resulting from water pollution have reached 60,000 (OECD 2007). Half of these deaths are among rural children who develop diarrhea from drinking contaminated water.

Anecdotal evidence suggests that people living along major rivers and large lakes suffer higher than normal rates of cancer, tumors, and spontaneous abortion, as well as diminished IQ, and the cause is believed to be high levels of contaminants in the soil and water (Lu and Bates 2007). In 2007, China's Ministry of Health reported that between 2005 and 2007 cancer rates from pollution rose 19 percent in urban areas and 23 percent in rural areas (Economy 2007).

Pollution problems have sparked a growing number of protests, mainly in rural areas, but urbanites are also increasingly organizing to protest the presence of dirty industries in their neighborhoods. The State Environmental Protection Administration (now the Ministry of Environmental Protection[4]), China's environmental watchdog agency, reported that 51,000 pollution protests took place in 2005 (Lu and Bates 2007). One catalyst for many protests is that farmers have suffered increasing losses because they cannot sell their "toxic" harvests (Economy 2004). The number of class action suits against polluters is also growing, and with the help of Chinese environmental groups and lawyers, some pollution victims are winning their cases.

Over the past decade, the Chinese central government has responded to these severe environmental problems by passing more progressive pollution control laws and setting higher environmental protection targets and investment into the tenth and eleventh Five-Year Plans. This growing push to address environmental problems has both domestic and international drivers. At a domestic level, the government has increasingly acknowledged the need to ameliorate the impacts of environmental degradation, a major side effect of modernization. Recent instances of industrial pollution have resulted in widespread discontent among those who bear the environmental costs of modernization but rarely enjoy its economic benefits. There is also a significant economic incentive for the government to solve China's environmental woes. Government officials estimate that the country loses 9 percent of its total annual GDP as a result of environmental degradation. As China has joined international institutions, it has been required to act on several environmental accords. Moreover, publicized instances of cross-border pollution, such as the Songhua River toxin spill near the Russian border in November 2005, have led to increased international pressure for China to solve its environmental problems.

The Chinese government began welcoming environmental assistance from international NGOs, multilateral banks, and governments in the early 1980s. China's growing greenhouse gas emissions have been a major driver of clean coal and energy-related projects. In addition, many international organizations have been carrying out work to cover a broad range of environmental issues, particularly biodiversity, water protection, and urban air pollution. International green NGOs have played a unique role in changing the policy dynamics around environmental policymaking and implementation, for such groups have been able to act as a "glue" bringing together Chinese government, research, and NGO communities to work together on solving some environmental problem or designing a policy. The numerous projects carried out by international NGOs, while not always easy to replicate nationwide, have played an important role of demonstrating to both government officials and environmental activists in China a more multi-stakeholder policy dynamic. In the early years, international NGOs have played a key role as incubators for Chinese NGOs through either partnerships or direct funding support (Turner and Lü 2006). Notably, a number of Chinese environmentalists who created their own NGOs initially worked for international green groups.

Green-group activities

After Friends of Nature's registration in 1994, other environmental groups followed suit, and today green groups make up the largest sector of NGOs in China. Chinese government sources have estimated the number of environmental groups to be nearly 5,000, but such government numbers provide an incomplete picture. Official figures do not account for those groups that are unregistered, such as volunteer organizations, nature clubs, internet-based groups, and student environmental associations at universities. Environmental groups have not generally tested the limits of their autonomy. Rather, they tend to proceed by taking small steps, staying well within the guidelines the central government has set for them. For example, a number of groups have echoed the concern of citizens that dam building has detrimental consequences for local economies, ecologies, and human health. Most groups are not organized in opposition to dams in general – or the government agencies implementing them – but instead advocate smart dam construction, suggesting that several smaller dams can yield more efficient energy returns than one large one. Recent green-group work has focused on proposed dams on the Nu River in Yunnan Province. In stark contrast to the growing number of citizen protests (some even violent) around pollution problems in China (Lu and Bates 2007), environmental NGOs generally have opted to push for enforcement of existing laws, such as calling for public disclosure of environmental impact assessments (Tan 2006).

While most Chinese green NGOs have been undertaking activities in the relatively "safe" areas of environmental education, recycling, and campaigning to protect the habitats of endangered species, some groups are pushing open the limited political space granted by the government and are pursuing activities that sometimes lead the government – in most cases local officials – to push back. These Chinese green groups have engaged in activities, such as networking and creating branch offices, that go beyond what the government envisioned under the strict registration regulations. Even when they operate within areas that the central government deems acceptable, such as monitoring local government and industries, these NGOs have had an effect that the government did not intend: increased capacity and overall success have emboldened some groups to undertake national campaigns to stop abuses of the ecosystem by local (and, indirectly, national) government (for example, the anti-dam campaign on the Nu River). In this section, we offer a short illustrative sampling of Chinese environmental NGOs that have successfully struck a balance between pushing against the limits of official restrictions while (more or less) maintaining government approval.[5] Most of the groups we shall highlight have been highly dependent upon international financial or training support. We have divided these NGOs into four categories, which are not mutually exclusive: (1) empowering citizens and checking local governments, (2) pressuring and "greening" local businesses, (3) sparking policy or legal changes, and (4) partnering with the news media in national campaigns.

NGOs empowering citizens and checking local governments

Green Watershed is an environmental NGO focused on integrated watershed management in the Lancang-Mekong River Basin in Yunnan Province. Founded by Yu Xiaogang in 2000 with the assistance of Oxfam America as part of a Mekong River watershed management project, Green Watershed has joined together villagers and local government officials in the Lashi Lake area to create watershed management committees. Green Watershed now facilitates the Lashi Watershed Management Committee, which runs dialogues among a broad range of government and community stakeholders to evaluate options for watershed development and protection. This bottom-up policymaking has attracted positive attention from provincial and central governments, and is being touted as a model for other areas.

In response to the national debate on building dams on the Nu River (Nujiang), one of China's last wild rivers, Green Watershed led an initiative to show villagers in the Nujiang basin how dam building could affect their communities. In May 2004, Green Watershed arranged for fourteen citizen representatives from the proposed dam sites in the Nujiang basin to visit villages near Manwan Dam (finished ten years ago on the Jinsha River) and Xiaowan Dam (currently under construction along the Lancang River). This "village-to-village" exchange enabled villagers near the Nujiang to see firsthand the detrimental effects of large-scale hydroelectric dams on remote rural communities. Following the visit, Green Watershed provided these villagers an opportunity to voice their concerns through Chinese news media sources (Hu with Yu 2005). By February 2005, less than a year after Green Watershed began its campaign, Chinese premier Wen Jiabao intervened and put a halt to the proposed dam project. But, as we discuss in the final section of this chapter, Green Watershed's success and the apparent approval of its work by the central government have not protected its leader from the wrath of provincial and local government officials, who have a separate set of conflicting interests.

ENGO pressure to green Chinese businesses

Few Chinese NGOs have pressured Chinese businesses to improve their environmental performance, much less partnered with them. One notable exception is the Institute for Environment and Development (IED). An early entrant to the Chinese NGO community, having registered in 1994, the IED aims to raise public awareness of environment and development issues through public education, information dissemination, research, and community involvement in sustainable development projects. With its strong network of environmental experts and experience in community education initiatives, IED was a natural choice for a Department for International Development (DFID; the United Kingdom) project designed to improve production processes within small- and medium-sized enterprises (SMEs) in Liaoning and Sichuan Provinces. In 2003, the IED acted as a liaison to help SMEs understand the concept of corporate responsibility and worked with DFID consultants and SME managers to develop plans for industry communication with local communities. In 2004, the IED facilitated a roundtable meeting with Chinese industry and government officials to introduce the concept of corporate social responsibility and highlight the potential role for industries in protecting the local environment.

The Institute of Public and Environmental Affairs (IPEA), led by activist Ma Jun, has embarked on an ambitious project to publicize a dynamic, up-to-date list of industries that pollute water and air throughout China. Using publicly available data, the IPEA has consolidated previously disparate data in one easily accessible website for ordinary citizens to monitor industries in their own backyards and, if necessary, pressure the polluters or relevant government agencies to resolve the situation. International companies frequently use the databases to check out their suppliers, particularly on the extensive water pollution database, which as of the summer of 2008 contained 19,000 records (interview with Ma Jun, 2008). A growing number of Chinese businesses have approached the IPEA to inquire whether they could demonstrate how they had lessened their pollution, which led Ma Jun to create a new initiative to oversee official audits as the criteria for removing companies from the database (interview with Ma Jun, 2008).

The IPEA's work has attracted widespread positive attention in the domestic news media, as well as praise from the central government, which in recent years has passed regulations pushing for more transparency in environmental information (Moore and Warren 2006). It merits mention that IPEA staff post only official government data, for to collect data themselves would be too risky; local governments often find such anti-pollution activism highly threatening. Evidence of this risk is found in the example of two environmental activists who were arrested after engaging in anti-pollution activities: Wu Lihong, following many years of criticizing local officials on pollution in Lake Tai, was sentenced in 2006 to three years in prison. Tan Kai was in the process of forming a green group in Zhejiang to monitor pollution when he was sentenced to eighteen months in prison (Salaverry 2007). These arrests have most likely put a damper on groups wishing to focus on anti-pollution efforts, but it merits mention that Chinese government agencies have generally avoided directly punishing and controlling ENGOs, in part because most of the ENGOs are providing services that help protect the environment and pose no direct threat to government authority.

One intriguing new development of Chinese ENGOs greening Chinese business emerged in the summer of 2008, when Green Watershed and seven other Chinese NGOs launched a Green Banking initiative (*Economic Observer weekly/SynTao* 2008). The eight, mainly Beijing-based, NGOs recognized the China

Industrial Bank as the first recipient of their award for integrating social responsibility and sustainable development into its strategy. This bottom-up initiative to encourage banks to give "green" loans to Chinese companies fully supports a top-down MEP program that requires banks to stop lending to companies that are on its ministry's polluter blacklist (Larson 2007).

NGOs pushing legal or policy changes

In 1998, Wang Canfa – a law professor at Beijing Politics and Law University – set up a decidedly unique NGO to help empower pollution victims in the courts. Through a broad range of activities, the Center for Legal Aid to Pollution Victims (CLAPV) aims (1) to raise consciousness of environmental law and rights of the public, (2) to improve the capacity of administrative agencies and judicial bodies that preside over environmental conflicts, and (3) to promote enforcement of Chinese pollution control laws. The CLAPV has few full-time staff and instead depends on ninety-five volunteer members – including law professors, teachers, graduate students, and lawyers – to do research work, advise lawmakers, and help pollution victims.

In the mid-1990s, a number of amendments to environmental laws added provisions extending to citizens the right to sue for damages from pollution. Pollution victims in China tend to be rural citizens, who are often unaware of their rights and unable to navigate a case through the complex court system. Since its inception, the CLAPV has brought seventy-four cases to court, boasting more wins than losses (Xu and Wang 2006). Although the CLAPV's groundbreaking activities – providing information to pollution victims, operating a legal advisory hotline, and helping victims file lawsuits – have often irritated local governments and industries, its work is legal and still within the bounds of NGO registration. The CLAPV's particularly strong autonomy is partly due to the fact that it is registered through a university, which is allowed more space than non-university-affiliated groups. In arguing so many cases successfully, the CLAPV is setting legal precedents and empowering citizens to fight for their rights in courts. Moreover, since many of the CLAPV's members possess strong legal backgrounds, they have been able to advise Chinese lawmakers about improving environment legislation. The CLAPV has been a key partner for international law organizations that aim to strengthen environmental governance in China; most notable has been the American Bar Association's trainings on public hearings for environmental impact assessments and work on environmental information disclosure (Moore and Warren 2006).

Some Chinese NGOs resemble environmental policy think tanks, like the South–North Institute for Sustainable Development (SNISD). The SNISD was created in 1997 by Yang Jike, a former member of the standing committee of China's National People's Congress (NPC). With the help of its high-level connections and multiple international NGO and foundation partners, the SNISD has become quite effective in disseminating environmental and energy policy research to influential policymakers. Its influence is captured well by a recent project in which the National People's Congress's Environment and Resource Committee requested that the SNISD undertake research on nature reserves to help inform a new protection law for nature reserves. The SNISD was chosen over government research centers in order to ensure fairness and impartiality in the legislation.

NGOs' leading national campaigns

Like NGOs in the West, some of the most prominent Chinese green groups dedicated their first national campaign to the protection of endangered species. In 1995, a year after it was founded, China's first environmental NGO, Friends of Nature, disseminated to the news media vivid photos that depicted how overlogging in western Yunnan Province was destroying the habitat of the endangered snub-nosed monkey. FON became the first NGO to compel the state-controlled news outlets to devote significant coverage to an environmental issue. The group did not stop there. FON also wrote letters to top leaders warning that continued destruction of the forests would all but doom the monkey. National government leaders responded by ordering locally specific logging bans and setting up a compensation system for the rural citizens whose livelihoods were affected by the new restrictions.

FON led another well-publicized 1999 campaign to protect the Tibetan antelope. The now well-established NGO alerted the news media, partnered with other NGOs to publicize information about the dangers to this rare species, and wrote a report for the national Environmental Protection Administration and the Forestry Ministry.[6] This report stressed the need for the central government to coordinate and substantially expand the anti-poaching efforts in Tibet, Qinghai, and Xinjiang, as well as provide more funding, weapons, and authority to anti-poaching patrols. FON recommended a crackdown on poachers in all three regions. The central government adopted the recommendations and carried out a month-long covert anti-poaching effort in the regions – the largest-ever coordinated police action to protect wildlife in China. As was reported in *Friends of Nature Newsletter* (1999), the campaign "resulted in the arrest of more than a dozen groups of poachers, confiscation of 500 to 600 Tibetan antelope skins, and was a big psychological blow to the poachers, who were taken by surprise."

FON and its NGO partners used the news media quite well in these two campaigns by feeding journalists stories and pictures. More recently, Chinese NGOs and news journalists have become partners in far more politically sensitive anti-dam campaigns (Hu with Yu 2005). The most striking example was the effort to keep the Nu River (Nujiang) free from dams. In late 2003, several large-scale water and electricity companies possessing powerful connections to top leaders announced plans to build a thirteen-step series of dams on the Nu. In response, a broad coalition of Chinese NGOs was formed, including FON, Green Earth Volunteers, the Institute of Environment and Development, Global Village of Beijing, Beijing Brooks Education Center, Society Entrepreneur Ecology, Wild China, and Green Watershed, all of which have depended quite heavily on international funding for their operations. The members of this coalition dubbed themselves the "China River Network" and in collaboration with environmental journalists began an opposition campaign in the print, radio, and television media (Hu with Yu 2005). The scope of the reporting was striking, seeing that the Ministry of Propaganda has periodically banned the reporting of dam issues over the past few years. The critique in the news media brought the Nujiang dam issue to the public's attention and sparked debates in internet chat rooms and newspapers.

Challenges to NGO development

Uneven registration and funding difficulties

Over the fifteen years since civil society groups have been able to legally register, many environmental groups have taken advantage of the opportunity. By way of comparison, in a recent survey of NGO leaders from the HIV, environment, and gay and lesbian sectors, nearly three-quarters of respondents representing environmental groups were registered organizations, whereas less than half of NGOs from the other two sectors had obtained legal status.[7] But in all sectors, the process of registration has never been easy, leading many groups to operate in the legal gray area of "unregistered." When asked to rank the reasons why they have not successfully registered, respondents most frequently cited the "confusing" and "complex" nature of registration as the most important factor. The difficulty of registering is not a new revelation. But even more interesting is the second most frequently cited rationale: many respondents claim to already have a "close relationship with the government." They suggest that because they can engage in frequent cooperation with local government agencies, often at officials' behest, the drawn-out process of registration is unnecessary. From the local government perspective, provided these groups are behaving themselves and kept under the watchful eye of one or many government agencies, registration at a central or provincial level is thought to be a waste of time and effort (Kunming environmental health official, 27 November 2008).

While environmental groups make up the largest number of registered NGOs, those that opt not to register tend to face more fundraising difficulties than registered groups. The precarious funding situation of green groups may also cripple their continued development. In 2005, 81.5 percent of ENGOs received less than $6,200 in grant funding, which meant 60 percent of these groups did not have offices and 44 percent of the employees received little or no salary (Li 2007). Most environmental NGOs in China receive funding from foreign government aid agencies and international foundations or NGOs; the 2008 survey cited earlier in this chapter found that well over half of respondents receive 60 percent or more of their budget from overseas sources.

Opportunities for domestic fundraising have been traditionally scarce, owing to the lack of sufficient tax incentives to give and the tendency for Chinese donors to direct any donations to wholly government-run foundations. The resultant heavy reliance on outside funding poses at least two major problems to

Chinese ENGOs. First, international funding tends to support short-term projects rather than long-term capacity building. Second, as China's domestic economy continues to grow, the proclivity of international funders, foreign governments in particular, to support Chinese environmental NGOs might diminish (Li 2007). For example, Japanese overseas direct aid to China, which has never been a major source of funds for grassroots groups, has been decreasing.[8] Even the European Union, which has been increasing funding of environmental projects in China, mainly assists Chinese government-affiliated organizations, in part because many projects are highly technical and few Chinese grassroots groups can carry out the work (Edwards and Wang 2004).

Like NGOs in other polities, Chinese environmental NGOs lean on their own members and other domestic sources to keep their organizations afloat. This support often comes in the form of donated supplies, free office space, and volunteering of services. While useful, this brand of giving has its limits. Few NGO members are capable of making large donations, for most are students, young professionals, and rural residents who do not have large disposable incomes. Donations from the general public and grants from domestic sources are few and far between. Over 80 percent of respondents to the 2008 survey of NGO leaders believed that the domestic opportunities for funding in China were inadequate. These same respondents cited the "lack of a philanthropic culture" and "government policies" as the top two reasons for the limited opportunities. Indeed, the central government has promulgated very few tax policies that might encourage philanthropic giving (Gallagher 2004). More recent attempts to improve the environment for donations have fallen short. The National People's Congress and State Council adopted the "Public Welfare Donations Law" in 1999; the law included a tax exemption for donations by both corporations and private individuals. Although this development should have resulted in a windfall for Chinese NGOs, enforcement of the law has been difficult, owing to inadequate dissemination of changes in the laws and conflicts with other, pre-existing legislation (Zhang 2003). An additional effort to increase the benefits of donating – the 2004 Regulations on Administration of Foundations – has not resulted in significant domestic giving to Chinese grassroots groups, green or otherwise.[9]

Data on Chinese foundations are difficult to gather, but in 2000 the NGO China Development Brief reported that China had seventy-six national and approximately 1,700 provincial foundations. Most of these foundations are quasi-government entities possessing small endowments that were given by an interested government agency. Most foundations remain tightly linked to government agencies – often headed by retired senior officials (Chen 2004). Thus, it is not surprising that Chinese foundations usually act as fundraising or project-implementing agencies for state initiatives rather than provide grants to civil society organizations (China Development Brief 2000; interview with Dan Guttman, 2008).

Government-led attempts to encourage philanthropic giving not only have been of little benefit to green groups, but have perhaps even diminished funding opportunities for these groups (e.g. Lu 2003). The Chinese government has deemed two government-sponsored social groups, the China Youth Development

Foundation and the China Charities Federation, as preferred beneficiaries of the funding drive. Consequently, the primary donors – Chinese foundations and corporations – have funneled the bulk of their donations to these organizations in an effort to curry favor with the government and as a form of advertising. The result is that all other civil society groups, particularly ENGOs, have been effectively squeezed out of government calls for private giving.

As we have said, because domestic funding sources remain scarce, green groups continue to rely most heavily on overseas contributions. But while these sources are largely responsible for the creation and continued existence of environmental NGOs, group leaders have begun to express concern that the *form* of support severely restricts what the groups can do and will limit their long-term sustainability. When NGO leaders suggest that funding problems – not policy restrictions – serve as the biggest obstacle to their work, they do not stop at complaining about too few sources for support. They go further, noting that international donors have restricted their funding to "project-based" grants, and provide very few opportunities for "core" support. In the 2008 survey of NGO leaders, 15 percent of respondents reported that their entire budget was covered by project-based sources; nearly 80 percent relied upon project funds for 70 percent of their budget. Perhaps most shockingly, no respondents reported any level of core support exceeding 50 percent of their budget. The distinction between "project" and "core" funding sources is important because the former is usually highly restrictive; leaders report that many project-based grants provide no money for salaries or overhead. In numerous interviews, ENGO leaders expressed deep frustration that the current emphasis that international donors place on "capacity building" is misguided. One leader remarked, "Donors think that capacity can be built only in meetings," but wondered what use this kind of capacity can be with no staff members to attend them. Environmental NGO leaders almost uniformly contend that the vast majority of current funding sources that stress training and attendance in regional and international meetings, while appreciated and sometimes helpful, are too often the wrong kind of support for any kind of long-term sustainability for these groups.

And while NGO leaders are undoubtedly concerned about the kind of support being offered, some wonder if even these international funding sources will be around much longer. As China's economy continues to grow at a breakneck pace, and the government budgets for money-hungry projects like the space program and the 2008 Summer Olympics, the country will appear less like a developing nation that needs foreign aid. One prominent NGO activist expressed his concern to us in the summer 2003, noting that "after the 2008 Olympics, China will be viewed by the outside world not as a struggling country, and aid to NGOs will likely drop."

Infrequent cooperation and increased competition

Despite the limitations of both domestic and international financial support, environmental NGOs could still well achieve their goals by building strong ties and networking with groups inside and outside their issue area. Although there have been some successful national campaigns to protect endangered species and criticize dam building, cooperation among green groups is not as strong as it perhaps should be. According to the 2008 survey, ENGO leaders seem to understand that cooperation should be the best way forward; when asked if they agreed with the statement that other domestic NGOs were more competitors than partners, all respondents either somewhat disagreed, disagreed, or strongly disagreed. And yet, when asked how they might best meet their goals as an organization, leaders most frequently responded that their group was better off "working independently" than "cooperatively with other groups." These results more accurately reflect the dominant position gleaned from in-depth interviews.

To be fair, among the three NGO sectors studied in the 2008 survey, environmental groups boasted the most cooperation, but the numbers are not too encouraging. Only 25 percent of respondents reported cooperating (in any form) with other NGOs once a month. More than 60 percent claim to have cooperated with other groups only once a year. Cooperation with domestic groups outside of the environmental sector is even rarer. In sum, although green groups appear to understand that cooperation is something that is good in theory, it is not something that they have often embraced in practice. One explanation offered by prominent NGO leaders for this disconnect is a lingering concern among groups that the government is wary of too strong ties between groups, and if individual NGOs want to continue to engage in their own work unabated, they are best off keeping to themselves (anonymous interviews, Beijing, 4, 12, and 16 July 2008). Other factors potentially hindering cooperation could simply be linked to the capacity of China's ENGOs, which lack sufficient funding and have high turnover of staff.

Domestic NGOs are not alone in tackling China's environmental problems. In fact, international NGOs in southwestern China predated domestic groups. But while these groups have a relatively long history and significant financial and technical resources at their disposal, many domestic ENGOs appear reluctant to engage in frequent cooperation with them. Although there might be similar concerns about political blowback, in some areas of China (as we discuss later in this chapter), ENGO leaders are increasingly concerned that international NGOs might replace them as the primary force in the sector.

Decentralization and political space: local governments giveth and taketh away

Although the aforementioned limitations are large barriers standing in the way of group development, perhaps the most important determining factor for the continued existence of ENGOs is the expanding and contracting political opportunity for social organizations in China. As we argue at the beginning of this chapter, the initial political opportunity for these ENGOs to emerge and continue has been granted by a government that has been willing to take a calculated risk that empowering these groups with limited autonomy will result in a high social benefit at a relatively low political cost. In short, the government has allowed them to exist to fulfill a clear charge and provide a service that the government is either unable or otherwise unwilling to offer.

In the environmental sector, the government recognizes the value added of green groups, due to their ability to bring education efforts, technical expertise, and much-needed attention to a policy area where the government is deficient. However, as with NGOs in other sectors, their work as providers of social services is contingent upon their meeting the needs of society. When government officials see these groups as having either succeeded or failed, the groups' rationale for existing no longer continues. For many government officials, failure does not always mean that they do a poor job in serving society. On the contrary, it might mean that environment groups did a fine job protecting natural ecology, educating the public, or defending pollution victims. However, in providing these services, meeting these societal needs, these groups came into conflict with other important interests of the government.

And so, while the central government is using green groups to help support its environmental policy goals, the government simultaneously needs to balance this increased political space for such groups with the regime's own goals. Although environmental NGOs are less frequently the subject of political repression than groups from more politically sensitive sectors, they are not immune from the wrath of displeased government officials, particularly at the local level, as we describe in the Yunnan case study in the next section. In that section, we argue that although the central government has increasingly prioritized pollution control and natural resource protection, decentralization has enabled local governments to ignore central environmental protection laws. The central government's encouragement of ENGOs is but one policy strategy to help check local government evasion of environmental protection laws. However, ENGOs typically lack the power to become truly strong watchdogs because of the overwhelming power of local officials – a situation that in part parallels the weaknesses of the local environmental protection bureaus.

Although the central government has offered significant rhetorical support to ENGOs, lauding their success and enlisting their help in the most public of projects, Beijing has still been wary of allowing too prominent a role and too great autonomy to these groups. The successful bid to host the 2008 Summer Olympic Games offers a compelling illustration. The Chinese government gave prominent roles to two of China's best-known ENGOs in an effort to add legitimacy to its claimed devotion to the environment, the newest of the Olympic movement's principles. In this context, the Beijing Olympic organizing committee included Friends of Nature and Global Village Beijing as NGOs to engage in research, lead environment education efforts, and provide expert advice to the organizing committee. But when China was awarded the games, the green groups saw a marked drop in their involvement, losing their prominent position in favor of paid international consultants. The Chinese leadership viewed the private sector as far less a political threat than domestic social organizations (Hildebrandt 2002, 2003).

Concerns about how the central government might respond can sometimes dictate the kind of work in which ENGOs are engaged. As is noted earlier in this chapter, one of the biggest problems with air pollution has been the transboundary nature of the problem. And while a majority of international NGOs operating in China focus on the climate change issue, this has been a slow area of development for Chinese groups. Overall, Chinese ENGOs have not become heavily involved in transboundary pollution issues, in part because it often would put them in the position of directly criticizing the Chinese central government's policies. In the months running up to the 2008 Summer Games, some green groups in Beijing reported more frequent visits by Public Security Bureau officials, which sent a strong message that no one should cause trouble during the Olympics.

But on the whole, unlike groups in other sectors, ENGO leaders do not express too great a concern about the potential for central government officials to restrict them or engage in widespread crackdowns. Moreover, environmental NGOs seem to have an important ally in the central government in Pan Yue. On 9 February 2006, Pan Yue – the famously vocal (and surprisingly independent) vice director of the MEP – declared that "environmental protection issues are of public interest and are the least politically sensitive. [It is] the best area for experiments in socialist democracy and rule of law" (Reuters 2006).

ENGO leaders have expressed to us a great deal of contentment when it comes to the central government in general and the MEP in particular. Like most Chinese citizens, they reserve their criticism of the government for provincial and local officials. In fact, in over thirty interviews with green-group leaders conducted in 2007, nearly all respondents reported that the cause of the restrictive political environment is not the central government, but rather the provincial and local governments.

Quite ironically, however, it was political decentralization that helped herald the birth of environmental NGOs in China. When Beijing began to devolve some political authority to lower levels of government, innovative solutions soon emerged to deal with vexing social and economic problems. Most famously, increased economic freedom in special economic zones on China's eastern coast helped develop the regional economy and served as an important proving ground for Chinese market socialism, which has now spread throughout the country. Likewise, greater political discretion in China's southwest allowed for experimentation with international and domestic ENGOs to provide social services; this model, too, has been copied in other provinces, both near and far from the political center in Beijing. And yet, the increased political authority of local levels also makes solving China's environmental problems a more difficult task. The success of central government policies designed to address issues such as water pollution is contingent upon implementation by local government officials.

Although local governments, too, might be interested in protecting the environment, if environmental protection interferes with more important local considerations – such as economic development – central government policies frequently are left unimplemented. Even when efforts have been made to marry local economic goals to environmental protection, local government officials have been reluctant to play along. One notable failed effort to check local governments was a pilot green GDP program that rewarded officials for their environmental performance. Though widely supported by Chinese citizens, the program ended in 2007 because of opposition from local governments, which quickly discovered that most would be ranked quite low under the more important cadre evaluation system.

The increased power of local governments under decentralization, in addition to the reluctance to implement many environmental protection policies, has resulted in an increasingly contracting political space for ENGOs. As we discuss below in greater depth, even in provinces like Yunnan, where green groups were once thought to flourish because of local political discretion and innovative policies, other competing interests have led local government officials to grow increasingly wary of ENGOs.

Core to the central government's strategy has been implementing a broad array of environmental laws and increasing investment and clean-up targets in the Five-Year Plans, as well as encouraging international assistance in the areas of pollution control and natural resource management. The main constraint on implementing the laws and meeting the goals in the Five-Year Plans and international projects has been the inherently decentralized structure of the government; local governments have both the power and an incentive to favor economic growth over environmental protection. Beginning in 2004, the central government has amended, revised, and added teeth to its standards on car emissions and laws on energy conservation, environmental impact assessment, and water pollution control. The overall trend in environmental legislation, regulations, and pilot projects is to move away from command-and-control policies that depend on local government enforcement and instead use markets, information disclosure, public hearings, and incentives for officials and businesses to improve compliance with environmental protection regulations.

Another potentially promising "local government workaround" has been the MEP's new partnerships with Chinese banks and export regulators to put polluting industries on blacklists that prevent them from receiving loans or export permits. One promising sign that environmental protection has been given higher priority came in March 2008, when the Environmental Protection Administration was promoted to ministry status and given more funding and six new regional offices – all of which could increase its capacity to enforce environmental laws. ENGO leaders welcome these kinds of reform. In interviews in 2007, green-group leaders responded favorably (and enthusiastically) to the suggestion that the central government exercise even more discretion when it comes to environmental issues.

ENGOs in Yunnan: from haven to hell?

Yunnan Province provides a good example of China's relatively underdeveloped periphery and offers a stark contrast to its booming eastern coast. In the wake of political decentralization, Yunnan, like many other provinces, has been required to go it alone in solving many social problems. However, because the province's economy is significantly weaker than that of the eastern provinces, the local government's task of filling the gap where the central government has transferred responsibility is greater. Because the province is home to one of the world's "biodiversity hotspots," the ecological health of Yunnan has drawn considerable interest from international green groups, beginning with the arrival of the mammoth US-based ENGO The Nature Conservancy (TNC) in the mid-1990s. The Yunnan government's welcoming of such groups is exemplified in its signing of a cooperative agreement with TNC on the Great Rivers Project to protect the ecosystems of its main rivers – the first such provincial–international NGO agreement in China. The political environment was initially so positive that Yunnan became known as China's dynamic haven for ENGOs (Cooper 2006), attracting international funding and activists (Chen 2005). Yunnan officials were interested in marketing their province as "green," and one interest in cooperating with TNC and other international ENGOs was to help promote tourism – eco or otherwise – to the province. Many international ENGOs working in Yunnan have helped support or create domestic counterparts, which underscores how Yunnan, in theory, should be an ideal proving ground for the success and continued growth of Chinese ENGOs.

But our recent research in Yunnan suggests that this characterization might be severely outdated. The challenges to ENGOs we discuss earlier in this chapter are just as grave in Yunnan as in provinces that do not boast a history of welcoming non-governmental organizations. Most environmental groups have secured legal registration in Yunnan, but their financial situations are decidedly precarious. Early green groups in the province enjoyed strong initial institutional support from officials. But as the number of NGOs has grown in the country in all sectors, and interest in environmental ones has waned, this core support has quickly dried up. In some cases, this means that groups have had to change their activities to better match the priorities of the few project-based funding opportunities available from international donors. For example, Chinese ENGOs in Yunnan focus on biodiversity protection, which is more popular with international donors, while very few have gravitated to pollution issues, which is a topic more groups are focusing on in other areas of the country. In interviews in Yunnan Province in 2007, many ENGOs reported that Yunnan green groups have diminished in size and scope; once large, lively NGO offices are now veritable ghost towns. Several ENGOs noted that in Yunnan, the market for social organizations is far better in some sectors, such as HIV/AIDS, which has become a major new target for international funding (as discussed in Chapter 8).

Long-time Chinese ENGO leaders in the province have pointed to the diminished opportunities for institutional support as the primary reason for the recent contraction in the number of domestic groups in Yunnan. But amid a perceived decline in the number of domestic NGOs, international environmental groups appear to be thriving in the province. Local ENGO leaders express a great deal of concern that while the international green groups sometimes do great service toward protecting the environment, the common feeling is that domestic groups are being squeezed out by international NGOs, which tend to take financial and human resources that might otherwise go to domestic groups.

Finally, the central government has encouraged civil society groups to help address many of the problems stemming from the country's rapid economic development, but powerful local governments have not always granted NGOs as much political space. The Yunnan government did support green groups in the 1990s as a way to promote tourism and investment in the province, but provincial and sub-provincial officials have not been as comfortable with more aggressive ENGOs, which has led them to decrease political space for ENGOs in the province. In short, while environmental issues are a problem in Yunnan, economic development remains a larger need. In the 2008 NGO leader survey, Yunnan-based respondents reported that their best and closest relationships were not with sub-provincial agencies, but with either provincial or central governments. Local ENGO leaders extol MEP's work on the environment, while criticizing the local government's lack of implementation and increased hostility to their environmental work. Nowhere has this disconnect between environmental protection policies at the center and economic priorities at the local level been more apparent than in the case of Green Watershed, discussed earlier in this chapter and at greater length by other scholars (Mertha 2008).

Green Watershed and its leader, Yu Xiaogang, led the push against dam construction on China's last wild river, the Nujiang. Having attracted the attention of international media, the campaign succeeded in forcing the government to suspend the project. But in doing so, Yu also attracted the ire of local governments, which saw their own economic interests negatively impacted by the suspension of the project. The Yunnan provincial government tried to close down Green Watershed through legal channels, but ultimately the NGO's sponsor defended Yu Xiaogang's activities. The provincial authorities subsequently placed Yu under a travel ban and his passport was confiscated by local authorities.

Admittedly, Yu Xiaogang represents one of several well-known "envelope-pushing" green activists. However, like Dai Qing, the journalist who campaigned against the Three Gorges Dam, and Wu Lihong, who doggedly criticized local officials around Lake Tai, Yu is highly respected among green activists but is not a model many appear ready to emulate. The majority of NGOs in all sectors inside and beyond Yunnan rarely test boundaries.

Other ENGO leaders in the province point to Yu's case to emphasize the negative implications of unchecked local authorities in China's highly decentralized political system. Other ENGOs in the province also have moved to decidedly safe activities that do not run the risk of conflicting with important local economic priorities. But even this might not be enough. One ENGO leader in Yunnan (anonymous, August 2007) has worked to create local water user associations. Local governments have allowed the ENGO to continue this work, and officials have become involved with the water associations. The ENGO leader is convinced that local government participation stems more from the desire to monitor the group than for concern about better water management, for local officials fear NGOs might undercut the influence of local officials on their constituents. In

Yunnan, the ENGO leader frankly concludes that when NGOs try to organize citizens, the "local government uses all means to destroy" the initiative.

Low rates of cooperation between ENGOs in Yunnan mirror what is found in the rest of China. Despite Yunnan's long history of NGOs, green groups appear to be ignorant of the NGOs in other sectors. In the provincial capital of Kunming, for instance, most ENGO leaders expressed surprise that other kinds of ENGOs even existed in the city (anonymous interviews, autumn 2008). And while ENGOs might be the province's oldest sector, the newer NGOs in Kunming (e.g. HIV/AIDS groups) are similarly ignorant of the presence of other organizations (anonymous interviews, September 2007).

Conclusion

While in the long term ENGOs will most likely continue to be among China's largest civil society groups, their ability to expand their effectiveness and wield greater political clout in the short to mid term is questionable. The urgent need for strong green NGOs stems from the continued weakness of the central government in pushing for strong enforcement of environmental laws, which means a continuation of poor air, water, and soil quality that will threaten human health and the economy, potentially causing more instability in the country. To the extent that these groups are engaged in work that complements the interests of local governments, ENGOs will continue to play a role in providing environmentally related services. But when the work of green groups conflicts with the changing priorities of provincial and local officials, as in the case of Yunnan, their role can become circumscribed.

Other difficulties loom large as well. Infrequent cooperation across the environmental sector will serve to keep the groups atomized and circumscribe their future growth. Inadequate and inappropriate funding opportunities keep groups from strengthening over the long term and tend to lead to fewer groups taking on ever fewer activities, with a concentration on the kinds of activities that are currently supported by the government or international donors. Other options for sustaining these groups and their activities might force us to reconsider our assumptions about NGOs. A handful of ENGOs have begun to flourish and actually have begun to raise their own money by selling goods and services. Some ENGO leaders suggest that their future existence depends upon essentially becoming a government subcontractor or a consultant firm that conducts NGO-type activities on the side (anonymous interview, September 2007).

While the obstacles facing Chinese ENGOs remain formidable, there are some reasons for optimism. Although laws making registration and fundraising easier do not appear to be on the horizon, in May 2008 new Measures on Open Environmental Information were put in place, which could provide a powerful tool for ENGOs to promote the public right to know (China Dialogue 2008; interview with Ma Jun, August 2008). For example, ENGOs may be able to obtain information necessary for better legal cases and expand their roles as true watchdogs on polluters. Even the apparent decrease in the number of ENGOs might be ultimately good in the long term, for those that persist will be stronger, more influential groups. And while political pressure might be heavy, the most dynamic of groups – such as Green Watershed, the CLAPV, and the IPEA – will not wilt away, for they are providing valuable services to those in the central government pushing for a better environmental governance system.

Notes

1 Department of Political Science, University of Wisconsin-Madison.

2 China Environment Forum, Woodrow Wilson International Center for Scholars. The authors thank Linden Ellis, Kimberly Go, and Jing Chen at the China Environment Forum for helpful input on earlier drafts of this chapter.

3 The China Environment Forum and its flagship publication, *China Environment Series*, have covered many environmental problems in greater depth (accessible online at www.wilsoncenter.org/cef). In addition, important academic literature on environmental problems in general (e.g. Economy 2004) and the work of Chinese green NGOs in particular (e.g. Ho 2001; Yang 2005) has grown significantly in recent years.

4 It was raised to the ministerial level in March 2008. To simplify the text, we use MEP throughout.

5 In this section, we cite groups by name because their work has been covered extensively in domestic and foreign media. However, the bulk of insights offered in this chapter, including survey results, come from recent research that was conducted with the understanding that subjects' identity would remain anonymous. Hence, we refrain from extensively citing the names of leaders or groups.

6 The National Environmental Protection Agency became SEPA in 1998 and was then elevated to the Ministry of Environmental Protection in 2008.

7 This survey of nearly 100 NGO leaders (representing twenty-six environmental groups, twenty-six HIV Groups and forty Gay and Lesbian Groups) was conducted in 2008 as part of a larger dissertation project (Hildebrandt 2009) examining three organized social groups sectors (environmental, HIV/AIDS, and gay and lesbian) throughout China. The project was funded by a National Science Foundation Integrated Graduate Education and Research Traineeship at the University of Wisconsin-Madison.

8 Japan's bilateral assistance to China was slashed to 121.2 billion yen in 2002, from a level of 214.4 billion yen just two years earlier (Sunaga 2004). Indicative of a continuing trend, overseas development assistance to China has been cut by 25 percent every year since 2002 (Katada 2005). Prime Minister Koizumi predicted that Japan would soon see China "graduate from Japanese ODA" (Masaki 2004).

9 A translation of the law is available at: www.npo.org.cn/en/member/law/detail.php?id=7.

References

Birnbaum, S. Elizabeth and Yu Xiubo (2006) "NGO Strategies to Promote River Protection and Restoration Goals," *China Environment Series* 8: 185–99.

Chandler, William (2008) "Breaking the Suicide Pact: U.S.–China Cooperation on Climate Change," *Policy Brief* 57, Carnegie Endowment: Washington, DC. Online, available at: www.carnegieendowment.org/publications/index.cfm?fa=view&id=19991&prog=zch (accessed 3 August 2008).

Chen Chao (2004) "China's Charities and Philanthropists," *China.org.cn* (24 April). Online, available at: www.china.org.cn/english/2004/Apr/94150.htm.

Chen Jie (2005) "NGO Community in China: Expanding Linkages with Transnational Civil Society," Working Paper 128, Asia Research Centre, Murdoch University.

China Development Brief (2000) "Foundation Law Will Raise Endowment Threshold." Online, available at: www.chinadevelopmentbrief.com/node/202.

China Dialogue (2008) "Which Way Forward for Chinese NGOs?" (1 July). Online, available at: www.chinadialogue.net/article/show/single/en/2156.

Cho, Jung-Myung and Giannini-Spohn, Suzanne (2007) "Environmental and Health Threats from Cement Production in China," A China Environmental Health Research Brief. Online, available at: www.wilsoncenter.org/topics/docs/cement_Aug31.pdf.

Cooper, C. M. (2006) "This Is Our Way In: The Civil Society of Environmental NGOs in Southwest China," *Government and Opposition* 41 (1): 109–36.

Economic Observer weekly/SynTao (2008) "Eight Chinese NGOs Announce the First Green Banking Innovation Award." Online, available at: www.syntao.com/E_Page_Show.asp?Page_ID=9244.

Economy, Elizabeth (2004) *The River Runs Black: The Environmental Challenge to China's Future*, Ithaca, NY: Cornell University Press.

—— (2007) "The Great Leap Backward?" *Foreign Affairs* 86 (5) (September/October). Online, available at: www.foreignaffairs.org/20070901faessay86503/elizabeth-c-economy/the-great-leap-backward.html.

Edwards, Alan and Wang Yongli (2004) "Sustainable River Basin Management in the Liaon River Basin," talk by EU officials at Tsinghua University, Beijing, as part of a China Environment Forum River Basin Governance Study Tour Meeting (14 July).

Friends of Nature Newsletter (1999) "Many Successes but Much More Needs to Be Done," issue 2. Online, available at: www.fon.org.cn/content.php?aid=7752.

Futrell, W. Chad (2007) "Choking on Sand: Regional Cooperation to Mitigate Desertification in China," *China Environment Series* 9: 57–61.

Gallagher, Mary E. (2004) "China: The Limits of Civil Society in a Late Leninist State," in Muthiah Alagappa (ed.) *Civil Society and Political Change in Asia*, Stanford, CA: Stanford University Press.

Hildebrandt, Timothy (2002) "Spray-Painting Change? Beijing's Green Olympics, NGOs and Lessons Learned from Sydney," *China Environment Series* 5: 80–5.

—— (2003) "Making Green in Beijing," *China Business Review* 30 (6): 16–21.

—— (2009) "Forging a Harmonious Middle Path? Organized Social Groups and the Chinese State," Department of Political Science, University of Wisconsin-Madison).

Ho, Peter (2001) "Greening without Conflict? Environmentalism, NGOs and Civil Society in China," *Development and Change* 32: 893–921.

Hu Kanping with Yu Xiaogang (2005) "Bridge over Troubled Waters: The Role of the News Media in Promoting Public Participation in River Basin Management and Environmental Protection in China," in Jennifer L. Turner and Kenji Otsuka (eds.) *Promoting Sustainable River Basin Governance: Crafting Japan–U.S. Water Partnerships in China*, Chiba, Japan: Institute of Developing Economies.

Katada, Saori (2005) "Toward a Mature Aid Donor: Fifty Years of Japanese ODA and the Challenges Ahead," in *Japanese ODA at 50: An Assessment*, Asia Program Special Report 128, Woodrow Wilson Center, Washington, DC.

Larson, Christina (2007) "Greening China's Banks," *China Environment Series* 9: 41–2.

Li Zhenyu (2007) "China's Grassroots Get Deeper", *EJ Magazine*. Online, available at: www.ejmagazine.com/2007a/greenchina.htm.

Lu Xiaoqing and Bates, Gill (2007) "Assessing China's Response to the Challenge of Environmental Health," *China Environment Series* 9: 3–15.

Lu Yiyi (2003) "The Limitations of NGOs: A Preliminary Study of Non-governmental Social Welfare Organizations in China," CCS International Working Paper 13, London School of Economics.

Masaki, Hisane (2004) "Japan's ODA at Crossroads," Japan Forum on International Relations. Online, available at: www.jfir.or.jp/e/column.041209-1.pdf.

Mertha, Andrew C. (2008) *China's Water Warriors: Citizen Action and Policy Change*, Ithaca, NY: Cornell University Press.

Moore, Allison and Warren, Adria (2006) "Legal Advocacy in Environmental Public Participation in China: Raising the Stakes and Strengthening Stakeholders," *China Environment Series* 8: 3–23.

OECD (2007) *OECD Environmental Performance Review: China*, Paris: Organisation for Economic Co-operation and Development.

Otsuka, Kenji and Turner, Jennifer (2006) *Reaching across the Water: International Cooperation Promoting Sustainable River Basin Governance in China*. Washington, DC: Woodrow Wilson International Center for Scholars.

Reuters (2006) "Pollution Test for China, Democracy Needed: Official" (9 February).

Salaverry, Daniela (2007) "A Community of Grassroots NGOs Protecting China's Rivers and Lakes," *China Environment Series* 9: 115–16.

Sunaga, Kazuo (2004) "The Reshaping of Japan's Official Development Assistance (ODA) Charter," FASID Discussion Paper on Development Assistance 3.

Tan Zuoren (2006) "Our Land Is under Siege," *China Rights Forum* 1.

Turner, Jennifer L. and Lü Zhi (2006) "Building a Green Civil Society in China," in Linda Starke (ed.) *State of the World 2006*, a Worldwatch Institute Report on Progress toward a Sustainable Society, New York: W. W. Norton.

Xu Kezhu and Wang, Alex (2006) "Recent Developments at the Center for Legal Assistance to Pollution Victims (CLAPV)," *China Environment Series* 8: 103–4.

Yang Yang (2007) "Pesticides and Environmental Health Trends in China," *A China Environmental Health Project Factsheet*. Online, available at: www.wilsoncenter.org/index.cfm?topic_id=1421&fuseaction=topics.item&news_id=225756.

Zhang, Ye (2003) *China's Emerging Civil Society*, Washington, DC: Brookings Institution.

Interviews

Interview, Beijing environmental NGO leader (20 December 2007).

Interview, environmental NGO leader (4 July 2008).

Interview, environmental NGO leader (12 July 2008).

Interview, environmental NGO leader (16 July 2008).

Interview, environmental NGO leader (12 September 2008).

Interview, environmental NGO leader (6 November 2008).

Interview, environmental NGO leader (14 November 2008).

Interview, Kunming environmental health official (27 November 2008).

Interview, Ma Jun (3 August 2008).

Interview, Dan Guttman (4 August 2008, Washington, DC).

Part III

Social welfare responses in crisis situations

6 The institutionalization of Buddhist philanthropy in China

André Laliberté[1]

Introduction

One of the remarkable illustrations of the development of civil society in China during the 1990s was the emergence of religious actors in social services provision (Tsai 2007; Eng and Lin 2002). One of the most path-breaking dimensions of this trend was the appeal launched by the Chinese Ministry of Civil Affairs (MOCA) to a transnational Taiwanese lay Buddhist philanthropic organization, the Tzu Chi Merit Society (*Ciji gongdehui*) to help some local governments provide aid and support following the 1991 flood disasters (Huang 2005; Laliberté 2003). This initiative was remarkable because it represented a departure from the international isolation that China had experienced after the massacre of 4 June 1989, heralded an improvement in relations with Taiwan, and suggested a new policy toward religious institutions. Although the acceptance of Tzu Chi in China in the wake of the severe floods may have seemed at the time a short-term government response to a crisis situation, it turned out in the end to represent a learning stage in a long-term strategy of supporting the development of China-based Buddhist charities. This chapter argues that the reliance on religious charities during the 1990s represents a new type of relationship between state and religion in response to challenges faced by central and local governments in the provision of social services.

This relationship between the state and Buddhist philanthropic associations was institutionalized on the basis of a complex structure that was previously established to separately monitor religious affairs and manage social policy (Ying 2006; Leung 2005; Potter 2003). The first tier of organizations includes the "government-organized NGOs" (GONGOs) sponsored by ministries and bureaus set up by the State Council and local governments to manage social services for the whole population and for targeted populations such as orphans, disabled children, and victims of natural disasters. Buddhist associations at the central, provincial, and local levels represent a second tier of organizations that have to report to bureaus for religious affairs or bureaus for minorities and religious affairs at corresponding and higher levels of administration. NGOs and independent charities, some of which have connections in Hong Kong, Taiwan, or abroad, represent a third tier of association. This third tier, established independently of the official Buddhist associations, has expanded significantly in the past two decades (FS 2007; Gen 2006; Fang 2001).

To provide context to this evolution, the chapter first identifies some of the major post-1989 challenges facing the Chinese regime that bear on its strategy of reliance on Buddhist charities, and underlines the crises experienced by local governments in 1991 and 1992 following a succession of natural disasters. The chapter then describes the nature of Buddhist philanthropy in China. It first highlights the role of Tzu Chi in the early 1990s as an opportunity for the state to learn about the potential for provision of social services by religious organizations, and then describes networks of Buddhist charity associations at the provincial and local levels that were subsequently established in the late 1990s. The third section makes the point that the state's decision to encourage Buddhist charitable work became more than just expediency in response to an emergency; it evolved to become the result of a concerted state strategy. This is demonstrated by pointing to the development of an elaborate structure to promote Chinese Communist Party (CCP) religious work, and by outlining the context of social policy for which Buddhist charities contribute. The final section of the chapter identifies the limitations of relying on Buddhist charities in social service provision.

The challenges of the post-1989 recovery, changing cross-strait relations, and responding to natural disasters

Chapter 1 defined crises as major changes in the environment of a collective characterized by three necessary and sufficient perceptions on the part of decision makers: threat to basic values, urgency, and uncertainty. The events that led to the Tiananmen massacre of 4 June 1989 have certainly represented such a major crisis for China, to the extent that the values defended by the CCP were challenged by society, the situation was critical, and the regime appeared unsure of its future. Although this crisis came to a resolution in 1992, the country experienced challenges of varying intensity and scope to its governance in the fifteen years that followed, approaching crisis levels. Some challenges, such as the confrontation with Falun Gong in the summer of 2000 (Ostergaard 2004; Keith and Lin 2003; Ching 2001) and the 2003 SARS outbreak (Schwartz, Chapter 7 of this volume; Kleinman and Watson 2006), were national in scope and reverberated around the world, but the state responded quickly – albeit harshly. Others, like the tension across the Taiwan Strait, approached crisis levels but did not threaten the regime (Clough 1999; Zhao 1999; Austin 1997). Some other challenges, such as floods and typhoons, did not directly affect the central government, but were perceived quite differently by local governments. In some dramatic cases, local authorities experienced such natural disasters as crises. The following summarizes these three types of challenges in turn. This discussion illustrates that the acceptance of Tzu Chi in China helped diverse levels of government address different forms of challenges throughout the 1990s.

The crisis of governance that was triggered by the students' demonstrations in the spring of 1989 and that continued until 1992, during which time the CCP remained divided over the continuation of Deng Xiaoping's reforms, finally came to a resolution when Deng offered the population a new social contract in which political debate would be sacrificed in exchange for increasing liberties in the private sphere. Ensuring that this policy could be pursued represented the major challenge faced by the government in the following years (Yang 2001: 28; Chen 1995: 155–60). The success of Deng's policy was premised on the ability to break the international boycott that had followed the events of 1989, and, for that reason, opening China to international relief organizations, whether religious or not, was conceived as beneficial. Deng understood that the People's Republic of China (PRC) had to recover the economic ground it had lost on the international stage if it wished to avoid a future crisis arising from lost foreign direct investment and access to international markets for Chinese goods. CCP leaders not only were looking for investment from Japanese and Western businesses, but also hoped to tap into the vast reservoir of wealth controlled by overseas Chinese worldwide, including compatriots in Hong Kong, Macau, and Taiwan (Thunø 2001).

The situation of Taiwan represented a particular challenge for the CCP. The deepening of democratization on the island after the lifting of martial law in 1987, in stark contrast with the authoritarian clampdown in the mainland, made the prospect of reunification less attractive than ever to the Taiwanese. Having moved away from dictatorship, Taiwan found the "one country, two systems" policy proposed by Deng Xiaoping in 1978 increasingly unpalatable. Elections in 1992 for the legislative Yuan – Taiwan's parliament – saw the pro-independence Democratic Progressive Party (DPP) make significant gains, further decreasing the likelihood of China achieving its goal of peacefully recovering Taiwan (Corcuff 2002; Tien 1996; Tsang 1993). However, other processes gave some hope to the Chinese leaders. The Singapore meeting between Wang Daohan and Koo Chen-foo, who represented two NGOs that were negotiating on behalf of the Taipei and Beijing governments, constituted an important breakthrough in relations between them. This meeting appeared to signal a thaw in the relations between Taiwan and China, thereby improving the investment atmosphere for Taiwanese businesses interested in mainland China (Goldstein 1999). In this context, welcoming Tzu Chi to the PRC was tantamount to a show of goodwill by China to its Taiwanese compatriots, and a clear signal that just as charities were welcome, so too were Taiwanese businesses.

Slowly improving cross-strait relations were again strained in 1995 and 1996, when the People's Liberation Army launched military exercises off the coast of Taiwan (Clough 1999; Zhao 1999). Taiwanese leaders responded to China's actions with assertive diplomatic campaigns aimed at obtaining international recognition while they let pro-independence sentiments on the island grow (Cabestan and Vermander 2005: 32–50). An additional brief period of tension developed in 2000 when the pro-Taiwan independence candidate Chen Shuibian won the presidential election. These dramatic changes in the domestic political situation in Taiwan threatened to make the goal of recovering the island increasingly difficult for the PRC (Cabestan and Vermander 2005: 167–74). Despite these developments, Taiwanese businesspeople continued to live in China, and volunteers from Tzu Chi continued their charitable activities, suggesting that the Chinese central authorities believed that cross-strait relations represented a manageable challenge.

Finally, China experienced a series of localized crises of governance as a result of a number of natural disasters. Floods in particular, by destroying vulnerable areas, were not only impoverishing residents of those areas, but also exposing the lacunae of local governments' crisis response capabilities. While natural disasters did not threaten the central government, they represented serious crises for provincial governments and major catastrophes for local governments in areas affected by the disasters (Nickum 1998). In 1991, central China experienced major floods that affected millions of people (Shankman *et al.* 2006). Although this was not an unprecedented event (Smil 2004: 77), the development of the country made the economic consequences of the natural disasters increasingly costly. By welcoming associations like Tzu Chi in such contexts, local governments were proving how far they were willing to go to show their concern for the welfare of the people under their care: they were ready to overcome old political enmities with the Taiwanese, and they were also showing flexibility in welcoming an association with a religious identity, despite the CCP's traditional ideological reservations concerning religion.

This new openness toward religion was put to the test by the end of the decade. A challenge to the CCP's authority appeared to emerge in 1999 when a peaceful demonstration by members of Falun Gong, a religious organization that sought recognition as a sixth official association in China (the five officially recognized religions are Buddhism, Taoism, Protestantism, Catholicism, and Islam), was followed months later by brutal repression against many *qigong* organizations (Ostergaard 2004; Keith and Lin 2003; Ching 2001). This act of defiance by a religious organization did not reach the severity of the 1989 demonstrations and did not compel the CCP to make major changes to its policy. On the contrary, as the following section illustrates, the challenge that some religious organizations (such as Falun Gong) represented, far from leading the state to retrench from its policy of relative openness to religious charities, only reinforced state efforts to co-opt Buddhist philanthropic societies and encourage their development. To understand the state's thinking, the following section elaborates on the activities of Buddhist charities through history, and in particular since the beginning of the reform in 1978. This overview will help us appreciate the benefit the state sees in reviving these organizations.

The re-emergence of Buddhist philanthropy in the reform period

Buddhist philanthropy: an ancient tradition with many forms

One important aspect of Buddhist institutions since the Ming dynasty is the emergence of the role played by lay people in the survival of their religious tradition, from the sustenance of the clergy to the printing of scriptures to gain merit (Ch'en 1964). By the end of the Qing dynasty and at the beginnings of the Republican period, Buddhism owed its survival to such initiatives by lay people (Welch 1968). At that time, the lay people were influenced by reformist monks such as Taixu, who encouraged them to get involved in society and elaborated a theological innovation known as "Buddhism for the human realm" (*renjian fojiao*), which argued that salvation should come from charity and involvement in the social and political trends of the time. In that respect, Buddhism, as a tradition, came to represent much more than an association of monks remote from mundane realities and aloof from politics (Pan 2001; Pittman 2001).

This type of social activism has existed in Taiwan since the 1960s and has remained alive in some of the overseas Chinese communities (Huang 2005; Chandler 2004; Laliberté 2004; Jones 1999; Huang and Weller 1998). A very interesting feature of this social activism, from the perspective of authoritarian governments, is that it does not incorporate political demands. This is a politically conservative movement, unlikely to mobilize populations in favour of political change. Therein lies its attractiveness for authoritarian states such as the PRC today, and the Republic of China (ROC, or Taiwan) before the end of the 1980s. It is no doubt this kind of behavior that has encouraged the CCP to trust that the revival of Buddhism in the PRC would not represent a threat to the regime. Still, this revival remains closely monitored.[2] While members of the Buddhist monastic community may offer training for aspiring monks and become involved in fund-raising, they may not get involved in education, cannot run clinics or hospitals, and cannot administer orphanages, or homes for elderly people. Lay people, however, can perform these activities.

When, after the 1991 flood, the MOCA called upon international NGOs and "compatriots" in Taiwan and Hong Kong to help local governments in distress, local Buddhist associations were still recovering from the Cultural Revolution and lacked the resources to provide the kind of help that religious charities had provided during the Republican era. Monastic communities were trying to rebuild their institutions and educating a new generation of monks and nuns. Lay people lacked a leadership to which they could turn (Birnbaum 2003). In addition, during the 1980s Buddhist institutions had adopted the philosophy of "allying Chan and rural labor" (*nong chan bing zhong*), which emphasized self-sufficiency for the monastic community (Ji 2004). For the Chinese central government, the appeal to associations from outside China offered the opportunity to learn about the potential and limitations of relying on charities, including those established by religious institutions. The 1991 flood represented a catalyst and a major incentive to learn from outside and foster the development of local organizations.

A new beginning: the Buddhist Tzu Chi Foundation in the PRC after 1991

The Yangtze River flood of 1991 represented an enormous tragedy for the Chinese population, and the CCP decided then to turn to the international community for support. This appeal to the international community contrasted with the defiant attitude the country had displayed only two years before when the People's Liberation Army was ordered to shoot students in Tiananmen Square. The CCP also appealed to "compatriots" in Taiwan and Hong Kong, thereby suggesting that the Chinese side wanted to put an end to tensions across the Taiwan Strait. Many international charities responded to the appeal. The Tzu Chi Foundation, a major transnational charity headquartered in Taiwan, was invited in this context. The Tzu Chi Foundation was remarkable because it was a Buddhist organization and the largest philanthropic body in Taiwan. That same year, 1991, Tzu Chi had launched international relief operations in Bangladesh. In the years that followed, it established its presence among overseas Chinese communities around the world, and visited a number of locations throughout China. With only a few exceptions, a majority of the sites visited by Tzu Chi were located in impoverished districts affected by floods, droughts, typhoons, and other natural disasters. The activities of Tzu Chi focused on emergency relief, the reconstruction of villages, and support for the building of schools (Tzu Chi 1999, 2000, 2005).

Tzu Chi's status was unusual compared to international and Chinese domestic NGOs because of the ambiguous situation of Taiwan. Tzu Chi could not be considered an international NGO because of its Taiwanese origins, the view of the PRC's government being that Taiwan is part of China. Because of its ambiguous status, however, no provincial government within the PRC has jurisdiction over Tzu Chi, which in practical terms means that the association is not a domestic one. Its presence in China resulted from the invitation given by the central government, which has in turn instructed provincial and local governments to cooperate with Taiwanese compatriots. As a result, volunteers from Tzu Chi do not benefit from much maneuverability and must closely follow the instructions of local authorities. Because of these constraints, the association has been unable to establish independent institutions and has been forced to rely on the goodwill of local actors, ranging from Party cadres to People's Liberation Army (PLA) officials in order to perform its humanitarian work (Tzu Chi 1999). Clearly, events over the years have shown that the PRC's authorities are interested in learning as much as possible about the potential benefits they can derive from Buddhist charities by letting Tzu Chi perform its activities despite the vicissitudes of relations with Taiwan.

Despite escalating and threatening PRC rhetoric following Lee Teng-hui's 1995 visit to the United States, Tzu Chi members were operating the distribution of relief to peasants in Anhui the following December. Notwithstanding missile exercises by the PLA over the waters next to Taiwan in the summer of 1996, Tzu Chi's members were ready to give a hand to locals in Quanqiu and Tongling Counties in Anhui to construct schools a few months later (Tzu Chi 1999). However, these activities gradually declined in visibility and importance in the late 1990s. Volunteers from the association were not forbidden by the PRC to visit China, but often obstacles came from Taiwan itself: many people on the island were upset by the threatening tone used by some of the CCP leaders during the election of 2000 and looked unfavourably upon the activities of the charity on the mainland (Huang 2005).

Once China had started to recover from the international isolation that followed the Tiananmen massacre, and its economy picked up again, the necessity to engage with an organization like Tzu Chi appeared less compelling. Although Tzu Chi volunteers in China helped communities in many provinces, the scale of its activities turned out to be rather modest relative to the enormous needs of the population: the missions organized by Tzu Chi lasted a few weeks and involved a few dozen people for areas where thousands of individuals were affected by natural disasters (Tzu Chi 1999, 2000, 2005). The possibility for Tzu Chi to expand its activities was limited by both the reluctance of many Taiwanese to support the PRC, and the residual resistance of many CCP cadres to accept that a religious organization – and a Taiwanese one at that – could be active in China. In the end, and contrary to what volunteers from the Buddhist charity had expected, the presence of Tzu Chi in China did not affect relations with Taiwan one way or the other: the island and its government, far from moving closer to China, were drifting further away from the project of reunification. In the end, however, it turned out that the initiative of the MOCA in 1991 represented the first stage of a more far-reaching development: Tzu Chi's presence in the PRC offered useful lessons about the potential for Buddhist charities based in China.

Recent development: the rise of local associations

Tzu Chi has always required its volunteers to remain politically neutral and has largely focused on impoverished areas – an approach that has proven especially helpful from the perspective of leaders governing China's impoverished areas. The success of Tzu Chi's approach has, since the late 1990s, encouraged other volunteer organizations to adopt a similar approach, one that combines involvement in the provision of social service with avoidance of any political advocacy. The contribution of Buddhist charities from within the PRC that I discuss next illustrates this trend. Hong Kong, because of its linkages with overseas Chinese communities, has played an important role as facilitator in the development of these charities. For example, since 2000 a major Buddhist organization with a liaison office in New York led by a lay person, the Hong Kong-based Gracious Glory Buddhist Foundation (*Cihui fojiao jijinhui*), was set up to provide relief in cooperation with Buddhist temples in the PRC. In 2006, it claimed to run poverty relief projects in twenty provinces totaling 120 million yuan (Xu 2005). Another Buddhist association based in Hong Kong, the Fuhui Charity Foundation, has helped finance schools in twenty provinces, and also provided financial assistance to orphanages, physically handicapped people, rural medical clinics, and communities in need of emergency relief.[3] In general, Buddhist philanthropic associations from Hong Kong are not suspected of harbouring political views that are unpatriotic, and the loyalty of their political leadership is trusted. As a result, these organizations are increasingly welcomed in the PRC.

After 2000, Jiang Zemin spoke often of religion as a phenomenon that would exist even in a socialist society, thereby supporting the development of religious affairs (Ying 2006: 349). This view endorsed the initiatives that had been already undertaken and quietly tolerated by local authorities. Hence, the Hebei Buddhist Philanthropic and Merit Society (*Hebei fojiao cishan gongdehui*), with the help of the Cihui Foundation, has already established a province-wide charity in Zhao County. The charity was founded in 1995 with the blessings of a well-known cleric in the province, Ven. Jing Hai, who was instrumental in rebuilding a major Buddhist center in Hebei province, the Cypress Forest Chan temple (*Bailin chansi*). Although abandoned for decades even before the Cultural Revolution, the monastery has emerged as a major pilgrimage center in north China, and a destination visited by Chinese and foreign scholars (Yang 2006). The charity, supported by the Bailin temple, focuses its energies on enabling poor children to go to school and on managing orphanages. It also publishes its own free magazine, the Wonderful Lotus (*Miaolianhua*). The help this charity received from the Cihui Foundation resulted from its founder's visit to the Bailin temple. The vice-chair of the Hebei Merit Society, Ven. Chang Hui, explained that his organization sought to provide charity in accordance with the theological innovations of Taixu, the same Buddhist monk who had served before as the inspiration for Taiwanese Buddhist charities.[4] Other provincial associations are following suit. For example, the provinces of Guangdong and Hunan each have their own Buddhist charitable foundations (*fojiao cishan jijinhui*).

These developments are not limited to provinces. Municipal and prefecture-level Buddhist associations are also establishing their own charity associations. Hence, the Shanghai Municipal Buddhist Association (*Shanghai shi fojiao xiehui*), a wealthy Buddhist association that is responsible for important locations such as the Jade Buddha Temple (*Yufo si*) and the Dragon Lotus Temple (*Longhua si*), has created its own charity foundation, the Shanghai Municipal Charity Foundation (*Shanghai shi cishan jijinhui*). Yet not all wealthy municipalities have their own Buddhist associations, and even when there are municipal Buddhist associations, they do not automatically create their own charities. On the other hand, some Buddhist associations in cities of lesser importance, such as Chengde, also in Hebei Province, have established their own Buddhist Charitable Foundation. These cases are representative of broader trends, but they do not flourish in equal strength in every province. The case of Hebei is interesting because the province was not a major center of Buddhist activity in the Republican period.[5]

Buddhist associations at even lower levels of administration, such as the district (*xian*) level, sometimes establish their own charities. Such is the case of the Lingchuan *fojiao cishan jijinhui*, in Shanxi Province. In some cases, it is even individual temples that are setting up their own individual charity. Such developments have been observed in Hubei Province, where the Wuzu temple in eastern Hubei[6] and the Zhanhua temple in Jingzhou[7] provide relief to the poor. These activities are not limited to the local population. Hence, Wuzu temple's volunteers distribute relief to migrant workers in faraway Wuhan. One striking characteristic that emerges from these observations, however, is the extent to which these activities are regional in scope, and not merely local. Although the activities appear haphazard and uncoordinated, the following discussion reveals that altogether they were part of initiatives launched at the highest level of government.

Institutionalizing the relationship between the state and Buddhist organizations

The framework for religious work

The CCP has put in place an elaborate structure of governance to control religion (Potter 2003). The Party's Central Committee is the leading organ that decides on religious policy and it mandates the State Council to implement its recommendations. This state control of religion did not break new ground after 1949, but merely continued what Don Baker called the "monopoly of rites" exercised by the state in imperial China (1997: 146). Although the CCP has relinquished a number of responsibilities in the economic realm since the beginning of the reform and opening policy, it still continues to enforce rigid control over religious policies. It still upholds a Marxist-Leninist worldview that Party cadres must strictly follow, and that remains premised on the withering away of religion: because its ideology promotes atheism, religious believers cannot join the Party. Furthermore, the CCP remains the ultimate authority determining what is considered an acceptable form of religion. The CCP has mandated a state organ under the authority of the State Council, the Bureau for Religious Affairs (BRA) (*zongjiaobu*), to take responsibility for administering the day-to-day workings of religious organizations. The BRA monitors the activities of the five religions recognized by the CCP: Buddhism, Taoism, Protestantism, Catholicism, and Islam. In addition, the BRA transmits Party instructions to religious leaders.

Since 1953, Buddhist clergy and lay people working in temples have been required to join the Chinese Buddhist Association (CBA), (*Zhongguo fojiao xiehui*), and under this umbrella organization are banned from expressing dissent from state religious policies. Yet over the years, the CBA has offered Chinese Buddhists an institutional channel through which to make demands on the state; the CBA represents the interests of monks and nuns in the administration of monastic property and it manages the training of future generations of monastic personnel. Although the CBA duly followed the strictures of CCP religious policy, this was not enough to protect it from the depredations of the Red Guards. During the late 1960s, Buddhist temples were sacked, lay people had to stop their activities, and monks and nuns were defrocked (Welch 1972). When Deng Xiaoping overturned the anti-Buddhist policies, the CBA experienced difficulty resuming its activities because, after ten years of turbulence, many older monks and lay people were too dispirited to resume their activities, and there was a shortage of young and qualified monks to manage the affairs of temples and transmit the precepts to future generations (Birnbaum 2003).

Other state organs have some influence on religious affairs in general, including on Buddhist organizations, albeit indirectly. The State Security Bureau, for example, exercises surveillance in temples and among lay associations. But besides this obvious extension of the state's effort to control religious organizations, other branches of government tend to support Buddhist institutions. For example, the National Tourism Administration favors the development of Buddhist temples and pilgrimage sites, and the MOCA supervises cooperation between Buddhist organizations and NGOs. Furthermore, as we shall see, the Chinese Academy of Social Sciences, via the Institute of World Religions (*Shijie zongjiao yanjiusuo*), encourages a better understanding of Buddhist organizations and advises policymakers on the potential contributions of these organizations to society.

State control also varies across regions and across levels of governments. Despite the remaining legal restrictions mentioned above that limit the activities of religious institutions, many local governments have preferred to look the other way, ignore the rules, and adopt a more liberal policy. Others are simply lax about enforcement. All provinces and most prefecture and district governments have set up their own bureaus for religious affairs, monitor their own Buddhist associations, and, as already mentioned, encourage the development of Buddhist charities and foundations in the area under their jurisdiction.

The evolution of religious policy

Party leaders have all left their personal imprints on religious policy. Mao Zedong wished for the eradication of religion, which he viewed as a remnant of "feudal society." He believed that it was necessary to accelerate religion's demise, and, after an initial policy of tolerance, launched campaigns to curtail any influence religious organizations might have. After Mao's death and the fall of the Gang of Four, Deng Xiaoping overturned this policy because he realized that Mao's approach had failed to eliminate religious belief, and also because he saw an instrumental value in temple reconstruction – as mentioned in the first section – for attracting overseas investment. As a result, the relationship between Buddhist associations and the state improved gradually after the end of the Cultural Revolution. Although no official commitments were made, changes in religious policy were gradually implemented following the 1989 crisis (Luo 1991). The events that led to the Tiananmen massacre revealed a series of problems: inflation, an increasingly precarious situation in the labor market, and corruption within the Party. In addition, there began to be expressed the wish to create a "socialist spiritual civilization." Although the "spiritual civilization" project did not directly reference religion and remained extremely vague, it legitimized the quest for morality, ethics, and meanings, all values customarily associated with religion (Bays 2004; Spiegel 2004).

Concerned by the vitality of religion in general, the expansion of Christian churches, and, after 1999, the emergence of Falun Gong, Jiang Zemin adopted a different approach. He adopted a policy of "accommodation" and "rule by law," which was meant to tighten state surveillance of religious institutions while appearing to recognize the legitimacy of religion and respect religious freedoms (Leung 2005). Along with these repressive measures, Jiang was nevertheless actively encouraging the rebuilding of Buddhist temples (Yang 2006). So far, Hu Jintao has seemed to move along the path opened up by Jiang. He has not changed his predecessors' policy of repression against "heretical sects" and non-recognized churches, and he supports the development of Buddhism and the other legal religions. Although his appeals to "harmonious society" may give the impression that he wants to promote the rehabilitation of Confucius, Hu remains committed to the CCP's materialist ideology.

The regulation on religious affairs approved by Wen Jiabao in November 2004 and voted by the National People's Congress (NPC) in 2005 restated that religious organizations should not "destroy social order, harm the bodily health of citizens, interfere in the State educational system, or harm the national interest, the public welfare of society or the lawful rights of citizens" (article 3), and reiterated that religious organizations shall not be controlled by foreign interests (article 4).[8] In one important respect, however, the 2005 regulations represent a new development, as articles 34 and 35 authorize religious organizations to perform activities that were previously forbidden. Hence, article 34 states that religious organizations and venues can run social welfare services. Article 35 allows religious organizations and venues to receive donations from domestic or foreign organizations or individuals. By contrast, article 40, in declaring that activities that "infringe upon citizens' personal or democratic rights, obstruct the orderly management of society, or encroach upon public or private property constitute a crime," sets limits to tolerance for religious organizations. However, article 40 is sufficiently vague to enable religious organizations to try different approaches (Ying 2006).

In sum, the CCP under Jiang and Hu has not abandoned its basic principles – belief in the superiority of science over religion – but these leaders have left their mark on legislation to ensure that the development of the religions tolerated by the state would be framed within a more secure environment. These policy shifts have some important consequences for the development of Buddhist philanthropy. Following the tumultuous 1980s, policymakers changed their view of Buddhist associations as "parasitic institutions" on Chinese society. Instead, they began a renewed push during the period of reform and openness where they have actually come to see the Buddhist associations as cultural assets to be preserved, and as a form of cultural capital with the potential to attract foreign investors (Ji 2004). As the development of tourism and foreign investment have encouraged the prosperity of some temples in the 1990s, many Buddhist leaders in turn have come to realize that they must give back to society by sponsoring philanthropy.[9]

Providing an intellectual justification to changes in CCP "religious work"

This evolution in the state attitude toward Buddhism took time, and the acceptance of religious philanthropy still faces some formidable obstacles, some of which come from the epistemic communities of intellectuals who advise the state on policymaking. In the 1980s, most of the intellectuals advising the state lacked training in the social sciences because of the Cultural Revolution's limits on education. As a result, few intellectuals questioned the view that religious organizations had no role to play under socialism (Luo 1991). To bestow positive attention on religion represented a major ideological shift, with potentially divisive consequences within the Party between reform-minded members and more doctrinaire Marxists. Strong social pressures made changes of perspective toward religion difficult to contemplate for most intellectuals who had been socialized, taught, and trained in the truth-claim of historical materialism, and in the knowledge that the policymakers they advised expected them to support that view. The strong commitment to historical materialism meant that any reconsideration of this worldview was bound to elicit resistance from Party intellectuals who had invested so much in it (Feng 2005; Gong 2000).

Chinese public intellectuals were trained in the mold of historical materialism, and religion was not considered a topic relevant to social science except for historians, or for anthropologists looking into the folklore of minority nationalities. Because of this general lack of interest in the study of religion outside of the narrow confines of history and ethnography, very few social scientists paid any attention to the place of religion in contemporary Chinese society.[10] The participation of religious actors in the delivery of social services, unsurprisingly, was even less likely to receive attention from them. Public intellectuals justified this lack of interest on the grounds of the widely held Mao-era belief that the CCP represented the vanguard of society, and that under its stewardship, religion was expected to vanish as a social force (Tang 2001; Gong 1998, 2003). As a consequence of this reasoning, there could be no discussion of the positive role religious organizations could play in socialist society.

Yet just a few years after the demise of the Gang of Four, the seeds for a reconsideration of this policy were sown. The realization that Maoism was of itself a quasi-religion, the resilience of ancestor worship manifested in the preference for sons over daughters, the persistence of popular beliefs and rituals in the countryside and even in the cities, despite official campaigns of denunciation, intellectuals' criticism, and the prejudice of many others, convinced CCP cadres that it would be better to exploit the persistence of religious tendencies to their advantage. In the 1980s, these views were rare, but in the early 1990s there emerged some discussion of the feasibility and effectiveness of letting religious institutions help the state manage social services within the context of debates on NGOs, non-profit organizations (NPOs), and charities.

In the late 1990s and at the beginning of the twenty-first century, Chinese social scientists started debating views that would have been unthinkable only a decade before. The change was at first incremental. Scholars began discussing the generally positive contribution of religious values to society (Dong 2000; Song 2000) but few went beyond general statements such as remarks about the benefit the state could derive from the compassionate orientation of contemporary Buddhism (Pan 2001), or the compatibility of religion with socialism (Li 2000). Others, like Liu Jitong (2005), went further and praised Chinese Protestant churches for their social services. During the same year, the issue of religious participation in the provision of social services became a major topic of discussion at a conference on religion and social ethics convened by the cultural institute Xinde in Shijiazhuang.[11] This evolution of the intellectuals' attitudes toward religious institutions, especially toward wealthy institutions like the Buddhist monastic orders, can be understood in the context of the transition toward a market economy, and the impact of the latter on social policy.

The evolution of social policy

After it took power, the CCP refused to let religious associations, or any other independent association, constitute an independent social force and itself maintained a monopoly over the provision of social services. During the first three decades of the new regime, traditional philanthropic societies, often linked with communal and ancestral temples, were targeted by campaigns launched against "feudal traditions" (Perry 2002: chapter 9). The goal of these campaigns was to eliminate any alternative to the work unit or the public administration for the provision of social services, thereby depriving of legitimacy any potential challenger to the state. Not only did this strategy deprive any competitor of authority, it also reinforced the instruments through which the CCP could assert its control over society. These campaigns were largely successful, if we measure success by the number of independent organizations that vanished after these efforts at state control. If we consider increases in basic literacy, public health, and life expectancy, the campaigns can also be viewed as achieving major accomplishments. But these advances had also to be assessed in the context of the Great Leap Forward's famine (Teiwes and Sun 1999), the chaos and stagnation of the Cultural Revolution (Bonnin 2004), and the resilience of poverty three decades after the founding of the PRC (Chen and Wu 2004; Li Changpin 2002).

When Deng Xiaoping launched his reform and opening policies, the mass campaign approach was jettisoned, and the Party-state increasingly called on civil society to become actively involved in economic reform. The suppression of independent social organizations and the taming of religious associations may have helped the CCP assert its control over society during the first decades of the new regime, but this policy of repression became a liability when the CCP decided to turn to civil society to support its policies of development and its proposed reforms in the means by which social services are delivered (Wang 2004).

As economic reforms have progressed and the state-owned enterprises' welfare system has increasingly unraveled, social discontent and instability have increased (Shambaugh 2000; Perry and Selden 2000). The authorities have responded by reconsidering their opinion that religious institutions should be kept away from any involvement in society. Many state officials were aware that the withdrawal of the state from social services provision risked exposing millions of people to the uncertainties of unemployment, poor health, or worse, and that neither corporate philanthropy alone nor self-help through such actions as the purchase of health insurance could alleviate the problem. For millions of people, the development of market forces had made access to education and health care increasingly difficult. Faced with this situation, decision makers and public intellectuals have come to recognize that resorting to civil society organizations, including religious associations, could help the state achieve some of its objectives. As a result, civil society organizations have come to enjoy an unprecedented degree of leverage to make political demands.

Yet the process remains haphazard. Many officials in the security apparatus continue to distrust religious associations. They believe that religious philanthropic societies have ulterior motives and are used as cover for illegal activities (Li and Fu 2002). There are no rules that state unambiguously what activities religious associations may legally practice, nor whether philanthropic association must sever relations with religious associations to which they may be affiliated. Current legislation remains unclear on whether religious associations can carry out more than strictly liturgical activities, such as the upkeep of temples, churches, and mosques, and the performance of rites. Pending the adoption of a new law on religion, the updated regulations on religious affairs adopted in 2004 by the State Council have remained equally unclear. While the regulations do not explicitly forbid religious institutions from offering social services such as the provision of disaster relief, support for orphanages, or sponsorship of schools, lack of clarity means that religious institutions lack the confidence that they can establish more durable institutions.

Religious philanthropy: how important a complement to state-provided social services?

The activities of the Buddhist associations discussed thus far represent the tip of the iceberg. Fieldwork and ethnographies by anthropologists have uncovered evidence that within China itself, charities and philanthropic organizations affiliated with the five officially recognized religious associations were involved in offering social services provision even before the legislation granted them this possibility (Tsai 2002, 2007; Eng and Lin 2002). Religious traditions with coreligionists abroad have been especially able to benefit from their transnational networks to attract even more resources. This is particularly true for Christian churches, which have managed to use the wide reach of their organizations in the West, in other Asian societies, and in the global Chinese diaspora to provide support for their activities. Christian associations have a long tradition of providing services in health care and education in China, and some of them managed to maintain a presence throughout the difficult years of the Cultural Revolution under the umbrella of the Three-Self Patriotic Movement and the China Christian Council (Kindopp 2004; Cheng 2003; Madsen 2003). Besides the house churches that are not registered with the authorities, many overseas organizations belonging to a great number of denominations bring to bear the resources they can mobilize from coreligionists in wealthy societies to provide relief.

In addition to these institutionalized forms of officially supported social service provision by recognized religious associations, other types of religious actors have become involved. Eng and Lin (2002), Tsai (2002, 2007), Feuchtwang (2000), and Dean (1998) have documented the provision of social services by traditional networks of temples that have been revived in the countryside. As the authors of these studies themselves readily admit, however, these ethnographies cover limited geographic areas and are not easily generalizable. It remains unclear whether these detailed ethnographies illustrate a widespread trend or simply local exceptions. Until local governments are encouraged to document such activities and to diffuse the information to outsiders, it will remain difficult to give an exact account of the extent of religious actors' involvement in the provision of social services. Yet the point is that besides Buddhists, other religious associations, even those that do not benefit from state recognition and support, have become involved in social services provision.

The activities of religious philanthropy may be underestimated because local cadres are reluctant to admit the presence of such activities for fear that reliance on these organizations would betray their incompetence in doing effective political work in materialist or atheist social service provision. In addition, deep-seated prejudices against these traditions that predate 1949 make it embarrassing to many to admit the resilience of these traditions. Finally, Party cadres are still educated in a materialist ideology that disparages the expression of any form of religious observance, and that considers "superstitions" to be even worse than the recognized religions. Despite these obstacles, there is evidence that some Buddhist institutions do offer important services, acting as channels for wealthy philanthropists who want to sponsor the construction of schools in impoverished areas. The Cihui Foundation, for instance, uses its connections among overseas Chinese in North America and Hong Kong to fundraise and finance its philanthropic activities. As the evidence from Tzu Chi's headquarters documents, for more than fifteen years some of these organizations have sponsored schools for impoverished children, helped build homes for elderly people, and, finally, have provided disaster relief services (Tzu Chi 1999, 2000, 2005).

It is clear that these kinds of activities must first receive the blessings of local Party cadres, but it is equally clear, from the documents distributed by diverse local Buddhist associations, that the CCP is not playing a major role in approving this provision of services. The need for social services remains daunting, whereas the resources available to Buddhist institutions are far too limited for them to exercise a significant political impact in China. Buddhist institutions are struggling to rebuild their temples,[12] train new generations to replace the elderly monks and nuns, and manage the institutions that survived China's Cultural Revolution (Birnbaum 2003). In addition to these constraints, the legislation on religious institutions remains ambiguous about the right of religious personnel to offer social services.

Because of the two obstacles discussed above, Buddhist institutions cannot offer services in education, health care, or even humanitarian relief on a mass scale in ways that the Catholic Church does in Catholic countries. One could also argue that even were Buddhist institutions able to muster the human resources to offer these services, they would hesitate to mobilize the resources lest they attract unwelcome attention from the Security Bureau. Any indication that Buddhists could organize a great number of people independently of CCP directives would probably be seen as a threat. This is one of the lessons people must have drawn from the emergence of Falun Gong and the repression it has suffered as a result of its growth and mobilization for the seemingly innocuous demand for legal recognition (Ostergaard 2004).

The context of the PRC also differs significantly from Taiwan when Tzu Chi was founded. In Taiwan, the central and local governments encouraged Buddhist institutions and Christian churches to run their own hospitals and universities. State officials in Taiwan encouraged religious organizations to provide such services because state provision of services, in particular in health care, was limited in some regions. Expectations that health care could be provided by the private sector, including religious organizations, arose naturally in that context (Li Shiwei 2002; Wang 1999). In the PRC, the reverse was true throughout the Mao era: the state was expected to deliver social services via the communes and the work units. Although post-Mao reform policies have been aimed at undermining this order of things, expectations remain high in the population about the role of the state. This remains particularly true for civil servants as well as workers in state-owned enterprises (SOEs). In sum, in the PRC, powerful vested interests will make it difficult to implement national policies of reliance on charities in the realm of social service provision, despite some success at the provincial and local levels.

Finally, Buddhist monasteries represent unlikely institutions to set up a systematic delivery of social services to more than limited numbers of poor people. First, as mentioned above, monks are busy trying to rebuild their institutions. Second, there may not be enough Buddhist activists in China to influence public policy in a decisive way. Even though Buddhism represents the largest of the five officially recognized religions in the PRC, even the most generous censuses do not count more than a sixth of the population as Buddhist.[13] Finally, not all of these Buddhist devotees are committed to delivering social services. Many who visit temples as tourists or reside there for a retreat are going there for a variety of reasons, including some that are strictly religious and that could not be confused with mundane considerations.

Conclusions

Although the acceptance by the state of Buddhist lay philanthropies may look on the surface like a short-term response to crisis situations, in the end it represents a long-term negotiated process. To be sure, the Tiananmen massacre and the dramatic changes in Taiwan represented major crises for the CCP's claim to legitimacy that precipitated important policy changes in 1991 and 1992, but the seeds of cooperation with religious philanthropies had been planted long before. The response to the crisis of 1999 confirmed that the Party-state apparatus had adopted a long-term strategy: while repression of Falun Gong was launched, cooperation with mainstream religious organizations was not only maintained, but expanded.

The institutionalization of the relationship between the state and religious philanthropic associations has built on previously established structures. The first tier of institutions is the network of NGOs that have been created with the help of the Ministry of Civil Affairs to develop expertise and provide social services to targeted populations such as orphans, disabled children, and victims of natural disasters. Some of these institutions have lost legitimacy because some of them, such as Project Hope,[14] were plagued by financial scandals. This first tier of institution, known as government-organized NGOs (GONGOs), was too close to the Party-state, and therefore unlikely to attract the support of people with religious connections. The second tier of institution includes the network of Buddhist associations at the central, provincial, and local levels, and their relationships with bureaus for religious affairs at corresponding and higher levels of administration. Although they were not originally asked to provide any social services, the government expected these institutions to provide cultural capital that might be converted into financial assets to attract investments and financial support from philanthropists. The effectiveness of these institutions is also limited because they are seen as too close to the government. The legal uncertainty about the activities that religious institutions can undertake prevents many religious leaders and clerics from showing too much initiative. The third tier of institutions is made up of the charities established by lay people, often in cooperation with 'compatriot associations' in Hong Kong or Taiwan, or with overseas Chinese. These organizations cooperate with the two other tiers of organization but remain independent. As we have seen, Tzu Chi and the Cihui are more successful because their connections abroad afford them some financial autonomy, and they benefit from their greater distance with the state.

Although it may look as if these charities established by religious institutions are taking up responsibilities that the state is relinquishing, the available evidence suggests that these claims are exaggerated. As the cases of the Tzu Chi Foundation and the Cihui Foundation have demonstrated, the state, at different levels of government, has the final say in authorizing the presence of such organizations in the areas of its jurisdiction, and its support remains essential in ensuring the success of relief provision by these charities. The services offered by Buddhist associations are limited in scope, and they cannot represent a substitute for comprehensive provision of social services. These philanthropic associations do not even advocate on behalf of the people they help. They provide relief to the poor but they do not design poverty alleviation programs; still less do they criticize policies that could reinforce poverty.

At best, these organizations represent an auxiliary to the state. To the extent that the definition of civil society in China adopted in this book includes NGOs that cooperate with the state to achieve common objectives, those Buddhist institutions, and religious institutions in general, represent an important component of PRC civil society. However, because of the constraints within which they operate it is also clear that they are unlikely to get involved in anything like a process of democratization, as civil society did in Eastern Europe decades ago. On balance, the state need not fear the philanthropic activities of Buddhist associations, because their reach remains highly limited. Moreover, these associations are unlikely to use the opportunity of providing social services to advance their own goals of sustaining religious activities lest doing so jeopardize their fragile situation vis-à-vis the state. Only time will tell whether this equilibrium can be sustainable, and only more research will inform us whether the same is true for associations affiliated with other religious traditions.

While at the national level Buddhist associations have been constrained by legal uncertainties, local governments in many cases have encouraged greater freedom of action because local authorities have recognized the benefits they could gain from the activities of these associations. Buddhist associations have gained from the state's recognition, and even its support for the rebuilding of their institutions. At the local level, this support has extended to cooperation in providing certain social services as a direct result of the 1991 floods. As a consequence, while they remain constrained at the national level, Buddhist charity associations enjoy greater possibility for growth and the consolidation of their institutions at the local level. This evolution suggests that crises of governance at local levels have provided non-state associations an opportunity to carve for themselves some autonomy for the pursuit of their activities. However, Buddhist associations have thus far remained cautious, not translating this growing local-level autonomy into political demands.

Notes

1 The author would like to thank the Social Sciences and Humanities Research Council of Canada for the financial support that make the research for this chapter possible. The author teaches political science at the School of Political Studies, University of Ottawa, Canada.
2 My stay in one temple in 2006 allowed me to observe that although one cannot join the CCP if one is a religious believer, no rule prevents CCP members from working within monasteries, where they can monitor activities among the monks.
3 The Fu Hui Charity Foundation has a list of the schools it sponsors at the following link: www.fuhui.org/llearn/school_list.htm.
4 Interviews 26 and 27 in Shijiazhuang (Hebei), in May 2004.
5 This can be inferred from the data on Buddhist activities provided by Holmes Welch in his major study of Buddhism prior to 1949.
6 Interviews 18, with administrative personnel of the Wuzu temple (7 May 2004), and 19, with a monk of the Wuzu temple (7 May 2004).
7 Interview 4, with the temple abbot, Jingzhou (22 April 2004).
8 The regulation was listed as decree no. 426 and was due to take effect in March 2005.
9 Interviews in Wuzu temple (Hubei), Jiuhuashan (Anhui), Bailin temple (Hebei), spring 2004.
10 This is of course changing with the emergence of new scholars and the publication by bodies such as the Chinese Academy of Social Sciences of journals focusing on religious studies. Other regional academies and institutions, such as the Shanghai Society for the Study of Religion, and the Institute for the Study of Religion of the Shanghai Academy of Social Science, are also emerging.
11 References online to that event were available until 2006 but since then the link has been shut down.
12 Many of the temples visited in 2004 and 2006 were at various stages of reconstruction. That was the case even in Buddhist pilgrimage sites such as Jiuhuashan, in Anhui.

13 The official figure until 2005 was 100 million Buddhists. Recent revisions mention twice that number, which is still only one-sixth of the population.

14 Interviews in Wuzu temple (Hubei), Jiuhuashan (Anhui), Bailin temple (Hebei), spring 2004.

References

Austin, Greg (ed.) (1997) *Missile Diplomacy and Taiwan's Future: Innovations in Politics and Military Power*, Canberra Papers on Strategy and Defence 122, Canberra: SDSC, RSPAS, Australian National University.

Baker, Don (1997) "World Religions and National States: Competing Claims in East Asia," in Susanne Hoeber Rudolph and James P. Piscatori (eds.) *Transnational Religion and Failed States*, Boulder, CO: Westview Press, 1997.

Bays, Daniel H. (2004) "A Tradition of State Dominance," in Jason Kindopp and Carol Lee Hamrin (eds.) *God and Caesar in China: Policy Implications of Church–State Relations*, Washington, DC: Brookings Institution.

Birnbaum, Raul (2003) "Buddhist China at the Century's Turn," *China Quarterly* 174 (June): 428–50.

Bonnin, Michel (2004) *Génération perdue: le mouvement d'envoi des jeunes instruits à la campagne en Chine, 1968–1980* [Lost Generation: The "Sent Down to the Countryside Movement" in China, 1968–1980], Paris: Presses de l'école des hautes études en sciences sociales.

Cabestan, Jean-Pierre and Vermander, Benoit (2005) *La Chine en quête de ses frontières: la confrontation Chine–Taiwan* [China's Search for Its Frontiers: The China–Taiwan Confrontation], Paris: Presses de Sciences politiques.

Chandler, Stuart (2004) *Establishing a Pureland on Earth: The Foguang Buddhist Perspectives on Modernization and Globalization*, Honolulu: University of Hawa'ii Press.

Chen Feng (1995) *Economic Transition and Political Legitimacy in Post-Mao China: Ideology and Reform*, Albany: State University of New York Press.

Chen Guidi and Wu Quntao (2004) *Zhongguo Nongmin Diaocha* [China Agriculture Research], Beijing, Renmin Wenxue Chubanshe.

Ch'en, Kenneth (1964) *Buddhism in China: A Historical Survey*, Princeton, NJ: Princeton University Press.

Cheng, May M. C. (2003) "House Church Movement and Religious Freedom in China," *China: An International Journal* 1 (1): 16–45.

Ching, Julia (2001) "The Falun Gong: Religious and Political Implication," *American Asian Review* 29 (4): 1–18.

Clough, Ralph N. (1999) *Cooperation or Conflict in the Taiwan Strait?* Lanham, MD: Rowman & Littlefield.

Corcuff, Stéphane (ed.) (2002) *Memories of the Future: National Identity Issues and the Search for a New Taiwan*, Armonk, NY: M. E. Sharpe.

Dean, Kenneth (1998) *Lord of Three in One: The Spread of a Cult in Southeast China*, Princeton, NJ: Princeton University Press.

Dong Jiangyang (2000) "Shilun Zongjiao zai Dangdai Shehuizhong de Qingshen Pipan Gongneng" [Exploring Religion's Vital Critical Function in Contemporary Society], *Shijie Zongjiao Yanjiu* 3: 126–33.

Eng, Irene and Lin Yi-Min (2002) "Religious Festivities, Communal Rivalry, and Restructuring of Authority in Rural Chaozhou, Southeast China," *Journal of Asian Studies* 61 (4): 1259–85.

Fang Litian (2001) "Renjian Fojiao de Jieshuo yu Renjian Zhengdao de Shijian" [The Scope of "Buddhism for the Human Realm" and the Practice of the Right Way in the Human Realm], Proceedings of the conference Renjian Fojiao Xueshu Yantaohui, Taipei, 8–10 January.
Feng Tiance (2005) *Zongjiaolun* [Religious Debate], Jinan, Shandong: Renmin Chubanshe.
Feuchtwang, Stephan (2000) "Religion as Resistance," in Elizabeth J. Perry and Mark Selden (eds.) *Chinese Society: Change, Conflict and Resistance*, London: Routledge.
FS (Fojiao Shijie) (2007) "Tianjin Fojiao Cishan Gongde Jijinhui Fu Minzu Diqu Weiwen" [Tianjin Buddhist Charity Foundation Applies to Set Up in Nationalities Areas]. Online, available at: www.folian.cn/news/Detail.asp?ID=4066.
Gen Tong (2006) "Zhongguo Fojiao Cibei Jishi de Linian yu Shijian" [The Theory and Practice of Karma and Serving Society in Chinese Buddhism], Proceedings of the conference *Shijie Fojiao Luntan* [World Buddhist Forum], Hangzhou, 13–16 April.
Goldstein, Steven (1999) "The Cross-strait Talks of 1993 – The Rest of the Story: Domestic Politics and Taiwan's Mainland Policy," in Shuisheng Zhao (ed.) *Across the Taiwan Strait: Mainland China, Taiwan, and the 1995–1996 Crisis*, New York: Routledge.
Gong Xuezeng (1998) *Zongjiao Wenti Gailun*, Chengdu: Sichuan Renmin Chubanshe.
—— (2000) *Zongjiao Wenti Ganbu Shiben* [The Religious Question for Cadres], Beijing: Zhonggong Zhongyang Dangxiao Chubanshe.
—— (2003) *Shehuizhuyi yu Zongjiao* [Socialism and Religion], Beijing: Zongjiao Wenhua Chubanshe.
Huang Chien-yu, Julia (2005) "The Compassion Relief Diaspora," in Linda Learman (ed.) *Buddhist Missionaries in the Era of Globalization*, Honolulu, HI: University of Hawai'i Press.
Huang Chien-yu, Julia and Weller, Robert P. (1998) "Merit and Mothering: Women and Social Welfare in Taiwanese Buddhism," *Journal of Asian Studies* 57 (2): 379–96.
Ji Zhe (2004) "La Nouvelle Relation état–bouddhisme" [A New Relationship betweeen the State and Buddhism], *Perspectives Chinoises* 84 (July–August): 2–10.
Jones, Charles Brewer (1999) *Buddhism in Taiwan: Religion and the State, 1660–1990*, Honolulu: University of Hawai'i Press.
Keith, Ronald C. and Lin Zhiqiu (2003) "The 'Falun Gong Problem': Politics and the Struggle for the Rule of Law in China," *China Quarterly* 175 (September): 623–42.
Kindopp, Jason (2004) "Fragmented yet Defiant: Protestant Resilience under Chinese Communist Party Rule," in Jason Kindopp and Carol Lee Hamrin (eds.) *God and Caesar in China: Policy Implications of Church–State Tensions*, Washington, DC: Brookings Institution.
Kleinman, Arthur and Watson, James L. (eds.) (2006) *SARS in China: Prelude to Pandemic?* Stanford, CA: Stanford University Press.
Laliberté, André (2003) " 'Love Transcends Borders' or 'Blood Is Thicker Than Water': The Charity Work of the Buddhist Tzu Chi Foundation in the People's Republic of China," *European Journal of East Asian Studies* 2 (2): 243–62.
—— (2004) *The Politics of Buddhist Organizations in Taiwan, 1989–2003: Safeguarding the Faith, Building a Pure Land, Helping the Poor*, London: RoutledgeCurzon.
Leung, Beatrice (2005) "China's Religious Freedom Policy: The Art of Managing Religious Activity," *China Quarterly* 184 (December): 894–915.
Li Changpin (2002) *Wo Xiang Zongli Shuo Shihua* [Words I Would Like to Tell the Premier], Beijing, Guangming Ribao Chubanshe.
Li Li'an (2000) "Cong Dangdai Zongjiao de Jiben Xingtai Kan Zongjiao yu Shehuizhuyi Shehui Xiang Shiying de Jige Texing" [Looking at the Characteristics of Religion's

Adaptation to Socialist Society from the Perspective of Contemporary Religions' Elemental Forms], *Shijie Zongjiao Yanjiu* 1: 13–21.

Li Shiwei (2002) *Taiwan Zongjiao Yuelan* [Readings on Taiwan's Religions], Taibei: Boyang Wenhua.

Li Shixiong and Fu Xiqiu (2002) *Religion and National Security in China: Secret Documents from China's Security Sector*. Online, available at: http://religiousfreedomforchina.org/English/docs/Final_20Report.htm.

Liu Jitong (2005) "Jiji Shiying yu Fuwu Shehui: Zhongguo Jidu Jiaohui Cishan Fuwu Xianzhuang yu Zhengce Kuangjia Yanjiu" [Actively Adapt to and Serve Society: Research on the Present Condition of Christian Charitable Service and Policy Framework in China]. Online, available at: www.chinasocialpolicy.org/Paper_Download.asp?Paper_ID=146&Paper_Lan=ch.

Luo Zhufeng (1991) *Religions under Socialism in China*, trans. Donald E. McInnis and Zheng Xi'an, with an introduction by Donald E. McInnis and a foreword by Bishop K. H. Ting, Armonk, NY: M. E. Sharpe.

Madsen, Richard (2003) "Catholic Revival during the Reform Era," *China Quarterly* 174 (June): 469–87.

Nickum, James E. (1998) "Is China Living on the Water Margin?" *China Quarterly* 156 (June): 880–98.

Ostergaard, Clemens (2004) "Governance and the Political Challenge of Falungong," in Jude Howell (ed.) *Governance in China*, Lanham, MD: Rowman & Littlefield.

Pan Guiming (2001) "Cong Taixu de 'Renjian Fojiao' Zhanwang xin Shijie de Zhongguo Fojiao" [Forecasting Chinese Buddhism in the New Century from Taixu's "Buddhism for this World"], *Shijie Zongjiao Yanjiu* 2: 108–11.

Perry, Elizabeth J. (2002) *Challenging the Mandate of Heaven: Social Protest and State Power in China*, Armonk, NY: M. E. Sharpe.

Perry, Elizabeth J. and Selden, M. (eds.) (2000) *Chinese Society: Change, Conflict and Resistance*, London: Routledge.

Pittman, Don Alvin (2001) *Toward a Modern Chinese Buddhism: Taixu's Reform*, Honolulu: University of Hawai'i Press.

Potter, Pittman (2003) "Belief in Control: Regulation of Religion in China," *China Quarterly* 174 (June): 317–37.

Shambaugh, David (ed.) (2000) *Is China Unstable? Assessing the Factors*, Armonk, NY: M. E. Sharpe.

Shankman, David, Keim, Barry D., and Jie Song (1996) "Flood Frequency in China's Poyang Lake Region: Trends and Teleconnections," *International Journal on Climatology* 26 (March): 1255–66.

Smil, Vaclav (2004) *China's Past, China's Future: Energy, Food, Environment*, London: Routledge.

Song Lidao (2000) "Dangdai Fojiao de Cibei Heping Lixiang" [The Compassionate and Peaceful Ideal of Contemporary Buddhism], *Shijie Zongjiao Wenhua* 4: 12–13.

Spiegel, Mickey (2004) "Control and Containment in the Reform Area," in Jason Kindopp and Carol Lee Hamrin (eds.) *God and Caesar in China: Policy Implications of Church–State Relations*, Washington, DC: Brookings Institution.

Tang Wenfang (2001) "Religion and Society in China and Taiwan," in Hua Shiping (ed.) *Chinese Political Culture, 1989–2000*, Armonk, NY: M. E. Sharpe.

Teiwes, Frederick C. and Sun, Warren (1999) *China's Road to Disaster: Mao, Central Politicians, and Provincial Leaders in the Unfolding of the Great Leap Forward*, Armonk, NY: M. E. Sharpe.

Thunø, Mette (2001) "Reaching Out and Incorporating Chinese Overseas: The Trans-territorial Scope of the PRC by the End of the 20th Century," *China Quarterly* 168: 910–29.

Tien Hung-Mao (ed.) (1996) *Taiwan's Electoral Politics and Democratic Transition: Riding the Third Wave*, Armonk, NY: M. E. Sharpe.

Tsai, Lily Lee (2002) "Cadres, Temple and Lineage Institutions, and Governance in Rural China," *China Journal* 48 (July): 1–27.

—— (2007) "The Struggle for Village Public Good Provision: Informal Institutions of Accountability in Rural China," in Elizabeth J. Perry and Merle Goldman (eds.) *Grass-roots Political Reform in Contemporary China*, Cambridge, MA: Harvard University Press.

Tsang, Steve (ed.) (1993) *In the Shadow of China: Political Developments in Taiwan since 1949*, Hong Kong: Hong Kong University Press.

Tzu Chi Merit Society (1999) *Ai zai liang'an jian huidang* [Love Extends Back and Forth across Both Sides of the Strait], Taipei: Ciji wenhua zhiye zhongxin.

—— (2000) *Bu hui da ai liang'an qing* [No Limits to the Feelings of Great Love across Both Sides of the Strait], Taipei: Ciji wenhua zhiye zhongxin.

—— (2005) *Dalu Zengzai* [The Mainland Quake Disaster]. Online, available at: www2.tzuchi.org.tw/tc-charity/html/ch-relieve.htm.

Wang Ming (ed.) (2004) *Zhongguo Feizhengfu Gonggong Bumen* [Non-governmental, Public Units in China], Beijing: Qinghua Daxue Chubanshe.

Wang Shunmin (1999) *Zongjiao fuli*, Taibei: Yatai tushu.

Welch, Holmes (1968) *The Buddhist Revival in China*, Cambridge, MA: Harvard University Press.

—— (1972) *Buddhism under Mao*, Cambridge, MA: Harvard University Press.

Xu Rongze (2005) "Jianshou Youshi Nuoyan, Shizhi Fupin Jikun de Qiye Daheng" [Holding Fast to a Promise, A Wealthy Entrepreneur's Fight to Alleviate Poverty], *Xianggang Nanhua Zaobao* (12 November).

Yang Dali (2001) "Rationalizing the Chinese State: The Political Economy of Government Reform," in Chao Chien-min and Bruce J. Dickson (eds.) *Remaking the Chinese State: Strategies, Society, and Security*, London: Routledge.

Yang Fenggang (2006) "The Red, Black, and Gray Markets of Religion in China," *Sociological Quarterly* 47: 93–122.

Ying Fuk-sung (2006) "New Wine in Old Wineskins: An Appraisal of Religious Legislation in China and the Regulations on Religious Affairs of 2005," *Religion, State, and Society* 34 (4): 347–73.

Zhao Shuisheng (ed.) (1999) *Across the Taiwan Strait: Mainland China, Taiwan, and the 1995–1996 Crisis*, New York: Routledge.

Interviews

Anonymous, Jiuhuashan (Anhui) (spring 2006).
Anonymous, Balin temple (Hebei) (spring 2004).
Anonymous temple abbot, Jingzhou (Hubei) (22 April 2004).
Anonymous, Shijiazhuang (Hebei) (May 2004).
Anonymous administrative personnel of the Wuzu temple (7 May 2004).
Anonymous monk of the Wuzu temple (7 May 2004).

7 The impact of crises on social service provision in China

The state and society respond to SARS

Jonathan Schwartz

Introduction

In 2003, the severe acute respiratory syndrome (SARS) epidemic began its spread across China. This potentially devastating infectious disease constituted a crisis for which the Chinese government was unprepared. Assessments of China's initial response to SARS pointed to numerous failures that were largely attributed to the inability of the state to provide sufficient public health support (Canadian Department of National Defense 2003). Perhaps unexpectedly, the negative assessments of China's SARS response changed over time, reflecting China's success in ultimately bringing under control a disease once expected to spread across the country, infecting millions. What enabled China to turn around what seemed to be a rapidly deteriorating disease control situation? Did non-state actors play an important role in China's effective SARS response? If so, what does the SARS case teach us about the impact of crises on relations between the state and civil society organizations in the realm of social service provision?

I open the chapter with a review of definitions of civil society and crises. I then analyze the Chinese infectious disease control infrastructure, its capabilities and reach. Then, following a brief description of the genesis of the SARS outbreak, I evaluate the different roles played by state and non-state actors in response to the outbreak. I conclude that, in order to control SARS effectively, the state was forced to increase its investment in, and attention to, public health issues even as it turned to a variety of non-state actors for assistance in what reflects a shifting dynamic in state–society relations in China's public health sphere.

Civil society and the non-state sector in China

As is noted in Chapter 1, many scholars argue that Chinese civil society is "state led," cooperating with the state to achieve shared goals. Other scholars argue that civil society in China is increasingly confrontational – working to undermine the state by taking on goals that challenge state domination. The Chinese state's view of civil society is that civil society is beneficial in terms of providing assistance and support to government initiatives at a time when state resources are in decline. However, the state also views with real concern the potential for civil society organizations to challenge ongoing Party-state domination (Perry and Goldman 2007: 17). Indeed, as Economy explains, "the key [for the Party-state] is not how the government tries to control NGOs, but how it could instead be subverted by them" (Cooper 2003). Thus, civil society organizations are broadly perceived by both scholars and Chinese officials as supporting the state while at the same time potentially subverting it.

The literature is replete with analyses of the growing role played by civil society in all aspects of Chinese public life (Frolic 1997; Otsuka 2002; Turner and Wu 2001; Knup 1998). NGOs, a key component of civil society in China, are identified by scholars as playing roles in environmental protection, social welfare, poverty alleviation, and health care. In general, the number and reach of NGOs has been expanding under the watchful eye of the state (Young 2003). This expansion in NGO numbers and activities has occurred in large part because, as Croll notes, in the state's efforts to compensate for its declining ability to provide social services, it views non-state actors as useful tools to supplement state funding, cushion hardship, and provide volunteer assistance to those in need. Thus, the state encourages NGOs to "fill gaps in vital welfare functions and respond to economic or physical hardship and natural disasters" where the state itself no longer has the capacity to do so (Croll 1999: 695).

In addition to the growing role of what Wang and Sun categorize as conventional social welfare or social service organizations to provide social services (see Chapter 1, and Wang and Sun 2002: 234–70), China has seen growth in what may be termed as non-conventional social service organizations. Important examples of non-conventional social service organizations are the residence committees (RCs) and their rural counterparts, the village committees (VCs). In 1954, China's Residence Committee Law was enacted. RCs are defined as grassroots, self-governing mass organizations (Article 11, China's constitution). Since the 1990s, the status of RCs as self-governing bodies has been established under Article 2 of the state's Organic Law on Residents' Committees (Wang 2002: 407). However, while described as self-governing bodies in the Chinese administrative structure, RCs are also dominated by it. In terms of the Chinese bureaucratic structure, RCs are appendages of sub-district offices, which in turn are subordinate to district and then municipal governments. Figure 7.1 illustrates the administrative position of RCs.

The role of RCs includes responsibilities to the state such as providing local police with information about activities in the neighborhood, helping to maintain the *hukou* (residence permit) system, helping to implement the one-child policy, facilitating government programs, and conveying information to residents about new government laws and policies. In some cases, such as enforcement of the one-child policy, RCs are viewed negatively by the public. However, in addition to such activities on behalf of the state, RCs have become increasingly active on behalf of the public. Thus, for example, RCs mediate in disputes, lead charity drives, act as sounding boards for residents' suggestions and complaints, and coordinate collective action in response to local problems (waste collection, inoculation drives, etc.) (Read and Chen 2008: 319–23; Wang 2002: 413). The

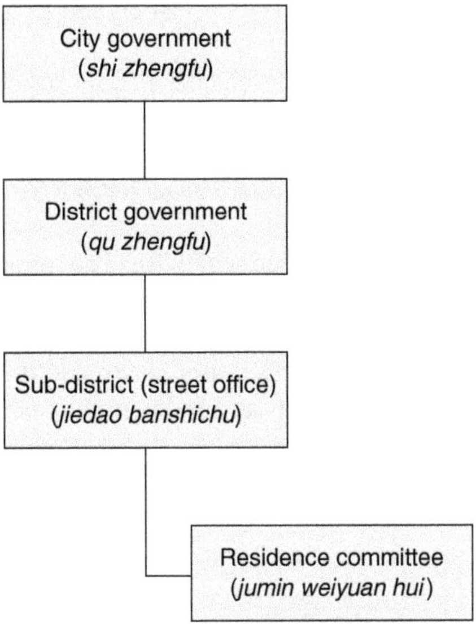

Figure 7.1 Administrative levels in Chinese cities.

majority of activists who volunteer their services to RCs receive no payment from the state.

With the passage of time, RC responsibilities have grown as the state has increasingly turned to them to provide better-quality and more extensive social services. With regard to disease outbreak prevention, RC roles have expanded in offering community services such as health, medical treatment, and sanitation (Wang 2002: 399, 408). With growing responsibility has come a shift as RCs have come to be viewed less as antagonistic to society and increasingly as providing a positive contribution in terms of social service provision.[1]

As with the case of RCs, in 1988 the National People's Congress passed a 1987 draft law that established elected VCs. These too were defined under the law as "mass organizations of self-government at the grassroots" (Manion 1996: 737; Worden *et al.* 1987; Organic Law of the Urban Neighborhood Committees 1990). Members of the VCs are supposed to be elected by their neighbors (though by and large this is not the case; rather, the Party selects representatives). These committees are not part of the state bureaucracy and are, in principle, autonomous in local affairs, though under the supervision of township governments (O'Brien 2001: 422). VCs are perhaps best described as a form of quasi-independent organization under the close supervision of the Party-state (China Ministry of Civil Affairs 2006; O'Brien 2001: 416). The township may issue directives to VCs, which must then help with their implementation.

And yet, as with RCs, the relationship is not purely one of top-down leadership (*lingdao guanxi*), with VCs acting as transmission belts for state policy. As in the case of RCs, the VCs enjoy limited autonomy of action, in particular in terms of welfare (Oi and Rozelle 2000: 522–3; O'Brien and Li 2006: chapters 3 and 6).[2]

While RCs and VCs share many similarities, in this chapter I focus largely on RCs. The number of RCs reflects their potential to play an important role in social service provision. Read and Chen estimate that there exist 90,000 RCs across China (2008: 315). In 1993 in Shanghai alone there were 2,400 RCs, each responsible for approximately 1,000 families.

RCs and their village counterparts are usefully described by Read as "straddler groups" – groups that bridge the divide between state and society (Read with Pekkanen 2009: chapter 1). These groups cannot be viewed as autonomous civil society organizations in the conventional Western sense, nor should they be dismissed as purely instruments of the state. Rather, as straddlers they serve a dual role that places them toward the "state" end of the state–society continuum described in Chapter 1.

Crises defined

As is noted in Chapter 1, we define crises as non-linear events that change existing patterns in a dramatic fashion. Crises are especially challenging to less developed countries (LDCs) since they often lack the resources to respond effectively. As a less developed country, China has faced a number of crises in the modern era. Among them, Zhong Kaibin identifies AIDS and the Songhua River disaster, and SARS as classic examples (Zhong 2007: 91). Thus, as is discussed in the section describing the SARS outbreak, SARS was a non-linear event that changed existing patterns in China. The outbreak took the Chinese Party-state by surprise at a time when it lacked the resources to respond effectively. I illustrate this lack of resources in the following section by evaluating China's reform-era public health system.

Transition and transformation of China's public health system

The capacity of a state to act effectively in one issue-area does not reflect its ability to do so in all issue-areas (Chung 1995: 487–508). Indeed, states tend to focus the majority of their resources on those sectors likely to produce the greatest rewards. In the case of China, this decision necessarily meant investment in sectors *other* than public health. In the reform era, the benefits of China's widely acclaimed Maoist public health sector were viewed as long-term, diffuse, costly, and technically complex (Bloom and Gu 1997: 352; Liu 2004: 532–8; Ronaghy and Salter 1974: 1331–3). Reformers preferred to sacrifice investment in public health in favor of job creation and infrastructure development. Investing in the latter offered immediate and obvious benefits that contributed to the wealth of the country and, by extension, to the state's legitimacy to rule (Banister 1998: 987; interview with Bekedam, June 2005).[3] As the central government withdrew support from the public health system, the system began to deteriorate rapidly, becoming, as Henk Bekedam, World Health Organization representative to China, notes, the "worst he has ever seen" (interview with Bekedam, June 2005).

In post-1980 China, responsibility for health services was shifted from the state to a market-driven, professionalized, and increasingly privatized system (Huang 2003: 10; Blumenthal and Hsiao 2005: 2). The center slashed funding for public health and medical care delivery while forcing local governments, enterprises, and individuals to pick up the costs. Reflecting the fragmented nature of the Chinese political system, having decentralized responsibility and slashed central government funding for public health, the state increasingly lost control over the quality and availability of health services (Kaufman 2006: 60; Zhong 2007: 91). Underlying and exacerbating the loss of central control over health care was the fact that the Health Ministry suffered from a bureaucratically inferior position vis-à-vis other central government ministries and provincial governments (Saich 2006: 93). As a result, local governments easily and often ignored numerous centrally mandated, yet unfunded, health regulations, instead focusing on locally identified priorities via horizontal interactions (Lieberthal 1992; Lieberthal and Oksenberg 1988).

Oksenberg's model of state–local relations provides a useful structure for understanding the functioning of China's new health care provision system. Oksenberg divides the political system into three: the core, intermediary institutions, and organizations in society and the economy (2002: 193–5).

The core is appropriately described within the context of the Fragmented Authoritarian model as enjoying enormous, yet shrinking, power that is concentrated in the hands of the Party-state. Core organizations exist at the central, provincial, prefecture and township levels. They retain a Leninist structure, though this structure is also influenced by Nationalist, Confucian, and Western institutional structures. The core retains tremendous power, including much of the means of production and, importantly here, the ability to mobilize (*dong yuan*) the public (though not to the same extent as during the Mao-era mass campaigns).

Intermediary institutions are linkage organizations that act between the core and the international community. Their role is to ensure that the core is not "contaminated" by outsiders, while enabling it to exploit the world for needed resources. Examples of such institutions include the China International Trust and Investment Corporation and the China Travel Service. Each of these organizations facilitates interaction with the international community without requiring direct core involvement (Oksenberg 2001: 25–7).

Finally, organizations in society and the economy are legal, semi-legal, and illegal organizations and associations such as religious organizations (official and unofficial), secret societies, government-organized NGOs, professional organizations, and unregistered organizations such as those in the environmental (see Chapter 5) and health spheres (see the discussion later in the chapter). These organizations have arisen in the social space made available by the core's shift to macro-control from its past micro-control of the Chinese system (Oksenberg 2001: 27–9; *People's Daily* 4 August 2004).

In practice, the core's shift has meant that the center assigns heavy responsibility for infrastructure provision, health services, and nearly all public services to governments at and below the prefecture levels (also members of the core). However, the transfer of responsibilities has not been accompanied by a transfer of adequate resources to fulfill the new responsibilities. Indeed, prefecture, county, and township governments are estimated to expend 55 percent of their budgets on health care and other public services, a percentage far exceeding the average for either LDCs (13 percent) or developed countries (35 percent) (World Bank 2005: 3).

Local officials are forced to grapple with seemingly contradictory expectations. On the one hand, they must adhere to central government directives (such as offering epidemic prevention services), while on the other they are expected to increase economic output and employment. Improvements in these latter spheres remain the key criterion for promotion. Not surprisingly, one encounters statements such as those by a virologist for the Guangdong Province Center for Disease Control, Bi Shengli, who notes that when faced with the SARS outbreak, local doctors were informed by local government officials that, owing to the economic threat of an epidemic, "[they] can only report two cases [of SARS] not twenty, or the local economy will be hurt," thereby causing a decline in revenue needed to provide social services (Garrett 2003). Faced with growing demand for social services and declining central support, local officials have increasingly supplemented their own efforts with support from non-state actors, Oksenberg's Organizations in Society and the Economy (interviews with Shapiro, May 2005; anonymous interviews in Shaanxi and Nanjing, June 2005).[4]

To summarize, in the reform era local governments lacked the incentive and capacity to compensate for declining central government investment in public health, with the result that a notable decline occurred in the quality and quantity of health care services and coverage across the country (Blumenthal and Hsiao 2004: chapter 5). In the period leading up to the SARS outbreak, the condition of China's public health system was poor. It suffered from long-term neglect by the core, bureaucratic weakness of its leading institutions, and insufficient funding. As a result, when SARS erupted, the Chinese leadership had at its disposal a weak public health system, one that was ill prepared to meet the challenges of a mysterious and contagious new and frightening disease.

Genesis of SARS in China

The first SARS case was documented by a local doctor in Foshan, Guangdong Province, on 16 November 2002. Following protocol, the doctor reported the infection case to a local epidemic prevention station (Kaufman 2006: 55–7).[5] With some delays, information regarding the epidemic moved from the local epidemic prevention station to the provincial health bureau and from there to the provincial government and provincial Ministry of Health. By mid-December

2002, provincial and national Ministry of Health experts had diagnosed the disease as viral. The disease continued spreading to other regions, including Beijing, Shanxi, Inner Mongolia, Guangxi, Hunan, Sichuan, Fujian, Shanghai, Shaanxi, and Ningxia. By 31 March 2003, 1,190 SARS cases had been reported. The number of cases peaked on 23 May with 5,285 reported cumulative cases and 303 SARS-related deaths (Quarterly Chronicle 2003: 862–5). With no new cases reported for two consecutive incubation periods, the government and the World Health Organization declared the epidemic in China officially over on 4 June 2003 (Quarterly Chronicle 2003: 866).

At the time of the outbreak, SARS was variously described by government officials and the domestic and the international media as "a greater threat than both the Asian financial crisis of 1997 and the flood disaster of 1998" as well as "the biggest shock to the [Chinese] system since Tiananmen" (*People's Daily* 25 June 2003).

The state's response

In the reform era, infectious disease control and, as noted, public health in general was given low priority by the state (interview with Lu, June 2005). This attitude changed dramatically as the leadership grew aware of the tremendous potential harm to China's population and economy that SARS represented (interviews with Bekedam, May 2005, and Lu, June 2005). However, owing to the fragmented nature of the Chinese political system, the central government had little capacity to force actions on local health bureaus. The local health bureaus, dependent on local government for approximately 90 percent of their financing, were unlikely to act against the interests of the local governments (Saich 2006: 92–3; interview with Bekedam, May 2005). Local governments were mostly concerned with maintaining calm and ensuring ongoing economic growth. The result was that there was little incentive for local and provincial health officials to disclose negative developments, and at the outset of the crisis the central government had little recourse beyond public exhortations of local and provincial units to enforce epidemic control initiatives.

Given the weakness of central–local interaction on disease control, it was unsurprising that the central government was slow to recognize the seriousness of the challenge SARS represented. Nor was it surprising that little action was taken in the early months of the epidemic (Davis and Siu 2007). Yet in a fragmented system such as China's, when an issue does become a priority, the state has the capacity to focus resources and direct pinpoint pressure to advance that priority. Numerous officials interviewed following the outbreak noted that SARS was not a public health issue, but rather a question of political will (interviews with Cheng, Li, Hong, and an anonymous Shaanxi provincial hospital physician, June 2005). When in mid-April the Minister of Health, Wu Yi, declared China's decision to make SARS prevention and control a top priority, the state did in fact effectively mobilize both the Party and the state bureaucracies (interviews with Bekedam and Shapiro, May 2005). Was this initiative sufficient to combat SARS?

According to Dr. Craig Shapiro, Health and Human Services Attaché to the US embassy in Beijing, SARS was a catalyst in changing the way the Ministry of Health functions (interview with Shapiro, May 2005). In May 2003, the central government established a national SARS control headquarters that reported directly to the State Council (the Cabinet) (Saich 2006: 94–5). The State Council also dispatched epidemic control experts from the center to inspect, supervise, and advise provincial and local officials on SARS control efforts. However, at least at the outset of the outbreak the main responsibility for addressing SARS was in the hands of China's new center for disease control (CDC) network. The CDC network functions as a subordinate component of the Ministry of Health bureaucracy that runs from the national level (the national CDC in Beijing) to the township level, as illustrated in Figure 7.2.[6]

The national CDC was established as a center of expertise to provide technical supervision and make recommendations following the model of the US CDC. By contrast, local CDCs replaced what were once epidemic prevention stations in providing public health services under the bureaucratic control of the relevant level of the public health bureaucracy. Thus, local CDCs are distinct from the national CDC, meaning they are responsible to the local department of health at the relevant bureaucratic level, with the national CDC largely responsible for

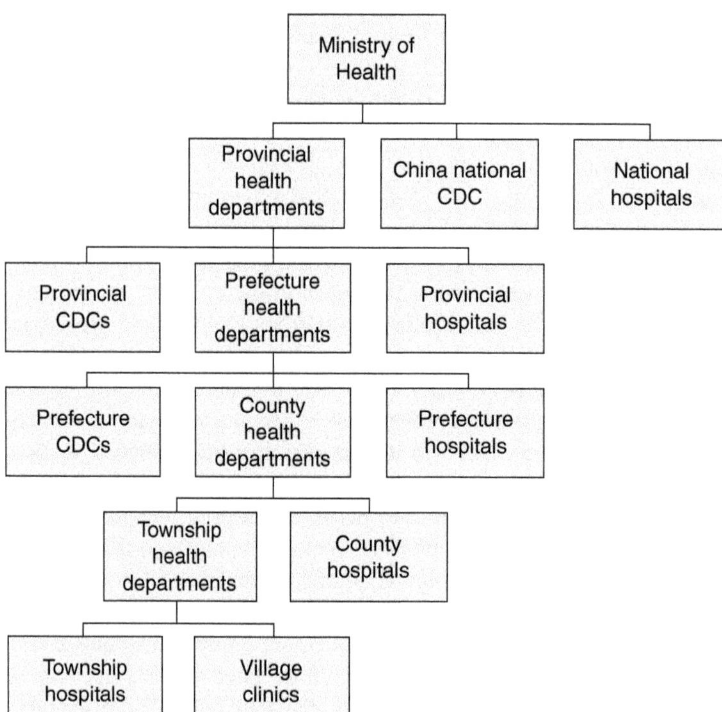

Figure 7.2 Structure of the Chinese center for disease control (CDC) network.

providing guidance. Local CDC responsibilities include reporting disease outbreaks, taking disease control measures, conducting limited research, and providing limited health education services. During the SARS epidemic, local CDCs were responsible for interviewing SARS patients, visiting homes and workplaces of SARS victims, performing disinfection of locations where SARS victims resided, collecting and analyzing SARS surveillance data, staffing SARS hotlines and information websites, and training government staff in epidemic response (WHO Beijing 2003).

To support SARS-related CDC activities, the central government made special allocations of funds for disease control that extended beyond the national CDC to the localities (*People's Daily* 29 August 2003). Among the results of this additional government funding were notable improvements to, and expansions of, infectious disease control facilities across the country. For example, Ditan hospital, one of two infectious disease hospitals in Beijing, had been slated for closure prior to the SARS epidemic. However, following SARS the closure was canceled, the hospital's budget was increased, and the hospital was designated for transfer to a new, more advanced facility outside the city center. A tour of CDC facilities in Shaanxi, Jiangsu, Beijing, and Shanghai provided additional evidence for central government and local assertions that, following the SARS outbreak, the central government made significant new investments in disease control (interviews with Cheng, Hong, Li, Yin, Zheng, and an anonymous Xi'an CDC director, June 2005).

Also exemplifying the central government's investment in improved disease control capacity, an extensive computerized reporting network was rapidly established to ensure that all potential cases of SARS would be efficiently and rapidly reported up the bureaucratic lines of control to the central government. The computerized system replaced the previous slower and far less efficient paper system in 75 percent of all township hospitals. According to Vice Health Minister Gao Qiang, a disease outbreak occurring anywhere across China will now be reported to the central government Ministry of Health within one day. This outcome is especially impressive given that many township-level hospitals lack other basic equipment, and in some cases even running water (interview with Shapiro, May 2005).

On 2 April 2003, the State Council established the Ministry of Health as lead agency to take control over the state response to the SARS epidemic (Quarterly Chronicle 2003: 866). The State Council also established provincial-level anti-SARS supervisory teams and crisis management mechanisms based on the "Plan for the Medical Circles Nationwide to Prevent the Epidemic of Severe Acute Respiratory Syndrome for the Year of 2003–2004" (*People's Daily* 23 August 2003). The plan focused attention on prevention in areas most vulnerable to a recurrence of SARS (e.g. health care facilities, rural hospitals and schools, and cities with large migrant worker populations). It also strengthened health education, monitoring, and treatment efforts in rural areas. Within this framework, the Ministry of Public Health established national expert groups, which were required to make a definitive report within twenty-four hours of receiving notice of potential clinical SARS cases from provincial or local-level officials. Similar expert groups were established at the provincial level. They too were expected to draw definitive conclusions about the severity of an outbreak, but were required to do so within twelve hours.[7]

In addition, while in the past there were few or no regulations on numerous public health protocols, in the wake of the SARS outbreak a flurry of new protocols and policies were introduced and passed from the center through the provinces on down the public health bureaucracy. These protocols and policies were developed in concert with field physicians, professors, and doctors, and came under the aegis of the Ministry of Health and the specially formed State Council working group (discussed earlier). Numerous additional policies were developed and implemented to prevent, control, and treat SARS.[8]

Despite the above-described reconcentration of power in the central government's hands (the core) and clear signals from the center to local governments to prioritize epidemic prevention in the face of the SARS outbreak, these initiatives of themselves proved insufficient. This is illustrated by the fact that in the midst of the response to the SARS epidemic, the central government removed the Chinese CDC from its leadership position because of its failure to control the outbreak effectively (interviews with Bekedam and Hu, May 2005).[9] The key challenge proved to be implementation (Schwartz 2003; interviews with Bekedam and Shieh, May 2005). In order to supplement government efforts, the state recognized the need for, and received, considerable support from non-state actors (Oksenberg's Organizations in Society and the Economy) (Wang 2003: 8). It is to the role of these actors that I now turn.

The non-state sector's response

Drawing on the Eastern European example, some scholars argue that in times of crisis, civil society organizations will step forward to fill a void left by the state. Thus, as in the cases of Hungary and Poland, faced with its lack of capacity to provide services, the state withdraws from social space that is then filled by non-state actors. While often working cooperatively with the state to achieve shared goals, this initially cooperative relationship may become contested as civil society organizations gain additional social space that they will later be unwilling to relinquish.

At least in the short term, the Eastern European dynamic has not been replicated in China. The SARS outbreak did not provide an equivalent opportunity for non-state actors to fill social space left open by the state in the social service provision sphere. Rather, the state largely took control, initiating anti-SARS mass mobilization campaigns and investing heavily to rebuild the public health emergency response capacity of the health sector (Greis and Rosen 2004: 17–19). Nonetheless, examples do exist of conventional NGOs (purely domestic ones as well as those working in concert with international NGOs) engaging in SARS-related activities. Assisting China's SARS prevention and control efforts were organizations such as the Chinese Red Cross and a range of voluntary

Buddhist, Taoist, Catholic, Protestant, and Muslim groups. These groups provided financial support as well as volunteers to local governments. Other examples include China's Family Planning Association (FPA), whose members participated in education, information dissemination, and survey work on the spread of SARS in rural areas. Also, members of the Huizeying Human Service Center in Beijing focused on helping medical workers and their families cope with the stress arising from work combating SARS (China Development Brief 2004).

In another example, the international NGO Amity collaborated with nine other Chinese NGOs (including the China Charity Federation) and the Asia Foundation to cooperate with government, health workers, and hospitals to mobilize resources (*Amity*).

In Shaanxi Province, the Research Association for Women, established in 1986, expanded its traditional focus on women's issues to develop and implement SARS-related programs. These programs included establishing community health education programs, creating a SARS prevention program for poverty-stricken rural mountainous areas, and organizing a workshop entitled "Surveying the Linkage of NGOs in China with Public Health after the Outbreak of SARS" (*Westwoman*).

The China Association for NGO Cooperation (CANGO) initiated a Henan Province-based project entitled "Promotion among Primary School Students on Knowledge of SARS Prevention and Healthy Life (2003)" (*CANGO*). A program aimed at migrant workers in the Beijing area was run by the Cultural Communication Center for Facilitators, and involved distributing disinfectant, face masks, and hygiene education flyers among migrant workers. These workers were considered especially vulnerable to SARS because their unofficial status meant they lacked access to the public health system (*Oxfam*).

According to Shannon Ellis, Civil Society Program coordinator of the Canada–China Cooperation Support Unit, numerous community-level organizations incorporated SARS prevention into their regular work. For example, AIDS organizations and those working with homosexuals drew on their experience in health training to educate about SARS infection control (interview with Ellis, July 2004). While additional cases of NGO contributions to tackling SARS exist, the relative paucity of such examples largely supports Gries and Rosen, who argue that the SARS outbreak did not provide an opportunity for non-state actors to *significantly* engage in social service provision (2004: 17–19). To a large extent, this reality reflects the complexity of establishing civil society organizations in China, an outgrowth of what Perry and Goldman describe as the Party-state's fear of "the specter of the former Soviet Union and its swift dismemberment in the wake of Gorbachev's bold political reforms" (2007: 17).

However, while only limited examples of conventional NGO engagement in SARS control can be identified, the activities of RCs (*jumin weiyuan hui*) and VCs (*cunmin weiyuan hui*) deserve attention. As previously discussed, while these are not conventional civil society organizations, neither can they be viewed as state organs.

During the SARS epidemic, there were numerous cases of these committees effectively implementing health regulations deriving from government officials. For example, in an effort to stop the spread of infection, state policies meant that between 20 percent and 30 percent of China's population were required to stay in their homes or place of employment for between two and three weeks (*geli*). While such a policy represents an excellent means to contain the spread of infectious disease, its implementation was clearly beyond the government's capacity. In order to implement the policy successfully, the state turned to RCs to keep track of all people entering or leaving their jurisdictions (interview with Bekedam, May 2005).

For example, when the Nantong city government declared a two-week isolation policy for all visitors from outside the city, enforcement was heavily dependent on residents' small groups, outgrowths of RCs. These groups monitored the arrival of visitors, contacted the visitors shortly after their arrival, and asked that they report to local clinics to be checked for signs of possible infection (interview with Lu, June 2005). In other cases, RC volunteers were trained to identify potential cases of infection. The training, provided by district hospital staff, was essential to enabling the volunteers to identify any of their neighbors, and visitors to their neighborhood, who might show signs of infection. Because of the existence of RCs and their volunteer staff, it became possible to implement the state policy that everyone arriving from a region of the country where SARS was known to exist would be checked for symptoms. The RCs ensured ongoing temperature checks by distributing free thermometers. Committee volunteers also distributed masks, disinfectants, and leaflets about prevention and control. They also purchased and distributed daily necessities for those in quarantine. Volunteers also reported potential infection cases to the district hospital via designated hotlines (interview with the anonymous director of a Shaanxi provincial hospital, June 2005).

Minhang District, Shanghai, exemplifies this process. In Minhang, RCs gathered 6,800 volunteers. Relying on no monetary incentives, the committees turned to active people in their communities, asking whether they would be willing to undergo SARS-related training. The training was conducted by community doctors (at the district level), who were in turn trained by the district CDC (interviews with CDC and public health officials, Shanghai, June 2005).

Clearly, the role played by the committees was central to effectively identifying potentially infected people, tracking their movements, providing information to public health officials on suspected cases, and ensuring that people remained informed of developments and policies relating to the epidemic. The organizations worked closely with the state public health network to identify, control, and treat cases of infectious disease.

However, it would be incorrect to assert that the committees in general functioned solely at the bidding of government officials. Many cases were reported of the committees acting in contravention of state policies. Thus, for example, numerous committees participated in sealing off their communities with roadblocks to protect their residents from potentially infected persons. These actions were widespread, reflecting the priority given by these committees to their own regions' safety even at the expense of central government expectations (interviews with Hu, Wingfield-Hayes, and an anonymous Shaanxi provincial hospital physician, May 2005).[10] Such activities point to the fact that while not wholly independent *of* the state, neither were these committees fully controlled *by* the state (Read with Pekkanen 2009: chapters 1 and 3).

Clearly, from the perspective of the committees the greater the perceived importance of directives from the state, the greater the likelihood that they would be implemented, reflecting the nature of these committees as closely tied to the state (Alpermann 2001: 46, 49–50, 67). However, as Wang notes, these committees have also been undergoing a process of transforming from intermediaries between the state and society into more fully non-governmental organizations, taking on activities in support of residents' interests vis-à-vis the state (2002: 414).

Thus, in the case of SARS the state successfully recentralized power in its own hands through heavy investment of financial, political, and legislative resources. This effort was supplemented by conventional civil society organization initiatives and, most importantly, by RCs and their village counterparts. Illustrating this dynamic is the Xi'an District's response to SARS.

Shaanxi Province, Xi'an City case study

Illustrating the combined effort involved in addressing the SARS outbreak is the response in Xi'an (interviews with an anonymous university hospital director, Xi'an city hospital, Shaanxi provincial CDC, June 2005). Shaanxi Province had twelve diagnosed SARS cases. Of these, only three originated within the province. Of the twelve cases, all but one were found in Xi'an City. These diagnosed cases combined with fifty-nine suspected cases for a total of seventy-one cases that required an epidemiological response.

During the course of the SARS outbreak, the central government Ministry of Health provided all provincial governments with guidelines on infectious disease reporting and control. The key documents were the 1998 Infectious Disease Law (revised in 2003), as well as the Food and Drug Safety Law and the PRC's Regulations on Public Health Emergencies (2003). The central government also rapidly updated the 1989 Infectious Disease Law to include SARS as a reportable disease (Wang 2003–4). The standards arising from this initiative were provided to the provinces through two bureaucratic lines of control: the Ministry of Health and the provincial government. Protocols and guidelines for SARS response were faxed and emailed from Beijing. Having received the central government guidelines, the provincial Ministry of Health was responsible for developing compliant protocols and regulations. Sub-provincial governments then adapted the provincial protocols and regulations to their local conditions.

To comply with central government requirements, the Shaanxi provincial government, along with the sub-provincial governments, required that all public health authorities, hospital staff, and administrators read and study the protocols and guidelines. The same was required of all enterprise and school officials.

Local authorities developed a quarantine (*jianyi*) system whereby transmission of infection was controlled by confining potentially exposed individuals to their homes. To limit movement of such individuals across the province and to identify possible SARS-infected individuals, the various levels of government established fever checkpoints at airports, train stations, and bus terminals, and along highways. In addition, in compliance with Ministry of Health guidelines, SARS headquarters were established at all levels down to the township to supervise and enforce implementation of government regulations. Local CDCs were responsible for investigating any clusters of suspected cases within two to seven days of having received notification. If a SARS case was confirmed, the patient was transported to a designated SARS treatment hospital by ambulance. Confirmation of SARS infection was made in a BSL-3 laboratory at the provincial or central level.[11] Any individual established as having had contact with a person diagnosed with SARS was placed under home isolation for twenty-one days.[12]

A key method for informing the local SARS headquarters about suspected outbreaks was a twenty-four-hour telephone hotline.[13] A person calling in had the option of identifying him- or herself or someone else as a potential case. To provide the public with information on how to identify potential SARS cases, the state relied on the mass media to saturate the airwaves with information on the disease.

During the SARS outbreak, all persons arriving at a hospital (for whatever reason) were checked for fever at a location outside the hospital proper. Anyone with a fever of 38 degrees Celsius or higher, without an obvious reason for the fever, was taken to an isolated fever clinic on the hospital grounds for further testing. Criteria for clinical diagnoses of SARS included a temperature exceeding 38.5 degrees Celsius, a positive X-ray finding of pneumonia, a decreased white blood cell count, antibiotic failure, and a history of exposure. Any people meeting these criteria were isolated. All patients exhibiting a fever and a history of exposure were isolated as well. Finally, all fever patients were kept under observation for twenty-one days.

While only the Xi'an Number Eight hospital was designated an infectious disease hospital (a new designation resulting from the SARS epidemic – previously it had been a tuberculosis hospital), other hospitals established infectious disease wards to accept patients. All hospitals accepted patients regardless of their ability to pay. According to interviewees, the hospitals received adequate compensation from the state for the patient care.

During periods when there are no ongoing epidemics, outbreaks of infectious diseases in Xi'an City are reported in compliance with the 1989 Infectious Disease Law. However, during an epidemic all potential infectious diseases are reported immediately, following procedures distinct from normal practices. Local VC/RC members, or individuals report by phone to relevant hospitals (i.e. township, or district, city, etc.). The hospitals fax daily reports on the number of patients seen and their diagnoses, along with certain syndromic findings, up the administrative chain of command to both government and health (hospital) administrators.[14] The county hospital (in rural areas – in urban areas the procedure is slightly different; refer to Figure 7.2) uploads the information into computers and forwards it to the provincial CDC and the township government (interviews with the director of Xi'an City hospital, June 2005). The reports are then forwarded daily to the central government Ministry of Health. These procedures were adhered to during the SARS epidemic, with the addition that daily reports were made even when no diagnosed fever patients existed. Every day by 4 p.m., the central government Ministry of Health received reports of the number of cases across the province (and the country) and posted this information on its website.

In order to protect patients and medical personnel from exposure, protocols on protective equipment use were implemented. All medical personnel wore masks (cotton, 12 layer, or, where available, N95S), hats, and gowns. Those working directly with potentially infected persons wore gloves, double masks, double gowns, goggles, and hats. Doctors and nurses assigned to infectious disease units were required to remain in the units for three months and were required to be available twenty-four hours a day. Their only contact with the outside was via telephone. After their three-month stint, they were quarantined in a hotel for an additional twenty-one days before returning home.

While acknowledging the importance of the procedures and regulations established by the CDC and Ministry of Health, all interviewees in the province emphasized the role played by non-government personnel in ensuring that cases of the disease were quickly identified and controlled. As was true elsewhere, interviewees in Shaanxi considered SARS a political problem requiring a political response. And while conventional NGOs played a role in the SARS response, VCs and RCs acting under the guidance and with the training of local CDCs and hospitals played an important role. The committee leadership designated and, with CDC assistance, trained committee members to take responsibility for identifying potential SARS cases. These members were responsible for monitoring their communities and notifying hospitals of people exhibiting indications of SARS. Because of the close ties within neighborhoods, the designated committee members were largely aware of all the comings and goings in their communities. Any person returning or visiting from an epidemic region would be checked by the committee members for symptoms. In addition, committee members conducted routine fever checks for all homes under their responsibility.

Xi'an International Studies University represented a microcosm of actions taken by the community to address the SARS epidemic. The university's main campus is located in the center of metropolitan Xi'an. The campus is enclosed by a wall with guarded gates. During the SARS epidemic, at the behest of the municipal government the university clinic director established a leading group for SARS (similar to the SARS headquarters discussed earlier) under the university RC. The RC worked collaboratively with the university administration, establishing a leading group that included the clinic director, the university Party general secretary, and the university president. Additional members included heads of all departments and the campus security chief.

Drawing on Ministry of Health regulations and the Shaanxi provincial and Xi'an municipal guidelines, the campus leading group categorized infectious diseases into three levels: basic (*yi-ban*), mid-range (*zhong-da*), and severe (*te-da*). Basic diseases were to be reported within twenty-four hours, mid-range within twelve hours and severe diseases within six hours. Although SARS was classified as mid-range early in the epidemic, the central government required that reporting on potential SARS cases occur every six hours. The reports went to the Yanta District Public Health Department, which uploaded the reports to the internet and sent them forward to the city government.

A specific set of measures was implemented by the leading group to ensure that individuals potentially infected with SARS could not enter or leave the campus. Thus, during the time of the crisis no students or faculty were permitted to leave the campus. No student who departed the campus for any reason (for example, in order to visit family elsewhere) was allowed re-entry to the campus until after spending fourteen days isolated in a building adjacent to the campus. All such students were kept under surveillance by the campus medical staff and had their temperatures checked four times daily.

Residents of the dormitories were regularly checked for fever. Any student exhibiting fever was isolated in the university clinic designated fever center for the extent of the SARS incubation period. The clinic was sealed off from the remainder of the health center and staffed by fully gowned, hooded, masked, and goggled nurses. Quarantine (*jianyi*) buildings were established for the university's fifty to sixty quarantined individuals. If after completing the quarantine period the individual exhibited no disease symptoms, he or she underwent a chest X-ray and, if the findings so warranted, was released to his or her dormitory. If, however, the patient's condition deteriorated while under observation, the patient would be sent by ambulance to the city's designated SARS hospital. Only one individual was ultimately suspected of having contracted SARS. As a general precaution the entire campus was disinfected.

Conclusion

The Chinese response to SARS illustrates the impact of crises on the roles of state and non-state actors in social service provision. In the period leading to the outbreak of the SARS epidemic, China's public health system was both weak and in decline. The Ministry of Health lacked influence, the CDC system had only just been established, the majority of China's citizenry had little or no health coverage, and the government was in the process of slashing financial support for infectious disease facilities. However, as China had yet to face a public health crisis in the reform era, there was little sense of urgency in government or within the public. Indeed, little urgency regarding China's epidemic prevention and control capacity was expressed at any level of government. Thus, the government's capacity to respond effectively to an infectious disease outbreak was poor and untested.

The SARS outbreak was a crisis that focused the spotlight on China's capacity to address the potential spread of a deadly infectious disease. Quite suddenly,

China's leadership and the world discovered that the Chinese state was unprepared to handle the crisis. While significant efforts were made to recentralize power in the hands of the central government Ministry of Health, an additional key to the effective SARS response was the activities and responsibilities taken on by a variety of non-state actors.

The SARS case describes a situation where social space once assumed to be under state control proves to be weakly controlled. Notably, as the SARS crisis grew, non-state actors gained an increased role – expanding into those areas of service provision once assumed to be state controlled. While conventional non-state, civil society actors did play a limited role in responding to SARS, the main contributors to the state's SARS control initiatives were the RCs and VCs – non-conventional non-state actors. These committees worked in close coordination with local CDCs and health bureaus to fulfill public health mandates beyond the capacity of state organs to independently fill. Ultimately, the result was a successful SARS response. The disease was limited in its geographical reach, brought under control, and eventually eradicated.

SARS represents a case where various non-state actors worked with the state to combat a crisis. This was a cooperative relationship that reflected efforts to achieve immediate shared goals. Post-SARS state initiatives to expand and enhance China's emergency response capacity continue to draw on this relationship, reflecting the state's ongoing effort to recentralize control over emergency health responses while also expanding its reliance on non-state organizations.

The SARS dynamic suggests that crisis situations enable non-state actors to increase their scope of activities. Unlike in the East European cases discussed earlier in this chapter, the SARS crisis has not as yet resulted in a contested relationship, but rather has brought a strengthening of the state's capacity to respond to infectious disease crises. To further evaluate the impact of crisis situations on state–society relations and social service provision, we must study additional crisis response cases. Given the growing threat of infectious disease pandemics, it seems likely that we will not be required to wait overly long. Indeed, as the next chapter, addressing the AIDS crisis, illustrates, crisis situations can have a direct impact on the balance between state and non-state actor social service provision. In responding to the AIDS crisis, the state drew lessons from the SARS crisis by expanding its relationship with non-state actors.

Notes

1 In 1999 the experimental *Shequ* were introduced. These have arisen instead of, and in parallel with, RCs. For a further discussion of *Shequ*, see Derleth and Koldyk (2004).

2 Especially in terms of services for the village such as welfare, culture, education, and public health. The extent of autonomy varies from village to village.

3 According to Bekedam, in his own pre-SARS outbreak discussions with Hu Jintao and Wen Jiabao he found that they recognized the existence of a funding shortage in public health, yet remained unconcerned.

4 Unfunded mandates are a key problem identified by public health officials across the country.

5 Epidemic prevention stations have been renamed centers for disease control. These are subordinate to the Ministry of Health bureaucracy. The epidemic prevention stations and now the CDCs are responsible for surveillance and other public health services.
6 The US Centers for Disease Control conduct epidemic investigations, research, training, and public education. However, they do not have institutions that spread from the center to the local level, nor do they provide medical care services, as is the case in China. Local Chinese CDCs fulfill many of the functions of US local health departments, and offices of epidemiology and infectious disease.
7 Three levels of epidemic severity are identified: Ordinary – reflecting a single SARS case within a reporting period; Serious – reflecting either a recurrent single case in one area or two or more cases within one prefecture or municipality; and Severe – reflecting two or more cases in one province, which will be seen as indicating that the disease is spreading.
8 The ministry designated SARS a contagious disease to be listed on the People's Republic of China Contagious Disease Prevention and Treatment Code. Those suspected of or confirmed as having SARS could be quarantined. Public security bureaus were made available to public health authorities where necessary to enforce quarantines. Public health departments across China have been required by the State Ministry of Health to organize rapid reaction drills in preparation for possible epidemics.
9 The CDC network was established two years prior to the SARS outbreak. The original plan was that the CDCs would be responsible for policymaking and technical work. However, the central government viewed the CDC system as having failed to respond to SARS effectively, with the result that the leadership role in responding to the outbreak was transferred to the Ministry of Health.
10 Cases of roadblocks were described by officials in each province visited during fieldwork.
11 BSL-3 is suitable for work with infectious agents that may cause serious or potentially lethal diseases as a result of exposure by the inhalation route. Examples of agents that should be manipulated at BSL-3 include *Mycobacterium tuberculosis* and *Coxiella burnetii*.
12 The length of quarantines changed as understanding of the SARS incubation period increased. Thus, while in the early stages quarantines lasted between ten and twenty-one days, they were eventually set at fourteen days.
13 The hotline existed before the SARS epidemic but was upgraded in response to SARS, with additional training for hotline workers. According to one township hospital official, during the epidemic the line was staffed by trained individuals who provided information and consultations, and took information regarding potential SARS cases. To illustrate its accessibility, the official successfully called the hotline during our interview.
14 Infectious diseases are categorized as A, B, C, with A being most severe and requiring reporting within six hours. B types must be reported within twelve hours and C types within twenty-four hours. Although SARS was originally categorized as a B-type infectious disease, reports of SARS were required within six hours.

References

Alpermann, B. (2001) "The Post-election Administration of Chinese Villages," *China Journal* 46: 45–67.

Amity Newsletter. Online, available at: www.amitynewsletter.org/index.php?issueNo=66 (accessed 18 March 2007).

Banister, J. (1998) "Population, Public Health and the Environment in China," *China Quarterly* 156: 986–1015.

Bloom, G. and Gu, X. (1997) "Health Sector Reform: Lessons from China," *Social Science and Medicine* 45: 351–60.

Blumenthal, D. and Hsiao, W. (2005) "Privatization and Its Discontents: The Evolving Chinese Health Care System," *New England Journal of Medicine* 353: 1165–70.

Canadian Department of National Defense Policy Report. Online, available at: www.forces.gc.ca/admpol/eng/doc/strat_2003/sa03_09_e.htm (accessed 1 February 2006).

CANGO. Online, available at: www.cango.org (accessed 11 October 2004).

China Development Brief (2004) "Split Appears among First Generation Chinese NGOs." Online, available at: www.chinadevelopmentbrief.com (accessed 13 February 2004).

China Ministry of Civil Affairs (2006) Document No. 23: *MOCA's Ideas on Improving Shequ Construction*. Online, available at: www.isanet.org/noarchive/derleth.html (accessed 5 February 2006).

Chung, J. H. (1995) "Studies of Central–Provincial Relations in the People's Republic of China: A Mid-term Appraisal," *China Quarterly* 142: 487–508.

Cooper, C. (2003) "Quietly Sowing the Seeds of Activism," *South China Morning Post* (10 April).

Croll, E. L. (1999) "Social Welfare Reform: Trends and Tensions," *China Quarterly* 159: 684–99.

Davis, D. and Siu, H. (eds.) (2007) *SARS: Reception and Interpretation in Three Chinese Cities*, Abingdon, UK: Routledge.

Derleth, J. and Koldyk, D. (2004) "The *Shequ* Experiment: Grassroots Political Reform in Urban China," *Journal of Contemporary China* 13: 747–77.

Frolic, B. M. (1997) "State Led Civil Society," in T. Brook and B. M. Frolic (eds.) *Civil Society in China*, Armonk, NY: M. E. Sharpe.

Garrett, L. (2003) "A Chinese Lab's Race to ID and Halt SARS," *Newsday* (6 May). Online, available at: www.phucla.edu/epi/bioter/chineselabsrace.html (accessed 7 November 2003).

Gries, P. H. and Rosen, S. (2004) "Introduction: Popular Protest and State Legitimation in 21st Century China," in P. H. Gries and S. Rosen (eds.) *State and Society in 21st Century China: Crisis, Contention, and Legitimation*, London: Routledge.

Huang, Y. (2003) "Mortal Peril: Public Health in China and Its Security Implications," Chemical and Biological Arms Control Institute. Online, available at: www.cbaci.org (accessed 6 July 2004).

Kaufman, J. (2006) "SARS and China's Healthcare Response," in A. Kleinman and J. L. Watson (eds.) *SARS in China: Prelude to Pandemic?* Stanford, CA: Stanford University Press.

Knup, E. (1998) "Environmental NGOs in China: An Overview," *China Environment Series* 1: 9–15.

Lieberthal, K. (1992) "Introduction: The Fragmented Authoritarianism Model and Its Limitations," in K. Lieberthal and D. Lampton (eds.) *Bureaucracy, Politics, and Decision Making in Post-Mao China*, Berkeley: University of California Press.

Lieberthal, K. and Oksenberg, M. (1988) *Policy Making in China: Leaders, Structures, and Processes*, Princeton, NJ: Princeton University Press.

Liu, Y. (2004) "China's Public Health-Care System: Facing the Challenges," *Bulletin of the World Health Organization* 82: 532–8.

Manion, M. (1996) "The Electoral Connection in the Chinese Countryside," *American Political Science Review* 90: 736–48.

O'Brien, K. J. (2001) "Villagers, Elections and Citizenship in Contemporary China," *Modern China* 27: 407–35.

O'Brien, K. J. and Li, L. (2006) *Rightful Resistance in Rural China*, Cambridge: Cambridge University Press.

Oi, J. C. and Rozelle, S. (2000) "Elections and Power: The Locus of Decision-Making in Chinese Villages," *China Quarterly* 162: 513–39.

Oksenberg, M. (2001) "China's Political System: Challenges of the Twenty-first Century," *China Journal* 45: 21–35.

—— (2002) "China's Political System: Challenges of the 21st Century," in J. Unger (ed.) *The Nature of Chinese Politics: From Mao to Jiang*, Armonk, NY: M. E. Sharpe.

Organic Law of the Urban Neighborhood Committees (1990). Online, available at: www.mca.gov.cn (accessed 19 February 2004).

Otsuka, K. (2002) "China: Social Restructuring and the Emergence of NGOs," in S. Shigetomi (ed.) *The State and NGOs: Perspective from Asia*, Singapore: Institute of Southeast Asian Studies.

Oxfam. "Migrant Workers: Working against SARS in Urban and Rural China." Online, available at: www.oxfam.org/hk/english (accessed 11 October 2004).

People's Daily (25 June 2003) "China's New Leadership Passes Test Presented by SARS." Online, available at: http://english.peopledaily.com.cn (accessed 20 February 2004).

People's Daily (23 August 2003) "Plan for the Medical Circles Nationwide to Prevent the Epidemic of Severe Acute Respiratory Syndrome for the Year of 2003–2004." Online, available at: http://english.peopledaily.com.cn (accessed 20 February 2004).

—— (29 August 2003) "Plan Put Forward by Ministry of Health for Prevention of SARS." Online, available at: http://english.peopledaily.com.cn (accessed 5 January 2006).

—— (4 August 2004) "Macro Control Proved to Be Timely and Effective." Online, available at: http://english.peopledaily.com.cn (accessed 4 August 2004).

Perry, E. J. and Goldman, M. (2007) "Introduction: Historical Reflections on Grassroots Reform in China," in E. J. Perry and M. Goldman (eds.) *Grassroots Political Reform in Contemporary China*, Cambridge, MA: Harvard University Press.

Quarterly Chronicle and Documentation (September 2003) *China Quarterly* 175.

Read, B. L. (2003) "State, Social Networks and Citizens in China's Urban Neighborhoods," unpublished thesis, Harvard University.

Read, B. and Chen, C. M. (2008) "The State's Evolving Relationship with Urban Society: China's Neighborhood Organizations in Comparative Perspective," in J. R. Logan (ed.) *Urban China in Transition*, Oxford: Blackwell.

Read, B. L. with Pekkanen R. (eds.) (2009) *Local Organizations and Urban Governance in East and Southeast Asia: Straddling State and Society*, Abingdon, UK: Routledge.

Ronaghy, H. A. and Salter, S. (1974) "Is the Chinese 'Barefoot Doctor' Exportable to Rural Iran?" *Lancet* 1: 1331–3.

Saich, T. (2006) "Is SARS China's Chernobyl or Much Ado about Nothing?" in A. Kleinman and J. L. Watson (eds.) *SARS in China: Prelude to Pandemic?* Stanford, CA: Stanford University Press.

Schwartz, J. (2003) "The Impact of State Capacity on Enforcement of Environmental Policies: The Case of China," *Journal of Environment and Development* 12: 50–81.

Turner, J. L. and Wu, F. (2001) "Development of Environmental NGOs in Mainland China, Taiwan and Hong Kong," *Green NGO and Environmental Journalist Forum*, Woodrow Wilson International Center for Scholars, Washington, DC.

Wang, D. (2003) "Chinese Leadership Signals Change," *Taipei Times* (2 January).

Wang, F. L. (2003–4) Guest Editor's Introduction, in F. L. Wang (ed.) *Chinese Law and Government* 36 (4) (July/August 2003): 6.

Wang, S. and Sun, B. (2002) "Zhong guo min jian zu zhi fazhan gai kuang" [Introduction to the Development of Civil Organizations], in K. Yu *et al.* (eds.) *Zhong guo gongmin shi hui de ying qi yu zhi li de bianqian* [The Emergence of Civil Society and Its Significance to Governance in Reform China], Beijing: Social Science Documents Press.
Wang, Y. (2002) "Self-Governance for City Residents and Changes in Community Management Styles," in K. Yu (ed.) *The Emerging of Civil Society and Its Significance to Governance in Reform China* [Zhong guo gongmin she hui de xingqi yu zhili de bianqian], Beijing: Social Science Digest Press [She Hui Ke Xue Wen Xian Chu Ban She].
Westwoman. Online, available at: www.westwoman.org (accessed 11 October 2004).
WHO Representative in Beijing (3 November 2003), Online, available at: www.cbc.ca/disclosure/archives/031118_SARS/docs/whobeijing (accessed 18 July 2003).
Worden, R. L., Savada, A. M., and Dolan, R. E. (eds.) (1987) *Country Study China*, Federal Research Division of the Library of Congress. Online, available at: www.country-data.com/frd/cs/cntoc.html#cn0356 (accessed 28 February 2008).
World Bank (January 2005) Conference on Mobilizing Urban Infrastructure in a Responsible Fiscal Framework, "Urbanization and Sub-national Financing Background Notes," Online, available at: http://worldbank.org/urban/mun_fin/uifpapers/bhattasali.pdf (accessed 3 February 2006).
Young, N. (2003) "Searching for Civil Society," *China Development Brief*. Online, available at: www.chinadevelopmentbrief.com/page.asp?sec=2&sub=3&pg=0&mp=1 (accessed 7 May 2005).
Zhong, K. (2007) "Crisis Management in China," *China Security* (Winter): 90–109.

Interviews

Shannon Ellis, Canada civil society project in China (June 2004).
Dr. Craig Shapiro, Department of Health and Human Services, HHS Health Attaché, US embassy, Beijing (26 May 2005).
Dr. Marie Shieh, Beijing United Family Hospital (26 May 2005).
Cheng Jun, Director Infectious Diseases, Di Tan hospital, Beijing (30 May 2005).
Dr. Hu Yonghua, Dean School of Public Health, Beijing University (31 May 2005).
Dr. Henk Bekedam, MSc, WHO Country Representative to China (31 May 2005).
Anonymous physician, Shaanxi Provincial People's Hospital (2 June 2005).
Anonymous director, Xi'an City CDC (3 June 2005).
Hong Bing Shen, Associate Dean, Nanjing Medical University School of Public Health (7 June 2005).
Dr. Li Jiequan, Director of the Nanjing Municipal CDC (7 June 2005).
Dr. Lu Yan, Nanjing City Chinese Medicine Hospital (7 June 2005).
Yin Qilin, Associate Director of the Nanjing Municipal CDC (7 June 2005).
Anonymous physicians, Nanjing Infectious Disease Hospital (7 June 2005).
Dr. Shen Hui Guo, Infectious Disease Control, Minhang District CDC (7 June 2005).
Dr. Zheng Yingjie, Department of Epidemiology, School of Public Health, Fudan University (7 June 2005).

8 The role of NGOs in China's AIDS crisis

Challenges and possibilities

Joan Kaufman

Introduction

In the taxonomy of social welfare proposed by Croll (1999) and elaborated on in Chapter 1, health services, including health education, fall into the category of social services. Public funding for China's health services, however, has been hard hit by the economic reforms of the past few decades, and serious gaps and inequities now exist, along with weak ability to respond to new challenges. In this chapter, I will explore this volume's dual themes of crisis and non-crisis drivers of civil society development in China. I shall examine how on the one hand new challenges to social service provision and on the other the crisis and threat of emerging infectious diseases have pushed the boundaries of NGO political space in China and created some new models for NGO service provision in collaboration with government.

Background

The global AIDS epidemic continues to worsen and is one of the leading development challenges of our era. Nearly 33.2 million people are infected with HIV/AIDS and there were 2.5 million new infections and nearly 2.1 million deaths in 2007 alone, with no signs of any slowing of the global epidemic (UNAIDS and WHO 2007: 1). Since the beginning of the global AIDS epidemic, NGOs have played a decisive role in the response, both for advocacy and for services. Advocacy groups such as ACT UP, representing gay men, have put pressure on governments and industry to increase funding and access for treatment and prevention programs. Groups representing people living with HIV/AIDS (PLWHA) have a mandated role in most international and national AIDS policy, program, and funding bodies (the principle of "greater involvement of people living with AIDS" – GIPA – promoted by UNAIDS. Services provided by AIDS NGOs, for outreach to gay men, condom distribution and promotion for sex workers, syringe exchange for injecting drug users, youth sex education programs, sex worker legal protection services, treatment and support to AIDS patients, AIDS orphans support programs, and many others, have been a key feature of successful AIDS responses in many countries. These groups have been able to reach and represent hard-to-reach and underrepresented groups with essential risk reduction education, recruitment for HIV testing and treatment, or assistance in accessing care and support and in representing their needs and perspectives in policy and program formulation. Once effective AIDS treatment became available in the 1990s, community groups and local NGOs became the backbone of AIDS treatment support in rural communities (Farmer *et al.* 2001) where trained medical personnel are scarce.

China's AIDS epidemic began in the early 1980s as a localized epidemic among needle-sharing intravenous drug users along the border with Myanmar (Kaufman and Jun 2002: 2339). China has been singled out as one of the five countries that will experience the most new infections by 2010, an estimated 10–15 million, because of the size of the population at risk and delays in early intervention (National Intelligence Council 2002). The government estimates that there are 650,000 HIV infections in the country, 203,527 of which are confirmed by testing, with 52,480 identified AIDS cases among them (Xinhua News Agency 2007b). HIV/AIDS is now found in all of China's thirty-one provinces, municipalities, and autonomous regions, with new infections growing at an estimated rate of 30 percent per year (Xinhua News Agency 2007b; Ministry of Health and UN 2006). Half of new infections are sexually transmitted, mainly among commercial sex workers, sexual partners of injecting drug users, and men who have sex with men.

While most infections are still among injecting drug (heroin) users, a separate epidemic among former paid plasma donors in central China accounts for a large proportion of identified cases. The proportion of infections among women has increased from 19.4 percent in 2000 to 27.8 percent in 2006 (Xinhua News Agency 2007b). In a number of locations in China, the epidemic is also beginning to expand into the general population. Half of all new infections are now sexually transmitted, and the sexual epidemic has the potential to expand rapidly because of the size of China's young population, changing sexual behaviors and norms, massive internal migration, high rates of STDs, inadequate knowledge about AIDS and perception of risk among the general population, and an emerging epidemic among hard-to-reach gay men, which has only recently been recognized.

The crisis leading to China's AIDS response

China's SARS crisis in 2003 was a turning point for the Chinese government's response to its HIV/AIDS problem (see Chapter 7). Because of the early failures and consequent embarrassment of the initial SARS response, the national leadership finally reversed course and began to address the AIDS crisis seriously. Wu Yi, a powerful vice premier at that time, was put in charge of the Ministry of Health after the firing of the Health Minister over the mismanagement of SARS. She translated the political capital mobilized for the SARS response first to the AIDS response and then to other emerging infectious diseases, especially avian influenza. (She has recently also been put in charge of food and product safety.)

China's failure as a global citizen as a result of SARS pushed the government to recognize the importance of global accountability on national public health crises and the need for an emergency preparedness and response mechanism for infectious diseases, which was established in 2005 at the MOH (Kaufman 2008).

As with SARS, a perception of crisis by Chinese government leaders led to action. Using Stern's definition of non-economic crisis (Stern 1999) provided by Shieh and Schwartz in Chapter 1, the AIDS situation in central China in 2000–2 precipitated a threat to basic values and created a sense of urgency and potential threat of civil unrest. The AIDS epidemic had been gaining momentum since the mid-1990s (Kaufman and Jun 2003: 2339). Even as HIV infections spread from southwest China to all of China's thirty-one provinces and autonomous regions throughout the 1990s and the extent of a tainted blood plasma collection epidemic in central China became known, the government continued to deny the severity of the problem, and only limited resources and attention were devoted to the response. The relatively small amount of funding of RMB 100 million ($12.5 million) in 2002 allocated by the central government was used almost entirely to build blood banks, with little devoted to prevention or treatment programs for the populations at risk. China's political culture of not reporting bad news (Peng 2006), evident during the SARS crisis as well as with recent avian influenza outbreaks, was certainly at play in the cover-up of emerging AIDS hotspots in central and southwest China. However, revelations by a retired doctor, Gao Yaojie, and a series of press reports (Rosenthal 2000; Southern Weekend 1999) on the severity of the epidemic caused by tainted blood donation practices in Henan Province exposed the government cover-up and began to publicize the plight of rural farmers, creating a flood of sympathy on the part of China's citizens. Previously, there had been little public sympathy for the victims of AIDS, mainly injecting heroin users or commercial sex workers, both highly stigmatized and illegal groups.

Henan's farmers and their affected children and elderly parents became the "innocent victims" that the AIDS crisis needed in order to gain public awareness and demand for action. As the extent of the epidemic in central China became known, rumors also began to circulate in the early 2000s via mobile phone text messaging and the internet that disgruntled AIDS patients were intentionally sticking people with infected syringes in public gatherings. Reports of such attacks in Tianjin caused a public panic and created a psychological crisis of fear. The pressure on government to respond, along with existing concern about the potential for a political crisis generated by demands for justice by infected farmers, pushed the government to take action (Jun 2006: 156). To address the plight of central China's AIDS-infected farmers, a free national AIDS treatment program was launched in 2003 by the Chinese government, called China Comprehensive AIDS Response (China CARES), focused at first on Henan and the six provinces bordering it (Wu *et al.* 2007: 685).

China CARES signaled the beginning of increased policy attention to AIDS. The government substantially increased funding ($100 million in 2005 and $185 million in 2006) (*China Daily* 2005), put in place proven interventions (such as drug substitution and syringe exchange for drug users, safe sex education, testing of blood supply) to control the epidemic, and signaled to local leaders that they would be held accountable for results. New national (State Council) directives and a new AIDS action plan were launched in 2006 (Decree No. 457 of the State Council: Regulations on AIDS Prevention and Control, 29 January 2006; China's Action Plan for Reducing and Preventing the Spread of HIV/AIDS, 2006–2010, State Council Office Document, 2006, No. 13). These documents indicated increasing political will to tackle the AIDS issue. As with SARS, political will and resources for mobilizing public health action were necessary to begin an overdue response (Kaufman 2005: 68).

The state recognizes its limits

However, even with this new-found political will to tackle AIDS through public service provision, the government is beginning to realize that it lacks the capacity to accomplish its goal. The SARS crisis in 2003 also exposed serious deficiencies in China's public health system, which has been weakened by insufficient funding, as well as decentralization and privatization, over the nearly three decades of market-oriented reforms. To refer again to Shieh and Schwartz's introductory chapter in this volume, the opening for NGO participation in China's AIDS response is occurring because the state has shed responsibility for public services in the health sphere and some of that role is being taken up by civil society organizations. Saich (2007) makes a similar argument about the need for new types of partnerships for social service provision, especially in areas like AIDS, where government is less able to reach beneficiaries than an NGO might be. It is increasingly clear to government that achieving its ambitious AIDS Action Plan goals must involve NGOs that can reach the populations most affected or at risk. Together with increased international funding for AIDS NGOs, this has resulted in some limited endorsement of the NGO role by the state and led to a proliferation of new grassroots organizations, especially groups serving gay men. As the epidemic becomes a sexually transmitted one and continues to expand among gay men (men who have sex with men, MSM) in urban areas, the northeast, and in places such as Shenzhen (one of China's most economically vibrant cities), the government is cooperating, formally and informally, with groups that have access to these high-risk men.

However, other high-risk groups for HIV/AIDS are falling through the cracks in government outreach efforts. Drug users and sex workers, two high-risk groups engaged in illegal behavior, avoid government services for fear of arrest. Economic migrants (miners, truckers, construction workers) are not easily reached because of their mobility, lack of workplace-organized AIDS education efforts, and their lack of entitlement to social services in the places where they work. Therefore, the climate of political will to tackle AIDS is providing a unique opportunity for AIDS NGOs to push the boundaries of local government's resistance to their existence by demonstrating their value as indispensable service providers, most particularly to these hard-to-reach populations.

In urban areas, numerous AIDS NGO groups have emerged to provide outreach and education to gay men through hotlines and in bars and bathhouses (AIZHI, Gay Men's Hotline, Friends Exchange, Chengdu Community Care Group). Patient support groups have formed, often affiliated with urban infectious disease hospitals (Mangrove, Ark of Love) or as vehicles for raising funds (Positive Art), or to provide anti-retroviral (ARV) treatment education and adherence support based on programs developed by Médecins Sans Frontières (AIDSCARE and China AIDS Info in Guangzhou). Other groups have been established either to raise money for orphan relief or to provide subsidies and services to AIDS-affected families (Chi Heng, AOS, Orchid).

Fewer groups exist to work with sex workers or drug users, both illegal, but groups that do operate fill important gaps by providing education and condoms to sex workers and miners (Panzhiyuan), male and female sex workers (Shanghai Le Yi, Chi Heng), drug treatment and rehabilitation for drug users (Daytop), or needle and syringe exchange distribution to injecting drug users (Kuming).

Few AIDS NGOs are based outside of cities, and most have difficulty operating in rural areas unless explicitly contracted by or supported by the local center for disease control (CDC). Those that do exist are usually groups of people living with HIV/AIDS (PLWHA) organized around technical services such as AIDS treatment support or AIDS orphan care. Such groups have formed in hard-hit areas in central China and Yunnan, and in some cases have become vocal advocates for better services or for providing relief and assistance to orphans and AIDS-affected families. These groups are often closely monitored by local government. Even with the increased privatization of the rural health sector in recent decades, health care provision is still organized and managed as a top-down process through government agencies, and there is little familiarity with independent service agencies working outside of health authority and local government control. Only a few local governments recognize the valuable role that NGOs can play in filling the social welfare service gaps in areas such as orphan care, treatment support, and community assistance to AIDS-affected households, even as these gaps worsen.

Continued poor understanding of and support for NGOs by local government leaders mean that the AIDS NGO role is hard to institutionalize at local levels. In urban areas, citizens have greater access to social welfare services and relief, either employer health insurance or urban social safety net programs. However, in rural areas safety net programs reach only the very poor. In both urban and rural areas, high-risk groups such as injecting drug users or commercial sex workers avoid government services, but in urban areas there are increasing numbers of peer outreach volunteer efforts and greater access to information on HIV prevention. However, there are fewer NGOs working with drug users or commercial sex workers in rural areas. Illegal drug use and prostitution have proliferated in rural Chinese market towns in recent years. Moreover, there is an intense stigma attached to homosexuality, partly related to the pressure for marriage and male offspring, so homosexual behavior is almost universally hidden in rural China, making it difficult to reach gay men with safe sex education messages. NGO outreach programs are needed to reach these at-risk groups at the same time that the political space for NGOs to operate remains very limited. NGOs remain distrusted by local government because of the perception by officials that they might be potentially counterrevolutionary groups, and in the case of AIDS precisely because they often provide services to these stigmatized and often illegal groups.

Civil society in China

China's overall NGO sector is unlike its counterparts in other parts of the world. In China's one-party state, the political space for NGOs to operate is still very restricted, and government remains the main service provider, even for services that in the rest of the world NGOs have traditionally played a major role in delivering. Paralleling the government service network, however, China's mass organizations and government-organized non-governmental organizations (GONGOs) operate through vertical hierarchies to local levels paralleling the government system. While numerous more independent social organizations (*shehui tuanti*) have emerged in China in the past decade, most of them operate as research, advocacy (*changdao*), or professional organizations, with relatively few actually delivering services (*fuwu*). But twenty years of fiscal decentralization and devolution of financing responsibility to lower levels has reduced the availability of social services, particularly health and education, in poorer areas (Saich and Kaufman 2005: 180), and some NGOs have begun to move into the breach, mainly in urban areas. There are now about 320,000 civil organizations in China registered with the Ministry of Civil Affairs (MOCA) (including *shehui tuanti*, *jijinhui* (foundations), and *minbanfeiqiye danwei* (private non-profit enterprises)). However, many civil organizations do not register with the MOCA (mainly community organizations, rural welfare and mutual help groups, religious groups) and there are probably about two million civil society organizations in China, including foreign NGOs, trade and science associations, charity groups, farmers' organizations, and doctor's organizations (Wang Ming 2006).

The working environment for Chinese NGOs is still beset by a climate of distrust (see Chapter 2). Original NGO laws were put in place in the 1950s aimed at eliminating counterrevolutionary organizations. The 1989 Law on Registration of Civil Organizations was aimed at identifying who the groups were, so as to restrict and control them, and this is still the major objective of laws today. The Eastern Europe and newly independent states (NIS) phenomena (Solidarity and the Orange Revolution) scared Chinese officials, and in 1990 the MOCA was expanded to set up a nationwide system to deal with NGOs. This was aimed at tightening the registration process to better control them. The "dual management" system was instituted, requiring a sponsoring organization and yearly re-registration. The main route for NGOs to operate legally in China is to register with the MOCA. Organizations must have a minimum of RMB 100,000 to register with the MOCA, and this serves as a barrier to many smaller organizations. Registration is not required for groups working at county level and below, providing some leeway for local groups but also little protection from local government authorities. Only one group working on an issue is allowed to register locally, and groups working on the same issue in different places are prohibited from coming together as a regional, provincial, or national organization. This provides a distinct advantage to GONGOs and mass organizations, for which these restrictions do not apply. The dual management system often acts as a hindrance to NGO operations, as some good organizations are unable to find sponsors willing to manage and take responsibility for them.

The other main route to legal operation for NGOs is to register with the Commercial and Industrial Bureau (as a commercial entity). Often, civil society organizations register with the Commercial and Industrial Bureau to avoid MOCA "dual management" restrictions. However, commercially registered civil organizations must pay 5 percent tax on any revenue, even if collected for charitable purposes – and all fundraising is considered as revenue. Increasingly, local groups are not registering at all and are letting another organization (usually a GONGO or well-established university-based program) "front" the money as a "pass-through" (a funds transfer agent) since some international funders do not require that NGO recipients be registered.

Current situation of AIDS NGOs in China

Shieh and Schwartz in Chapter 1 provide a functional typology of civil society organizations in China (Figure 1.1) and suggest that Chinese NGOs fall more into the sociological than into the political definition of civil society in terms of their relative levels of autonomy from the state and their shared goals. In their discussion, they state that the political definition of civil society identifies social organizations "as components of a social force in opposition to the state resulting in, or by nature a part of, the democratization process." In addition, the definition envisions democratization arising over time "as a result of individuals combining their otherwise disparate grievances against the state, and learning norms of democratic interaction in the process" (Chapter 1). I would argue that in the realm of AIDS at least some characteristics of the political definition exist, especially in the recent events surrounding election controversies related to China's Global Fund governance mechanisms (see pp. 167–9), through which Chinese AIDS NGOs have been learning norms of democratic interaction. Thus, in particular with regard to AIDS NGOs, the sociological definition is appropriate when combined with recognition of the precursors of oppositional civil society as described in the political definition of civil society.

China's AIDS NGO scene involves an increasingly independent GONGO sector, a set of active legal advocacy NGOs, some with international funding and links to global legal advocacy networks, groups representing PLWHA ("patient groups"), and a growing number of grassroots service NGOs with specific focus on most at-risk populations like men who have sex with men, migrants and youth. Because sex work and drug use are illegal, groups representing these populations are scarce and are usually led by a non-affected person or by government-affiliated groups at local levels. The visibility, legitimacy, and participation of all these groups have been strengthened in recent years by the funding provided by the Global Fund for AIDS, TB and Malaria (GFATM) and the mandated establishment of its civil society governing mechanism, the country coordinating mechanism (CCM), and controversies and subsequent actions in China surrounding the CCM. (See p. 167 for detailed discussion of the CCM mandate, controversy, and resolution.)

As with the overall context for NGOs in China, government remains the main service provider in the AIDS response, unlike in other countries, where NGOs play an important role in service delivery to marginalized groups. The government role has been mainly played by China's Center for Disease Control and Prevention's National Center for AIDS Prevention and Control (NCAIDS). The national CDC operates under the leadership of China's MOH. At the provincial and local levels, the provincial health bureaus and their affiliated CDCs have led the AIDS response with designated responsibility for carrying out the official China CARES program of free testing and treatment provision and HIV prevention activities (with substantial financial support from GFATM and other international donor programs), and are the main government counterparts for most international AIDS funding programs. Even though local CDCs are bureaucratically accountable to their own local governments (through local health bureaus), earmarked vertical funding from the GFATM through the CDC and health bureau system has increased their resources and independence to carry out technical work.

However, because government-funded services such as public health education have been significantly weakened in the past two decades under China's fee-for-service health system, which is focused on curative care, the need for greater local NGO involvement in China's AIDS response is clear, especially to reach groups that avoid government scrutiny. And because the AIDS epidemic is expanding faster than the political space for NGOs at the local level, local CDCs have been engaging in pragmatic partnerships with grassroots NGOs and defending that work to local government, therefore pushing the boundaries of what might normally be allowed. These pragmatic partnerships between local CDCs and grassroots NGOs are helping to improve understanding of the value of NGO roles, possibly to the benefit of all local NGOs in China.

A number of developments are driving this process: the changing and more independent role of GONGOs, limited tolerance for legal advocacy groups, and increasing collaboration between local government and service-focused grassroots NGOs, especially MSM groups. The tainted blood AIDS epidemic in Henan remains politically sensitive for provincial officials, who have not yet been held accountable for purported government involvement in the blood collection scheme of the 1990s. As a result, dissent and action by the many infected rural villagers or groups representing them are quickly quashed. The internet, especially listservs and online communities, has been a critical mechanism linking up groups around China, often for legitimate purposes sanctioned by government (such as, the GFATM's country coordinating mechanism (CCM) election process), and has played a networking function that the government's NGO registration process was in part set up to prevent.

China's main AIDS GONGO is the Chinese Association of STD and AIDS Prevention and Control (CASAPC). This national-level GONGO was established originally as an affiliate of the MOH, and its founding director was a former vice minister of health. In its early years, it received funding from the government, but this ended in 1998 when it lost its mandate to coordinate national AIDS activities after the establishment of the State Council Working Group on AIDS. The CASAPC is now playing a key role as a "pass through" for funding to all kinds of AIDS NGOs (registered or not) and considers any group working on AIDS as a legitimate member of its operational network (Kaufman 2006). It now collaborates with all types of local groups, patient organizations, and other groups to apply competitively for Ministry of Finance funds for projects. Like many other mass organizations and GONGOs, including the All-China Women's Federation, it is no longer fully subsidized by government and has had to compete for grant and other funding to carry out its activities. Given the close relationships with government and the approved national network of affiliates, this obviously puts it in an advantageous position compared to grassroots NGOs, which are restricted from setting up networks. In 2004, the CASAPC decided to become an intermediary to facilitate and coordinate the work of grassroots NGOs, and funnel money to unregistered ones if necessary. It has been playing this role for Global Fund projects since Round 3. Round 3 provides support for China CARES, China's own national community-based HIV treatment, care, and prevention program in central China (seven provinces where HIV had spread primarily through illicit blood and blood plasma donation practices: Anhui, Hebei, Shandong, Henan, Hubei, Shanxi, and Shaanxi). The four-year program (2004–9), totaling US$98 million, helps pay for ARV treatment, care, and support, and community-based behavior change communication and testing and counseling for resident PLWHA and their communities. There have been three additional approved Global Fund rounds for HIV/AIDS work (see pp. 163–9 for descriptions and amounts) and another one is currently being reviewed (Round 7, focused on migrant workers).

The China STD AIDS Association even serves as a bank account for six groups without bank accounts working at the local level. The association ran a small grants proposal workshop several years ago aimed at providing help on "rules of the game" for funding applications and then helped NGOs to implement projects and to evaluate their work. It put together an expert committee that facilitated the Global Fund Round 5 process. Currently it serves as a "bridge" organization for channeling funding to groups doing good work at the local level. Since 2000, it has held several AIDS NGO coordination meetings (in Zhuhai, Harbin, and Chongqing), with an increasing number of groups participating (six in 2000 and more than 100 in 2005).

Other national GONGOs to have carried out significant work on AIDS are the China AIDS Foundation, the Chinese Preventive Medicine Association, and the Red Cross. Mass organizations like the All-China Women's Federation and the Youth Federation also conduct many AIDS projects with their local affiliates.

Another set of independent AIDS NGOs (not GONGOs) can be described as legal advocacy NGOs, representing the rights of persons affected by AIDS in China, either patient groups or AIDS orphans, although many of these groups also provide services. These groups are most visible internationally. They are less well known within China, with their work rarely being covered in the domestic media, although they actively participate in domestic meetings and AIDS listservs. These listservs, along with group email mass mailings, have become more common in the past decade and provide an easy mechanism for sharing information about meetings and events, along with other information of interest. These online communities, although closely monitored by government, have also become an important "networking" mechanism in recent years in China for groups with limited budgets for travel to conferences, or in cases where actual gatherings might be politically sensitive. These include Wan Yanhai's group AIZHI Action, the earliest such NGO, which was instrumental in early public revelations about the Henan AIDS epidemic caused by the tainted plasma donation services. Wan's online newsletter published the first interview with Gao Yaojie, the retired doctor in Henan Province who first publicly revealed the severity of the epidemic and its cover-up in the province in the late 1990s. Groups like Li Dan's Orchid group working with Henan AIDS orphans also fall into this category of legal advocacy NGOs and have been periodically closed down by local or national authorities. These groups receive the most international exposure and have been recognized internationally with awards (the Jonathan Mann Global Health Award, the Reebok Human Rights award, etc.). They participate in international AIDS advocacy organizations (Amnesty International and Human Rights Watch) and post online stories and calls for action to global listservs.

Even with increasing collaboration with international groups promoting legal advocacy and human rights accountability for AIDS victims, the political space for these groups in China has generally been increasing. And yet, as with other NGOs and outspoken dissident groups, the political space contracts along with periods of political tightening on dissent, as in the climate surrounding the Party Congress in the fall of 2007 and the Olympics hosted by China in 2008.

In general, there is less tolerance for legal advocacy groups working in Henan Province, especially for groups representing demands from PLWHA, which are also mainly based in Henan. This is because the Henan government regards the AIDS issue as politically sensitive and continues to keep tight control over information about the severity of Henan's AIDS problem (Kaufman and Jun 2002). Wan Yanhai has been a special target of politically connected Henan Province officials, whom he has angered repeatedly with his revelations of government complicity in both the tainted plasma collection program and the subsequent cover-up in the province. Notably, he has been detained twice in recent years, but released after intervention and advocacy by China's own national health authorities, accompanied by international publicity and pressure. Similarly, Li Dan and Hu Jia, both original members of AIZHI before starting their own organizations, have been detained for their AIDS work in Henan. Gao

Yaojie, an elderly retired obstetrician and gynecologist, has also been detained and monitored, and in 2001 was denied a passport for travel to the United States to receive an award, although she was eventually permitted to attend an award ceremony in the United States in 2007 after considerable international publicity and pressure. Human rights organizations outside of China publicize these stories, often pressuring groups like UNAIDS (the Joint United Nations Programme on HIV/AIDS) and the Global Fund to censure the Chinese government and pressure the Chinese to relax their restrictions on dissent. But while these awards, detentions, and suppression of dissent dominate the international news media, there is usually limited publicity and public awareness in China of these controversies. However, within the AIDS NGO community, these actions are certainly noted and act as a deterrent to open dissent and exposure (especially to the international community) of China's problems dealing with its AIDS epidemic.

Local government and grassroots NGO cooperation on AIDS

Perhaps the most important development for AIDS NGOs has been the increasing collaboration between local government and service-focused independent grassroots NGOs in many areas with expanding epidemics and pragmatic local government leadership. Because of the political climate of support for AIDS work, these groups have spontaneously proliferated to fill gaps in services. The recognition of their value by local CDCs or civil affairs bureaus has helped them to continue and provided them protection. Examples include an AIDS orphan community outreach program in Fuyang Anhui (the AIDS Orphans Salvation Association) and local AIDS prevention outreach efforts to at-risk groups. This is especially true in urban areas for MSM groups and in rural areas of Sichuan and Yunnan, where local NGOs reaching out to sex workers, miners (Panzhihua in Liangshan, Sichuan), and other most at-risk groups are working in collaboration with local CDCs.

It is no coincidence that Yunnan and Sichuan are in the forefront of these efforts. The China–UK HIV/AIDS Prevention and Care Project, funded by the United Kingdom's Department for International Development (DFID) and technically supported by Family Health International, provided important early funding to NGO outreach activities and helped foster good working relations with local government. From the early 1990s, the Ford Foundation's China Office has also been providing support for independent AIDS NGOs and AIDS researchers in Yunnan, Beijing, and elsewhere. These projects helped document HIV risk behaviors and then built a backbone of technically strong independent NGOs working on HIV prevention for MSM, sex workers, and youth, and representing PLWA.

Independent MSM-led groups have proliferated in urban areas of many provinces, notably the northwest provinces, in Shanghai and Beijing, Chengdu, and Kunming. The past decade has seen rapid growth of MSM groups, from one university-led organization (Friends Exchange Project in Qingdao, Shandong) and several Beijing- and Hong Kong-based NGOs (the Beijing Tongzhi Network, AIZHI, the Chi Heng Foundation) promoting and carrying out HIV prevention outreach and condom distribution in bars, parks, and bathhouses. These organizations also use the internet and magazines for outreach to the numerous active local groups serving the gay community and communicating with each other online. The 2 percent national infection rates currently documented among MSM (5 percent in Beijing) have in some ways forced government agencies tasked with AIDS prevention to reach out to the growing number of locally spawned volunteer MSM groups, and there has been a resulting expansion of MSM groups nationally, often working in collaboration with local CDCs engaged in AIDS education outreach in urban areas (Wu *et al.* 2007: 687). Although legal, because of historical stigma and fear of exposure by MSM in China these groups are reluctant to identify themselves to government or government-affiliated agencies. Therefore, GONGOs, like government, have limited access to MSM populations and are increasingly relying on local volunteer groups to reach them. AIDS patient groups (often for hemophiliacs and people infected via blood transfusions) have also grown in China's large urban areas; originally affiliated with infectious disease hospitals and led by medical personnel, they are now becoming more independent. However, in rural China at the local level there are few such legitimate groups representing former plasma donors, and groups that do form are the ones most feared by local governments, which do not want to be held accountable for patient demands for financial or legal redress. Most local crackdowns related to the AIDS epidemic in Henan have occurred for such reasons.

Chinese NGOs and the Global Fund for AIDS, TB, and malaria

Perhaps no other situation has contributed to the growth and participation of AIDS NGOs in China's AIDS response so much as has the controversy surrounding the country coordinating mechanism (CCM) for the Global Fund to fight AIDS, TB, and malaria. The Global Fund was established in 2002 with a mandated governance mechanism that required the establishment of a group made up of civil society representatives (Global Fund 2007) to review, approve, and submit all applications, the "country coordinating mechanism" of CCM.

> CCMs are central to the Global Fund's commitment to local ownership and participatory decision making … their role does not stop with grant approval: once the grant is signed, they are also responsible for overseeing its progress during the implementation stage.
>
> (Global Fund 2007)

China has successfully competed for four rounds of Global Fund funding for HIV/AIDS, having signed grant amounts totaling nearly $180 million, thus far receiving nearly $84 million. The first award of $98 million for five years (2005–9), Global Fund Round 3, provided support for AIDS treatment, testing, and counseling in seven central provinces (Henan and surrounding provinces). The Global Fund Round 4 award of $64 million for four years (2005–9) was aimed at slowing the spread of HIV among most at-risk sex workers and injecting drug users (IDUs) in seven central and western provinces where HIV is spread through high-risk behaviors such as commercial sex and injection drug use: Yunnan, Sichuan, Guangxi, Hunan, Guizhou, Jiangxi, and Xinjiang. Global Fund Round 5 provided $29 million in support of a four-year program (2006–10) that focuses on rapid extension of proven HIV prevention interventions for sex workers and men who have sex with men (MSM) in eighteen cities within seven low-prevalence provinces: Chongqing, Gansu, Heilongjiang, Inner Mongolia, Jilin, Liaoning, and Ningxia. The five-year, $14.4-million Round 6 project, begun in 2007, aimed to mobilize NGOs in scaling up effective HIV interventions for sex workers, MSM, IDUs, and PLWHA in fifteen provinces: Henan, Beijing, Tianjin, Shanghai, Guangzhou, Guizhou, Yunnan, Hunan, Hubei, Xinjiang, Guangxi, Anhui, Gansu, Sichuan, and Chongqing. Round 6 was recently awarded but the principal recipient was changed from the originally proposed GONGO, China STD and AIDS Association, to the China CDC, which has served as the principal recipient for all other global fund awards.

While China did establish a CCM, it worked more as a rubber stamp for applications developed and executed by China's Ministry of Health and CDC. The CCM was mainly composed of international NGO representatives, Chinese pharmaceutical company representatives, and an officially endorsed Chinese PLWHA organization. Grassroots NGOs had limited voice in the process. Several years ago, an election was organized to formally elect NGO representatives. A well-known Beijing-based AIDS activist representing grassroots patient groups lost the election and claimed that it was rigged by the government and unfair. This precipitated a thorough review by the Global Fund, assisted by UNAIDS, and resulted in a new election that by all accounts was a uniquely transparent and accountable local election process, advertised and participated in by any interested AIDS NGOs in China (*Global Fund Observer* 2007).

This process on the one hand provided an opportunity for wide discourse and comment over the internet within China, and helped to network disparate groups around the country. Several widely attended local meetings (in Xi'an, Beijing, and Kunming) brought groups together, often for the first time, with UNAIDS and donor representatives to teach them how to conduct the elections. The election resulted in two elected representatives (Wang Xiaoguang from Daytop, a group representing injecting drug users, and Meng Lin from ARK of Love, a Beijing-based PLWA group) and two NGO committees, each constituted with eleven elected representatives from a broad spectrum of groups representing hemophiliacs, MSM, former plasma donors, and migrant workers. The group meets regularly (the author attended a full meeting in summer 2007) and has been actively involved in the writing and review of recent Global Fund applications focused on NGO and migrant worker issues; Round 6 of the Global Fund is 100 percent set aside to support Chinese AIDS NGOs.

The controversy and resolution served as a significant door opener for NGO participation in the AIDS response in China; helped to bring on board central government leaders, who now (at times grudgingly) accept the reality of Global Fund requirements; and has established a genuine mechanism for voice and input by NGOs into China's AIDS response. Global Fund Round 6 is seen by many as an important further mechanism to institutionalize the AIDS NGO role in China's AIDS response. However, a recent decision by the Global Fund and China's Ministry of Health to switch the principal recipient (e.g. prime executing agency) from China's main AIDS GONGO, the CASAPC, to the China CDC is seen as a signal that this process is being closely watched and controlled. Many grassroots NGOs, with their new mechanisms for voice and input, are also claiming that funding and work arrangements proposed in the winning proposal to the Global Fund have been revised and that they will be marginalized in implementation (*Global Fund Observer* 2007). A new independent NGO is being established in China, Global Fund Watch, to monitor future compliance with Global Fund rules. However, real participation and influence in government-organized work has a long way to evolve.

Other constraints also hinder the current work of grassroots NGOs. Lack of core operational funding is perhaps the greatest constraint. Despite large amounts of donor funds for AIDS in China (during the period from 2006 to 2010, an estimated total of US$365 million is expected from major external contributors), little reaches the bottom, and especially local NGOs. At the local government level, local NGOs operate within the vagaries of local government understanding and support. The main determining factors affecting the political space to operate are personal *guanxi* (connections) and good relations with local officials. While many groups have good operating collaborations with local CDCs, which are in charge of HIV prevention, the CDC is a weak player in local politics. Relationships with CDC and local government may be pragmatic and functional but they can just as easily be uneasy and bad-tempered. Many of these NGOs work with a largely volunteer network with frequent staff turnover. Usually started by a visionary champion willing to take risks and navigate local politics, most need capacity building on routine management processes like financial accountability, staff planning, fundraising, and program planning. Moreover, there is damaging in-fighting among groups, especially within the MSM community, with sometimes unfounded allegations publicized on list-serves. This basic lack of trust, compounded by desire for visibility and competition for scarce funding, has fragmented rather than unified groups working on similar issues, playing into the hands of central government by preventing the needed alliance building among these groups.

Conclusion

The SARS crisis in China, along with increasing public concerns and pressure, drove the government to deal more aggressively with its AIDS epidemic in 2003. Recent strengthening of the response is helping to open the political space for AIDS NGO involvement. In part fueled by successful partnership with urban

MSM groups, there has been greater acknowledgment at the central level of the need for AIDS NGOs and their role, but there has been little loosening up at the local level in central China, where concentrated numbers of AIDS patients live. Conflicts between victim/patient groups and local government agencies following the blood scandal have created a climate of distrust, and while there is less open conflict, numerous barriers restrict the work of local NGOs. In-fighting among MSM groups competing for funding and local ownership has also prevented the kind of alliance building that has characterized successful civil society movements in other countries.

However, at the same time, in some high HIV prevalence areas outside central China, pragmatic partnerships between local government centers for disease control bureaus and an emerging and increasingly networked set of grassroots NGOs, mainly unregistered, are helping to develop effective models for NGO participation in welfare service provision locally. Various restrictions are being circumvented, often with tacit approval from responsible civil affairs officials. These include official government NGOs (GONGOs) acting as pass-through organizations for funding to get around restrictive registration and control mechanisms. This non-registration approach is pushing the boundaries of NGO operation possibilities in China because there is overall endorsement by those working on AIDS and by recent policy statements endorsing the role of NGOs in the AIDS response. No one seems willing to close them down at the moment, despite their lack of legal status. The Global Fund CCM controversy and its resolution have also helped to begin institutionalizing mechanisms for NGO input into AIDS governance and discourses.

Despite this progress, many challenges remain. There is a lack of professionalism and management capacity within the sector, poor understanding of fundraising, along with a lack of trained staff and heavy turnover of volunteers. In-fighting between groups over funds, local ownership, and visibility has further inhibited needed coordination on advocacy and programs. But recent new influxes of donor funding with specific focus on NGOs and AIDS will help to build the capacity of the sector. The Global Fund Round 6 project is 100 percent set aside for NGOs, and a newly launched Gates Foundation-funded program is aimed at improving HIV prevention for at-risk groups, with greater involvement of the NGO community. However, for these initiatives to be successful, local government must open up to partnership with the NGO community and recognize that rather than being a threat, such partnership can help contribute to effective welfare provision in areas where the government can no longer fully provide services. This may translate into better understanding by local government of NGO roles in general and contribute to greater possibilities and legitimacy for other civil society organizations in China.

Bibliography

Bentley, J. G. (2003) "The Role of International Support for Civil Society Organizations in China," *Harvard Asia Quarterly* (Winter): 11–20.

Callick, R. (2007) "China to Give NGOs a Break," *The Australian* (28 May).

China Daily (2005) "Spending on China's HIV/AIDS Prevention Set to Double" (December 28).

China Development Brief (2001) "250 Chinese NGOs: Civil Society in the Making, a Special Report from China Development Brief."

—— (2005) "200 International NGOs in China, a Special Report from China Development Brief" (Beijing Civil Society Development Research Center).

—— (2007a) Editorial: "'GONGOs' Are Here to Stay, but Need to Reform and Open Up" (1 April), 11: 3.

—— (2007b) "HIV/AIDS: NGOs Proliferate as the Global Fund Steps In" (23 May). Online, available at: www.chinadevelopmentbrief.com/node/1109.

China Economic Net (2007) "Legal Reform Urged for More Play of NGOs in China's Fight against HIV." Online, available at: http://en.ce.cn/National/Politics/200705/02/t20070502_11241815_3shtm.

Croll, E. (1999) "Social Welfare Reform: Trends and Tensions," *China Quarterly* 159: 684–99.

DFID-China Office (2003) Civil Society Consultation Meeting on HIV/AIDS Programming in China, Beijing, 17 April. Department for International Development China–UK HIV/AIDS Prevention and Care Project.

Farmer, P., Leandre, F., Mukherjee, J.S. *et al.* (2001) "Community-Based Approaches to HIV Treatment in Resource-Poor Settings," *Lancet* 358: 404–9.

General Offices of the Communist Party Central Committee and State Council of the People's Republic of China (1996) "Circular on the Strengthening of the Management of Social Organizations and Non-governmental, Non-commercial Enterprises" (Central Office, No. 22, 8 August).

—— (1999) "Circular on the Strengthening of the Management of Civil Society Organizations" (Central Office, No. 34, 1 November).

Gill, B. and Okie, S. (2007) "China and HIV – a Window of Opportunity," *New England Journal of Medicine* 356 (18): 1801–5.

Global Fund (2007) "The Global Fund Overview for East Asia and the Pacific: Successes, Challenges, and Achievements to Date," Geneva.

Global Fund Observer (2007) "China Changes Course on Using NGOs as Grant Implementers" (October).

Guan, X. F. (2007) "NGOs Have More Room to Develop," *China Daily* (25 May). Online, available at: www.chinadaily.com.cn/cndy/2007-05/25/content_879965.htm.

Interfax-China (2007) "Bid Failure by China's Largest AIDS NGO Bad for All NGOs," (6 April).

Joint United Nations Program on HIV/AIDS (UNAIDS) and World Health Organization (2006) *AIDS Epidemic Update* (December).

Jun, J. (2006) "The Social Origins of AIDS Panics in China," in J. Kaufman, A. Kleinman, and A. Saich (eds.) *AIDS and Social Policy in China*, Cambridge, MA: Harvard University Asia Center Publications.

Kaufman, J. (2005) "SARS and China's Health Care Response: Better to Be Both Red and Expert!" in A. Kleinman and J. L. Watson (eds.) *SARS in China: Prelude to Pandemic?* Palo Alto, CA: Stanford University Press.

—— (2006) Dai Zhizeng's Presentation Summary in Report on the Tsinghua University, Harvard University, CASAPC – China AIDS NGO Training Workshop, China AIDS Public Policy Training Program.

—— (2008) "China's Health Care System and Avian Influenza Preparedness," *Journal of Infectious Diseases* 197 Suppl. 1 (2008): S7–S13.

Kaufman, J. and Jun, J. (2002) "China and AIDS – the Time to Act Is Now," *Science* (28 June) 296: 2339–40.

Kaufman, J., Kleinman, A., and Saich, A. (2006) *AIDS and Social Policy in China*, Cambridge, MA: Harvard University Asia Center Publications.

Lu, Y. Y. and Attawell, K. (2002) "Review of Primary Stakeholder Participation and NGO Involvement," UK–China HIV/AIDS Prevention and Care Project, unpublished independent report commissioned by the UK Department for International Development.

Ministry of Health, People's Republic of China, Joint United Nations Programme on HIV/AIDS (UNAIDS) and WHO (2006), *2005 Update on the HIV/AIDS Epidemic and Response in China* (24 January).

Mooney, P. (2006) "Rare Article Reveals Party Views on NGOs," *South China Morning Post* (1 September).

National Intelligence Council (2002) *The Next Wave of HIV/AIDS: Nigeria, Ethiopia, Russia, India, and China*, ICA 2002-04D.

Peng, Z. C. (2006) "Preparing for the Real Storm during the Calm: A Comparison of the Crisis Preparation Strategies in Managing Future Pandemic Influenza in China and the U.S.," unpublished paper, Harvard Kennedy School, visiting fellow.

Rivers, B. (2007) "China Changes Course on Using NGOs as Grant Implementers", *Global Fund Observer*, 77 (30 September).

Rosenthal, E. (2000) "In Rural China, a Steep Price of Poverty: Dying of AIDS," *New York Times* (28 October).

Saich, A. (2000) "Negotiating the State: The Development of Social Organizations in China," *China Quarterly* 161: 1–24.

—— (2007) "Changing Role of Government and Civil Society," unpublished PowerPoint presentation and lecture to Brandeis-Harvard China AIDS Policy Leadership and Management Course, Brandeis University (5 September).

Saich, T. and Kaufman, J. A. (2005) "Financial Reform, Poverty, and the Impact on Reproductive Health Provision: Evidence from Three Rural Townships," in Y. S. Huang, T. Saich, and E. Steinfeld (eds.) *Financial Sector Reform in China*, Cambridge, MA: Harvard University Asia Center Publications.

Southern Weekend (*Nanfang Zhoumo*) (2000) Issue of 30 November, devoted to AIDS in China.

State Council of the People's Republic of China (1998a) Regulations on the Registration and Management of Social Organizations in China, Order No. 250 (25 September).

—— (1998b) Temporary Regulations on the Registration and Management of Non-Government Non-commercial Enterprises, Order No. 251 of the People's Republic of China's State Council at the 8th Standing Committee Session (25 October).

State Council of the People's Republic of China (2004) Regulations on the Management of Foundations (trans. Jim Weldon), *China Development Brief*. Online, available at: www.chinadevelopmentbrief.com/node/301. In Chinese at the Ministry of Civil Affairs website: www.chinanpo.gov.cn/web/showBulltetin.do?id=15502&dictionid=1103.

—— (2006a) Regulations on AIDS Prevention and Control, Decree No. 457 (29 January).

—— (2006) *China's Action Plan for Reducing and Preventing the Spread of HIV/AIDS, 2006–2010*, State Council Office Document No. 13.

Stern, E. K. (1999) *Crisis Decision Making: A Cognitive-Institutional Approach*, Stockholm: Stockholm University Press.

Sun, J. W. (2004) "Door Opens for Creation of Civil Society," *Shanghai Daily* (23 August): 12.

UNAIDS and WHO (2007) *AIDS Epidemic Update* (December 2007) (UNAIDS/07.27E/JC1322E).

Wang, M. (2006) Presentation at Tsinghua Harvard CASTAPC AIDS Public Policy Training Program, Training Workshop on AIDS and NGOs, Beijing (15–17 July).

Wang, N. (2006) "China CDC," presentation at Tsinghua Harvard CASTAPC AIDS Public Policy Training Program, Training Workshop on AIDS and NGOs, Beijing (15–17 July).

Wexler, R., Xu, Y., and Young, N. (2006) "NGO Advocacy in China," a special report from *China Development Brief* (September).

Wu, Z. Y., Sullivan, S. G., Wang, Y., Rotheram-Borus, M. J., and Detels, R. (2007) "Evolution of China's Response to HIV/AIDS," *Lancet* 369: 679–90.

Wu, F. S. (2005) "International Non-governmental Actors in HIV/AIDS Prevention in China," *Cell Research* 15 (11–12): 919–22.

Xinhua News Agency (2006) "China Encourages NGOs Participation in Fight against AIDS" (23 March).

Xinhua News Agency (2007a) "Sichuan Calls for NGO Reform" (1 May). Online, available at: http://news.xinhuanet.com/english/2007-05/01/content_6052298.htm.

—— (2007b) "More Women Suffer from HIV/AIDS in China" (4 June).

Xu, H., Zeng, Y., and Anderson, A. F. (2005) "Chinese NGOs in Action against HIV/AIDS," *Cell Research* 15 (11–12): 914–18.

Young, N. (2007a) "How Much Inequality Can China Stand?" A Special Report from *China Development Brief* (February).

—— (2007b) "Personal Press Statement, China Development Brief," *Wall Street Journal* (11 July).

Part IV

Conclusion

9 Serving the people?

The changing roles of the state and social organizations in social service provision

Jonathan Schwartz and Shawn Shieh

Introduction

Our goal in this volume has been to identify and explain the changing nature of state–society interaction in the sphere of social service provision. In this volume, we explore the evolving roles of state and social actors in providing social services, we evaluate the impact of these changing roles on state–society relations in China, and, finally, we discuss how these changes impact social service provision. This dynamic is important to understand because the pace and direction of change have broader ramifications for the nature and development of Chinese civil society. Ultimately, through this volume we engage the debate over the nature of Chinese civil society, its direction, and its impact on China's existing system of government.

In the first chapter, we laid out the key hypotheses that guide the contributions to the volume. We hypothesize that social service provision in China is undergoing gradual change resulting from ongoing interactions between the state and civil society. However, this gradual change is being supplemented by more rapid changes arising as a result of crises that bring to light the incapacity of the state to provide sufficient social services. Furthermore, we suggest that these processes are best understood as expanding autonomy for a wide array of social actors even as these actors recognize the benefits of close ties to the state.

In order to explore these hypothesized developments, each of the chapters has been structured around a series of themes to ensure analytical continuity. The first theme describes the changing roles played by the state and social organizations in providing social services. The second theme describes the impact of these changing roles on state–social organization relations. The third theme describes how these changing roles are affecting China's social welfare regime. In this concluding chapter, we synthesize the arguments developed throughout the volume, and draw out the ramifications for our broader understanding of evolving state–society relations in China.

In the first section of this concluding chapter, we explore the lessons deriving from the contributions in terms of the three themes. In the second section, we consider the impacts of crisis versus non-crisis situations on the state–social organization relationship. In the final section, we draw general conclusions.

The themes

In this section, we consider the three themes and how each of the case studies fits within them. Throughout, we draw illustrative examples from the chapters but do not aim to be comprehensive. The first theme we consider is the changing roles in social service provision between the state and social organizations.

Theme 1: changing roles of the state and social organizations in social service provision

A key lesson arising from the contributions is that the state is playing a shrinking role in social service provision. The state's shrinking role is partly a result of a deliberate decision by the state to reduce its participation, but is also a reflection of growing needs and demands for social services that are a result of China's rapid reforms. Through their chapters, the contributors demonstrate that demand for social services has exceeded the state's capacity and willingness to provide them.

Thus, Keyser (in Chapter 3) notes that while the state claims full responsibility for orphan care, in fact it is unable and unwilling to provide it. The decline of state responsibility for orphan care has been largely caused by reform-era developments, for example rural–urban migration, the growing population with birth defects, and the growing number of street children. In particular, Keyser notes that certain populations of children fall outside the official definition of orphan and are therefore ineligible to receive state support. In other cases, cross-jurisdictional conflicts among government agencies result in some populations being left without support.

As with Keyser's case, Schwartz (Chapter 7) notes that the state lacks the capacity to address public health crises alone, without external assistance. Following from Schwartz's chapter, Kaufman (Chapter 8) notes that the state recognizes its continued inability to meet public health needs in the area of HIV/AIDS.

According to Schwartz and Kaufman, the state traditionally provides for health-related services. However, during the reform period this has changed. A clear example is in emergency disease response. As both Schwartz and Kaufman note, the state turns to social organizations for assistance in addressing health-related social services. For example, the state obtained the assistance of residence committees in quarantining, testing, and caring for ill and potentially ill SARS patients, while men who have sex with men (MSM) groups played an important role in cooperation with the state in providing services to HIV/AIDS victims.

Zhang and Smith (Chapter 4) conclude that the growing economy has expanded the need for worker protections far beyond those provided by China's only legal union, the All-China Federation of Trade Unions. Indeed, the ACFTU is not geared toward assisting the massive and growing migrant worker population. Social organizations have emerged to take on this role. Among other services, these organizations provide information on legal rights, provide safe gathering locations, and even offer mobile health services (as in the case of the Center for Women Workers Network).

Laliberté (Chapter 6) notes that after an extended period in which religious organizations were moribund, China's Buddhist (and to a lesser extent Christian) organizations have expanded their roles. Often with the assistance, collaboration, or even with direct initiatives of Buddhist organizations from outside of mainland China (e.g. Taiwan and Hong Kong). These organizations provide flood relief, reconstruction, and education facilities to meet the needs of populations in need of assistance.

These examples offer insight into the growing numbers of social organizations that are emerging across the country. The chapters reveal an astonishing diversity of organizations, including domestic, international, hybrid, quasi-state, religious, legal, and underground social organizations arrayed along a continuum from closely allied to the state to autonomous from the state (see Figure 9.1). In many cases, these organizations not only seek to fill roles abandoned by the state, but advocate to create new services that the state is unwilling to legitimize or fund.

That the state has recognized the benefits provided by these organizations is illustrated by state actions to strengthen the legal status of social organizations, civil non-enterprise units, and foundations by promulgating various regulations regarding registration and management.

As many of the chapters illustrate, decentralization has also enlarged the local government role in social service provision and in regulating social organizations. This trend is not necessarily beneficial to non-governmental social service providers. The chapters underline how local governments respond in very different ways to these organizations. In the sphere of religious charities, Laliberté argues that local governments have been more welcoming and tolerant of Buddhist (and Christian) charities than has the central government. This is most likely because these organizations have made tangible contributions to disaster response and poverty-relief efforts at the local level, but, as religious organizations, remain ideologically problematic in the eyes of the central government.

By contrast, in the spheres of HIV/AIDS and environmental protection it is the central government that has generally been relatively supportive of social organization activities, while local governments have sometimes been more hostile. Thus, Hildebrandt and Turner (Chapter 5) identify environmental NGOs (ENGOs) as filling a niche at the local level that is encouraged by a central government eager to address the challenges of rampant pollution but lacking the capacity to do so. By contrast, local governments are more often reluctant to enable ENGO activities because of concerns that better environmental protection will come at the expense of economic growth. The services being provided by ENGOs include empowering local citizens, keeping an eye on local governments, and pressuring them to adhere to China's environmental protection laws.

Theme 2: how state–social organization interactions have changed

The chapters in this volume reveal the growth of an increasingly diverse and vibrant NGO community whose interactions with the state can no longer be

State ⟷ Autonomous social organizations

Examples	Government agencies/public institutions	Mass organizations	GONGOs	Semi-GONGOs	NGOs
(Shieh)	Ministry of Civil Affairs	Communist Youth League	China Youth Development Foundation (Project Hope)	Beijing University Women's Legal Aid Center	Global Village Sanchuan Development Association (Qinghai)
(Schwartz)	Centers for Disease Control	Village and neighborhood committees			Huizeying Human Services Center
(Laliberté)	China Buddhist Association	Regional Buddhist associations			Tzu Chi – an international social service provider
(Hildebrandt and Turner)	Ministry of Environmental Protection	All-China Federation of Trade Unions		Center for Legal Advice to Pollution Victims (CLAPV)	Friends of Nature Green Watershed
(Zhang and Smith)					Shenzhen Institute of Contemporary Observation Shenzhen Migrant Workers' Association
(Kaufman)	Centers for disease control		Chinese Association of STDs and AIDS Prevention and Control (CASAPC)	Sun Village	AIZHI Action (AIDS) Orchid Group (AIDS orphans)
(Keyser)	Child welfare institutes	All-China Women's Federation	China Children and Teenagers Fund		"Grassland Home" The "Angel Moms"

Figure 9.1 State–social organization continuum.

Note

GONGO, government-organized non-governmental organization.

adequately captured by the corporatist model that views social organizations as an extension of state regulation. As Shieh discusses in Chapter 2, the state's corporatist efforts to control social organizations have been partial and haphazard. As a result, social organizations have grown outside the state's regulatory ambit, and modes other than regulation have become increasingly significant. Shieh distinguishes between two such modes, negotiation and societalization. Negotiation is a mode in which the social organization and state voluntarily collaborate with one another over social service provision, while societalization is a mode in which social organizations work outside of the state to provide social services.

Both modes, and especially societalization, are indicators of the growing capacity and autonomy of social organizations, reflecting an emerging civil society in China.

Schwartz describes a relationship largely dominated by regulation, with some room for negotiation. Thus, aside from a small number of NGOs the response to SARS was dominated by highly regulated institutions supplemented by collaborative efforts between the state and residents' committees. The SARS crisis does not reveal an immediate shift in state–society relations. Indeed, the state enhances its power and reach by collaborating with the residents' committees.

However, while no major changes occurred in state–social organizations relations during the SARS outbreak, in its aftermath the vulnerability and weaknesses brought to light by the SARS response led to awareness among government leaders and the public of the need for additional support. As Kaufman describes, HIV/AIDS well fits this situation. Regulation here is supplemented with negotiation and, to some extent, societalization. Thus, social organizations at the local and national levels are not only engaged in negotiations with the state on social service provision, but also engaged in networking with other social organizations.

As many of the chapters show, negotiation is a valuable mode for many NGOs. Thus, for example, Keyser describes negotiated arrangements regarding foster care between child welfare institutes (CWIs), social welfare institutes (SWIs), and international non-governmental organizations (INGOs), and Zhang and Smith describe negotiated arrangements between migrant worker NGOs and the Shenzhen ACFTU to provide services to migrant workers.

Laliberté's chapter is informed by a combination of regulation and negotiation. Regulation is clear in the decisions of the central government vis-à-vis the various religious social organizations and the constraints on their activities. However, while religious organizations are highly regulated in China, as Laliberté notes, the state invited Taiwan and Hong Kong Buddhist organizations into China to assist domestic social organizations and in order to break out of the post-Tiananmen incident isolation imposed by the international community. The negotiation is reflected in the nature of relations at the central and local levels, where governments seek assistance in providing social services such as school construction and disaster relief that are difficult for the state to provide.

Interestingly, by 2000 even the central government had recognized that religious social organizations can provide important services, enabling them to launch their own welfare operations. In 2005, religious social organizations received greater autonomy via legislation institutionalizing the right of religious organizations to raise money and provide social services.

Societalization is also becoming more prominent as NGOs seek international funding, and network with other domestic social organizations, intellectuals, and the media. Close ties are forming between many Chinese NGOs and the international community. Many NGOs discussed in this book rely heavily on international NGOs, corporations, and governments for funding, training, and other forms of assistance. While many Chinese NGOs have some ties with the state, they are also beginning to form ties with other domestic NGOs. Networks, both real and virtual, are emerging and playing an important role in developing NGO capacity. As discussed by Zhang and Smith, there are also close ties between intellectuals and NGOs. However, there are definitely limits, as Hildebrandt and Turner argue that NGOs tend not to network across sectors, partly because networks have been discouraged by the state and because these NGOs are often in competition with each other over scarce resources.

The crisis chapters highlight the need to view interactions between the state and social organizations over a sustained period. In the short term, crises underline the continuing importance of regulation as a mode. During crises, the state recentralizes control and mobilizes its own resources to address an issue of critical importance, while social organizations play a relatively minor role. Schwartz, Kaufman, and Laliberté suggest in their respective chapters, however, that, over the long term, crises in China have opened the door for greater participation by social organizations as the state recognizes that it cannot resolve crises alone and invites participation by both domestic and international organizations. In other words, what appears to be heavy-handed state regulation in the short term appears to evolve into a blend of regulation, negotiation, and societalization as social organizations enter the process.

We should emphasize, though, that the emergence of negotiation and societalization as important modes of interaction does not mean that social organizations are challenging or confronting the state. If anything, social organizations tend to avoid direct challenges or confrontation. As we argue in Chapter 1, the sociological definition of civil society, which regards the state and social organizations as engaged in collaborative, mutually beneficial activity, is more relevant to China than the political definition. The contributors generally support this view. Social organizations tend to value close ties with the state because those ties translate into legitimacy and resources. Societalization, which signifies greater distance from the state, is generally considered a less valuable option. When social organizations engage in societalization, they are careful to do so in ways that do not threaten the state. Any threat perceived by the state is likely to result in greater regulation and repression of the social organization.

Finally, it is important to distinguish the relationship existing between the central government and social organizations from the relationship that exists between local government and social organizations. As is mentioned earlier, central and local governments are not unified in their perception of social organizations. Where they perceive them as beneficial in relation to their own goals, governments will be supportive of social organizations' activities. However, when the activities are viewed as detrimental to government goals, that support can quickly evaporate. For example, Laliberté notes that local governments are quite supportive of Buddhist charities and organizations, whereas the central government views them with concern. By contrast, Hildebrandt and Turner note that the central government is generally highly supportive of ENGOs, while local governments strive to close them down when they challenge local interests.

Theme 3: how changes in social service provision roles have affected the quality and nature of social service provision in China

The third theme touches on a key question: have the ongoing changes in responsibilities for social service provision in China resulted in improved services? Whereas in the past, social services were recognized as being the responsibility of the state, and the state provided those services (whether through state-owned enterprises, communes, or Party-sponsored organizations like the Women's Federation), the reform era brought an end to the "iron rice bowl," often leaving citizens to fend for themselves as local governments scrambled, and often failed, to pick up the slack. This exemplifies a situation where social organizations move in to fill political space vacated by the decentralizing state. In other cases, social organizations are expanding to meet the demand of a changing population that has generated demand for new types of social services. In other words, the growing economy, rising wealth, and improved living conditions have resulted in a range of new demands for social services such as clean air and water, safe food, and high-quality education.

In many respects, social organizations are nimbler than the state, effectively identifying gaps in existing service as well as areas where demand is growing for new services. Zhang and Smith well describe this process in their discussion of migrant worker organizations stepping in to meet the needs of a sector of workers never even conceived of by the state and its union. In fact, all the contributors to this volume describe such a dynamic, though with some variations: demand for social services grows; the state is unable or unwilling to meet that demand (and in many cases is oblivious to the demand); social organizations step into the "breach" by providing the needed service.

Furthermore, these organizations are often willing to provide services to groups that are otherwise marginalized or ignored by society. For example, HIV/AIDS groups play an important role in providing services to shunned sectors of society, while migrant worker groups offer education and health and legal advice to another often-disdained segment of Chinese society.

Despite these real and important contributions to the provision of social services in China, it would be unwise to overstate the reach and influence of social service organizations. A drawback to relying on social service organizations to provide a growing palette of social services is the limited reach of these organizations. As described by Kaufman (AIDS organizations), Laliberté (Buddhist associations), Zhang and Smith (workers' organizations), Keyser (foster organizations), and Hildebrandt and Turner (green NGOs), and to a lesser extent by Schwartz (residence committees), these social service organizations cannot provide the extent and quality of service required by society. Constrained by regulations and inadequate membership, funding, and expertise, these organizations work most effectively as providers of services that supplement the state social welfare system.

The impact of crises on state–social organization relations and social service provision

One goal of this book is to explore the impact crises have on the roles played by the state and social organizations in providing social services. Though we are limited in drawing conclusions by the small number of comparative cases in our study, we nonetheless identify a number of important, if tentative, lessons. As Laliberté illustrates, major crises (in his study, the 1991 floods and the 1989 Tiananmen incident) drove the central government to turn to social organizations for assistance in addressing the emergency needs of recovery and reconstruction. The need for this assistance was made obvious by the state's clear inability to address fully the challenges arising from the crises.

In the SARS example, Schwartz reveals that when the state recognizes the immensity of the challenge it faces, it directs tremendous resources to addressing the problem. However, even with incredible redirection of resources and a new emphasis on disease response, the state was unable to resolve the crisis independently. Here the state turned to social organizations to supplement its efforts. Furthermore, the crisis drove home to the state its need for assistance in addressing a weakness – in this case, infectious disease control. The outcome becomes clear in Kaufman's chapter, where, faced with a major disease control challenge, the HIV/AIDS epidemic, the state has increasingly turned to social organizations to tackle the social service needs of the population.

In short, the crisis situations described in this volume illustrate the awakening of the state to the gaps in its ability to address social service needs. This awakening results in significant state investment, with expanding room for social organizations to contribute to providing relevant social services. Thus, in the longer term the crisis catalyzes a new relationship between the state and social organizations (through regulation, negotiation, and/or societalization), with the latter enjoying a larger role.

Lending further credence to this observation is the response to the Sichuan earthquake of May 2008. The massive state mobilization – including military and civilian organs – was heavily supplemented by social organizations (Yang 2008). Interestingly, when the state turned to outsiders for assistance, among the first organizations contacted was the Tzu Chi foundation, discussed by Laliberté (Chapter 6). This reflects the institutionalization of a norm of seeking non-governmental assistance in crisis situations.

By contrast, the relationship between the state and social organizations in non-crisis situations is best described as undergoing gradual change over time. This contrast seems clearest when comparing the child welfare and migrant labor chapters to the crisis chapters. In both of these non-crisis cases, NGOs began to emerge in the late 1990s and have grown fairly steadily since, even though neither the child welfare nor the migrant labor issue has assumed crisis proportions, thanks largely to international attention and funding. The lack of attention paid by the state to these two issues has created a difficult operating environment for NGOs, many of which are not legally registered.

General lessons

All the chapters in this volume share a number of commonalities that extend beyond the thematic similarities we have previously identified. These commonalities include (1) the tensions felt by social organizations between the wish for greater autonomy from the state, and the desire for closer ties with it; (2) the varied openness and recognition of need across levels of government and its effect on government willingness to work with social organizations; (3) the impact of international and quasi-international social organizations on China's state–social organization relations; and (4) the role of the mass media. In the following section, we explore these commonalities, drawing lessons for our understanding of state–social organization relations.

Social organizations seek greater autonomy, yet, simultaneously, closer ties to the state

A key commonality arising from the volume is the seemingly contradictory pulls that influence social organizations in their relationship with the state. The clearly expressed interest of social organizations in greater autonomy from the state is to be expected, given that these organizations seek to provide services without interference by bureaucrats or regulators who might limit their activities. However, both international and domestic social organizations have repeatedly expressed an interest in forming ties to the state at the central and/or local levels. Such ties are viewed by social organizations as fundamental to achieving their goals, for the state has access to resources, has status, and has reach that far exceeds that of even the best-organized and most highly regarded social organizations.

Openness and recognized need influence the willingness of government entities to work with social organizations

A second commonality arising from the volume relates to the impact of decentralization over social service provision in China. Decentralization has pushed the responsibility for social service provision down to the local level, in particular the sub-provincial level. As Zhang and Smith, Kaufman, Keyser, and Laliberté all note, the local governments often lack the will or the capacity to address the social service provision challenge with which they are confronted. Lacking the will and/or capacity, these governments may choose to turn for assistance to social organizations. Doing so would seem a logical, low-cost step for local officials.

However, in cases such as HIV/AIDS, religious charitable works, and migrant labor organizations, officials are often leery of requesting or receiving assistance. In some cases (such as HIV/AIDS and environmental protection), the central government realizes the benefit of cooperating with domestic and international social organizations, and yet local governments may remain reticent. Thus, activism by social organizations is dependent on the open-mindedness of local officials and the priority those officials choose to give the specific issue (often regardless of central government directives).

The role of the international community

We also note that the international community has an important role as creator and defender of political space. Owing to the desire on the part of the central and local Chinese governments for international aid and assistance, the international community (including international NGOs, foreign governments, and foundations) is able to leverage resources to increase the political space for activism by domestic social organizations. Indeed, we are struck by how many of the Chinese NGOs discussed in this book rely heavily on international funding. While largely viewed as making powerful and positive contributions, international organizations are also viewed as presenting domestic social organizations with difficult challenges. At times expectations of the international community can prove detrimental to the effective functioning of domestic social organizations. As Hildebrandt and Turner illustrate (in Chapter 5), domestic ENGOs have been constrained in their activities by priorities set abroad, and in some cases are forced to compete with international ENGOs for skilled volunteers and members.

The role of the media

By and large, this volume has not emphasized the role played by the media in social service provision.[1] However, we recognize the important role the media play in mediating the relationship between the state and social service organizations. Most obviously, the media are a tool of tremendous use to the state. Thus, the state draws on the media to inform the public and activate social organizations wishing to cooperate with the state, as we see during the 2008 Sichuan earthquake and in Chapter 7 (in connection with the dissemination of information on SARS).

The media are also a crucial tool for social organizations. The media protect and advance the goals of social organizations in a number of ways. These include informing and educating the public and leadership regarding the mission of social organizations; pressuring or embarrassing state entities guilty of legal or illegal behavior that social organizations are seeking to curtail; providing protection for social organizations through coverage of activities that might otherwise result in censure or even closure of the social organizations; and, finally, by publicizing social organizations' activities and thereby helping them attract potential members and donors. We see examples of these roles in Chapters 5 (drawing on the media to embarrass industries and local governments into adherence with the law), 8 (examining the internet and magazines as key tools for outreach and for providing information and support to those afflicted with HIV/AIDS), and 3 (with specific organizations such as Sun Village able to gain greater influence through their exposure in the media). By providing coverage of social organizations and informing the public and the leadership of the various activities taken on by social organizations, the media can protect the political space social organizations have obtained. Thus, it is not surprising to learn that many Chinese social organizations actively court the media and seek to include media personalities among their members, as in the case of Friends of Nature.

Concluding section: the direction of state–society relations in China

As we see repeatedly throughout this volume, the relationship between the state and society is undergoing significant change. We argue that this change can be best viewed as guided by regulation from above, negotiation between state and social organizations, and, finally, social actors acting independently of the state. Over time, and as a result of the state's decentralization process initiated in the reform era (post-1979), the state has expanded the political space available to social organizations through regulation and negotiation because it is increasingly struggling to fulfill the social service provision roles that were once its sole responsibility. In addition to the state's withdrawing from political space it once controlled, we also see the growth of new political space as new social services needs come into existence. Here again the state and social organizations engage in both negotiation and regulation in an effort to define their respective roles and responsibilities. However, these efforts are supplemented by activism that occurs outside the state, the third mode in the state–society relationship – societalization.

The process of shifting allocations of responsibilities and newly established responsibilities is described in the first part of the volume as occurring over time in a gradual fashion. However, this gradual change does not sufficiently describe state–social organization relations in China. As Part III illustrates, this gradual change is supplemented by crisis events that catalyze more rapid change. As is described in the "crisis" chapters, the state invariably responds to crises with massive allocations of resources and mobilization of state, Party, and military personnel and equipment. But, again as illustrated in these chapters, the state is aware that its own resources are insufficient. A 2008 example of the limitations of state mobilization is the massive snowstorms that paralyzed the country during Chinese New Year. Here the state initiated a mass mobilization of state resources to tackle the crisis. However, social organizations played little or no role. While the failure to engage social organizations cannot be viewed as the sole cause of what is widely viewed as a failed response (corruption, among others, should be viewed as a contributing variable), their lack of participation is notable (Zhang 2008).

The relationship between the state and social organizations reflects a steady process of increased social organization involvement in social service provision with occasional shocks (crises) that catalyze more rapid movement toward greater activity by social organizations.

Also arising from the contributions to this volume is the theme that the state (at the central, provincial, and local levels) remains the key actor for providing social services. The state is the main direct provider, and also functions as the key collaborator with, and provider of support to, social organizations wishing to provide social services. In addition, the state is recognized by both domestic and international social organizations as the main conduit for investment and advancing social service projects. Therefore, despite the growing benefits of cooperation between various levels of government and social organizations, we see here that the state retains a dominant position in social service provision.

In Chapter 1, we define civil society by drawing on a sociological definition. This definition recognizes that the state and civil society are not necessarily conflictual in nature, and that the state and social organizations can collaborate to achieve shared goals. While the ultimate outcome of the state–society interaction may be growing democratization, this is not a necessary result. The many examples of state–society interaction identified in this volume serve to support the relevance of this definition for the China case. Indeed, none of the chapters points to a growing break between the state and social organizations. In each chapter, we see efforts at pragmatic collaboration. The state collaborates because it is increasingly aware of its inability in reformist China to provide the social services that are its responsibility under the social contract (and because social organizations do bring additional benefits apart from providing social services, such as ties to international funding, expertise, and publicity). Social organizations collaborate because they recognize that the state has access to resources, power, and status that are highly beneficial to achieving successful social service provision outcomes.

As the Chinese state continues to decentralize decision making, local governments will feel the pressure to pick up where the center left off. Furthermore, services once provided by state-owned enterprises and communes are now devolving to local governments. The local governments, lacking sufficient resources but recognizing the importance of satisfying the demands by the public for social services, are bound to find a solution. Increasingly, the solution lies in developing a collaborative relationship with social service organizations. The result is a growing role, coupled with greater responsibilities for social organizations. While this process may be viewed as a stage in a path toward democratization, this study shows that such a progression is by no means inevitable.

Note

1 Ultimately, our goal has been to evaluate the state–social organization relationship. Therefore, we have limited ourselves to recognizing the important role of the media in enabling social organization activities. While it is outside the purview of this volume, we view the media's role in the state–social organization relationship as of great importance, representing an area worthy of further study.

References

Yang, Guobin (2008) "A Civil Society Emerges from the Earthquake Rubble", *Yale Global* (5 June). Online, available at: http://yaleglobal.yale.edu/display.article?id=10910 (accessed 6 June 2008).

Zhang, Yi (2008) "Icy Hand of China Corruption Bared," *Asia Times* (6 March). Online, available at: www.atimes.com/atimes/China/JC06Ad01.html (accessed 14 July 2008).

Index

eBooks – at www.eBookstore.tandf.co.uk

A library at your fingertips!

eBooks are electronic versions of printed books. You can store them on your PC/laptop or browse them online.

They have advantages for anyone needing rapid access to a wide variety of published, copyright information.

eBooks can help your research by enabling you to bookmark chapters, annotate text and use instant searches to find specific words or phrases. Several eBook files would fit on even a small laptop or PDA.

NEW: Save money by eSubscribing: cheap, online access to any eBook for as long as you need it.

Annual subscription packages

We now offer special low-cost bulk subscriptions to packages of eBooks in certain subject areas. These are available to libraries or to individuals.

For more information please contact webmaster.ebooks@tandf.co.uk

We're continually developing the eBook concept, so keep up to date by visiting the website.

www.eBookstore.tandf.co.uk

For Product Safety Concerns and Information please contact our EU representative GPSR@taylorandfrancis.com
Taylor & Francis Verlag GmbH, Kaufingerstraße 24, 80331 München, Germany

www.ingramcontent.com/pod-product-compliance
Ingram Content Group UK Ltd.
Pitfield, Milton Keynes, MK11 3LW, UK
UKHW020201200926
475702UK00004B/567
9780415452243